Dr. Jeanne Brooks-Gunn is Associate Director of the Institute for the Study of Exceptional Children and is a Research Scientist at Educational Testing Service, Princeton, New Jersey. She is also Assistant Professor of Clinical Pediatric Psychology, College of Physicians and Surgeons of Columbia University, New York City. Her work deals primarily with infant development, but she is also conducting research on adolescent girls: their sex-role development and their attitudes and experiences concerning early menstruation.

Dr. Wendy Schempp Matthews is a child psychologist with the New Jersey Department of Human Services and at the Arthur Brisbane Child Treatment Center in Ailair, New Jersey, and serves as a consultant for the Training Institute for Sex Desegregation of the Public Schools at Rutgers University. She is currently researching the fantasy play of young children and its relation to their social, affective, and intellectual development.

To my grandmother, Coyla Ramsdell Brooks,
who showed me that the only difference
between masculine and feminine is the spelling,
and to my husband, Robert Ward Gunn,
who, by dividing the chores, multiplies the love.

Jeanne Brooks-Gunn

To Avery, growing up.

Wendy Schempp Matthews

What does it mean to behave like a boy
or like a girl? Is there a social process
by which boys learn to become "masculine" and girls "feminine"? Exploring the
process of growing up male and female,
the authors reveal how facets of society
and biology influence the sex role each
individual acquires.

*Among the many topics this book explores
are:*

- what the differences *really* are between
  boys and girls at different ages

- how parents influence the sex-role development of their children

- what impact television, school, and
  peers have on a child's sex-role identity

- how children themselves view sex roles
  and what they think it means to be
  "masculine" or "feminine."

Highlighting this thorough and eye-open-
ing book with photographs, illustrations,
research findings, and personal anecdotes,
the authors give you information that can
help you raise and teach children in a way
that frees them from the constraints of
sex roles and encourages them to develop
as individuals.

HE & SHE

How Children Develop Their Sex-Role Identity

Jeanne Brooks-Gunn and Wendy Schempp Matthews

Prentice-Hall, Inc.   A SPECTRUM BOOK   *Englewood Cliffs, N.J. 07632*

Library of Congress Cataloging in Publication Data
BROOKS-GUNN, JEANNE.
    He & She.

    (A Spectrum Book)
    Bibliography:-p.
    Includes index.
    1.-Sex role.   2.-Child development.   I.-Matthews,
Wendy Schempp, joint author.   II.-Title.
HQ1075.B76   301.41   79-13187
ISBN   0-13-384388-2
ISBN   0-13-384370-X pbk.

Editorial/production supervision and interior design
    by Claudia Citarella and Donald Chanfrau
Cover and interior photographs
    by Ellen Eibel and Rosalie Mahaffey
Cover design
    by Muriel Nasser-Bernstein
Manufacturing buyer: Cathie Lenard

© 1979 by Prentice-Hall, Inc., *Englewood Cliffs, N.J. 07632*

A Spectrum Book

Printed in the United States of America

10   9   8   7   6   5   4   3   2   1

PRENTICE-HALL INTERNATIONAL, INC., *London*
PRENTICE-HALL OF AUSTRALIA PTY. LIMITED, *Sydney*
PRENTICE-HALL OF CANADA, LTD., *Toronto*
PRENTICE-HALL OF INDIA PRIVATE LIMITED, *New Delhi*
PRENTICE-HALL OF JAPAN, INC., *Tokyo*
PRENTICE-HALL OF SOUTHEAST ASIA PTE. LTD., *Singapore*
WHITEHALL BOOKS LIMITED, *Wellington, New Zealand*

CONTENTS

WHAT ARE LITTLE BOYS
MADE OF, MADE OF?

What are little boys made of, made of?
What are little boys made of?
    Frogs and snails
    And puppy-dogs' tails,
That's what little boys are made of.

What are little girls made of, made of?
What are little girls made of?
    Sugar and spice
    And all things nice,
That's what little girls are made of.

What are young men made of, made of?
What are young men made of?
    Sighs and leers
    and crocodile tears,
That's what young men are made of.

What are young women made of, made of?
What are young women made of?
    Ribbon and laces
    And sweet pretty faces,
That's what young women are made of.

(English Nursery Rhyme, early 1800's)

PREFACE

A staggering amount of research has been and continues to be conducted by biologists, psychologists, sociologists, anthropologists, and other natural and social scientists on the phenomenon of sex-role development. Be it that the political tides have produced the overwhelming attention given to this area of study, or that the research findings have in some way triggered the political tides, two facts are clear: there is a surge of interest on the part of the professional and layperson alike concerning the processes by which individuals acquire sex role; and there is a wealth of research that can serve interested persons as a resource for gaining the understanding they seek. As research psychologists, we, too, have participated in efforts aimed at acquiring further insight into children's acquisition of sex role as a developmental phenomenon.

Venturing outside our research laboratories to provide consultation services to day care centers, parent cooperatives, and public school systems, we have attempted to share recent findings with others. In doing so, we have been struck by the extent of interest in young children's sex-role development. Teachers, school administrators, guidance counselors, and parents have, in discussions of sex-role development, often lamented their ignorance of the topic. Frequently, consulting sessions would end with a crowd of inquiries by members of the audience or workshop about incidents in their personal experience, with requests for explanations, advice, reassurance, and references so that they might enlighten themselves on the commonplace but crucial phenomenon of sex-role acquisition. The overwhelming concern of so many individuals, as well as the scarcity of sources available to them, motivated us to formulate an account of children's sex-role development directed toward today's parents, educators, nurses, child-care workers, and students of child development.

In reading the book, you will find that we frequently give anecdotal as well as empirical evidence for the existence of sex differences, or differences in the way grown-ups treat boys and girls, or the role of media in sex-role development. We do this not just to liven things up, but to bring the process of sex-role development closer to you than laboratory-derived findings might. We hope that in reading our anecdotes, you will recall instances from your own lives with children and that you will see, as we saw more and more clearly as we wrote, that sex roles and sex-role socialization are pervasive phenomena in our society. Nary a nook, barely a cranny of a child's world is free of some subtle, or not-so-subtle, form of sex typing.

As our developmental account will make obvious, different features of personality or intellect differentiate boys from girls at different ages; different aspects of the child's world predominate in the socialization of those differences at different times; and the children themselves view sex roles differently as they move through different developmental stages. After a look at what sex roles are (Chapter 1), how sex roles operate in the context of our social system (Chapter 2), and after an overview of the biological foundations of sex roles laid in the prenatal and neonatal periods (Chapter 3), we discuss infancy (Chapter 4), the preschool years (Chapter 6), middle childhood (Chapter 7), and adolescence (Chapter 8 and 9), always reviewing the sex differences, the sex-role mediators, and the child's sex-role perceptions characteristic of the developmental period under consideration. Also, we devote some time to a discussion of the major theories of sex-role development (Chapter 5).

Our goal is to present a developmental account of the socialization of sex roles. If, in the process, we provide the reader with an understanding of socialization in general, or if our account proves instructive about how researchers proceed to ask and answer questions about the process of child development, then, as the French say, *tant mieux* (so much the better)!

ACKNOWLEDGMENTS

We would like to congratulate our previewers, Mary Jean Brooks of Family Services Association, Grand Rapids, Michigan, Robert Matthews of Rutgers University, Barbara Richardson of Cornell University, Diane Ruble of Princeton University, Carla Seal of Harvard University and Marsha Weinraub of Temple University, for reading their way through the roughest of our rough drafts, and to thank them most heartily for their comments. We also extend our thanks to the Training Institute for Sex Desegregation of the Public Schools, Rutgers University, for opening the doors of their library and steering the way through an extensive collection; to Karin Frey, for her remarks upon reading the final draft; and, to Michael Lewis, for his encouragement and support.

Especially, we thank Linda Worcel, who performed the arduous and sometimes frustrating task of editing, referencing, and proofreading.

And finally, we thank the many parents and educators who, in asking us what they could read on the subject of sex-role identity, originally inspired us to write this book.

CREDITS

SEX ROLES
What Are They?

chapter one

Once upon a time there was a man, and his wife cooked. One day his wife said, "I'm tired of cooking," so they switched jobs. She went out to his field to pick corn, and he cooked. He cooked some dough, the dough began to rise and rise and rise. It got on the babies. The babies cried so much that the china rattled. It broke. And when she came back it was a big mess. The end.

Miss Jones worked for a building company; she worked very hard but she was careless. Every time she was in charge of a group, she was very strict to them. One day Miss Jones was working on a building. She said to her troopers, "If you don't work, I won't pay you one cent," and she started to work. She wanted to show the other workers how fast she was. So she took a gidder (girder?) and instead of screwing and bolting it in hardly, she just took a screw and stuck it in. When the building was done, she had forgotten she had done this and she decided to live in it. So one day in the middle of summer Miss Jones was having a nap. All of a sudden she felt there was an earthquake. She went downstairs and left the house. When she got out of the house it didn't shake any more. Then all of a sudden she remembered what she had done, and the building collapsed. Well, Miss Jones didn't get hurt but she had learned a lesson. The end.

(Guttentag and Bray, 1976, pp. 277-278)

These two tales, told by a precocious 6-year-old, illustrate how early children discern the scripts society has written for its male and female members. Tracing a child's acquisition of sex role from conception, through birth, infancy, preschool, middle childhood, and adolescence, this book asks the question: What story will a child be writing about his or her life as a function of his or her sex?

We wonder: Is the notion of sex role so confining that children can see only set courses of action for boys and girls, for men and women, and for themselves? Does the notion of sex role become increasingly confining with age? Can children do what the teller of the next tale did, namely, break loose from the confines of sex role and envision other possibilities? (The implication that the heroine was successful only because she could not attract a man betrays this child's still sex-typed views about women and work.)

Once there was a lady. She couldn't find anyone to marry so she just had to work alone. She couldn't work at a woman's job to be a secretary and things like that 'cause she just didn't want to. She decided to become a mechanic. She did very well at the job and became president of that working firm and lived happily ever after.

(Guttentag and Bray, 1976, p. viii)

SEX ROLE DEFINED

Just what is a sex role? Jeanne Block defines it as "a constellation of qualities an individual understands to characterize males and females in his [or her] culture" (1973, p. 512). The child whose tales began this chapter understood corn-picking and cooking as activities which characterize males and females respectively. Included in the constellation of qualities are not just activities but personality features, role relations, social position, and a host of abilities and behaviors—all thought to differentiate the sexes (Angrist, 1969). Some of the qualities are indisputable: women have childbearing capacities, men do not. But other qualities presumably differentiating the sexes are the subject of continued debate and wonder. Seeking to settle the issue of which sex is the better, 8-year-old Sylvia went straight to the top and asked:

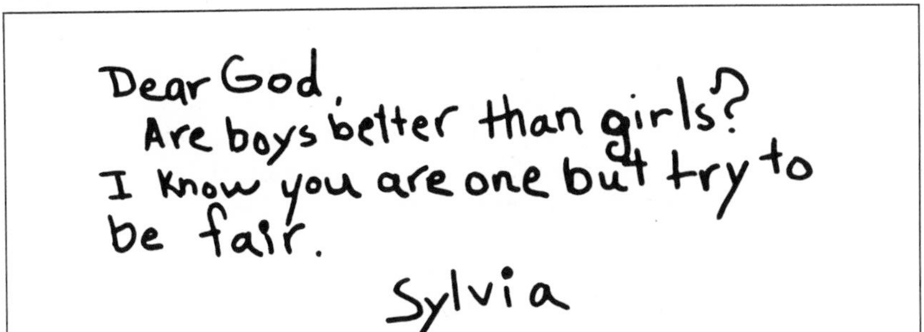

Dear God,
Are boys better than girls?
I know you are one but try to be fair.

Sylvia

Figure 1-1. (Reprinted from Children's Letters to God, *Eric Marshall and Stuart Hample. Copyright © 1966 by Eric Marshall and Stuart Hample. Reprinted by permission of Simon & Schuster, a Division of Gulf & Western Corporation and the Sterling Lord Agency, Inc.)*

This book was written for people like Sylvia who still wonder who is better in math and in reading, who is more creative, aggressive, dependent, competitive, and affectionate. We do not purport to act as Sylvia's higher source. All we can do is share with the reader the answers that a number of fields, but particularly developmental psychology, have been able to come up with after extensive investigation and research. In each developmental period—neonatal, infancy, preschool, middle childhood, and adolescence—we review the evidence for and against sex differences that are thought to characterize that age span. When all the results are in, we can look again at the definition of sex role and ask whether all or any of the qualities people in our culture understand to characterize males and females actually do.

Once we separate the substantiated sex differences from the unsubstantiated ones (i.e., the ones that prove not to be differences at all), we can further ask how sex role differences came about. Are biological or social forces to account for them? If biological, exactly what takes place? If social, what contributions do culture, parental socialization practices, and social attitudes make to sex-role differentiation? If *both* biological and social forces are at work, how can we describe the interaction leading from a simple *sex* differentiation (like men having beards and women not) to *sex-role* differentiation (like men working outside the home and women inside)? Taking an historical perspective on sex-role differentiation, social scientists have considered the idea that the biological or physical differences between the sexes lay at the base of sex role, propelling men and women into different social roles (D'Andrade, 1966). Men, on the average stronger than women, assumed whatever roles required strength, such as hunting large game; women, being uniquely equipped for bearing and nursing children, assumed whatever roles enabled them to stay close to home.

Whatever the bonds that tied men to some roles and women to others, they exist no more. Individuals no longer have to rely on muscle power to bring in the bacon nor on breasts to nurture the baby. Indeed, men never did bring home all the bacon. Hunting, for which the male's superior strength was well-suited, was never the main food source for early people; women, who gathered berries, dug roots, or planted gardens, provided at least half of the food supply. Except for actual childbearing, contemporary adult roles are virtually interchangeable among the sexes (although it is and always will be the case that some individuals are better suited to some tasks than others).

Any biological basis of sex-role differentiation is not only inadequate justification for current sex roles, but is apparently insufficient justification for past sex roles as well. For example, anthropologist Margaret Mead, in her study of New Guinea societies (1935), found a very distinct division of labor on the basis of sex, but strength had little to do with it. Specifically, she found men working in the fields planting yams and women working in the fields planting sweet potatoes. While the distinction between yams and sweet potatoes might elude *us,* it is critical to the natives of New Guinea. Yams, for them, are highly valued and serve ceremonial functions in their culture. Sweet potatoes, however, are just ordinary, everyday fare. Their sex-typed division of labor, it seems, is based more on social than physical or biological factors. As in many cultures, the male activity is more valued and accorded higher status, even when the male and female activities differ not one bit!

We shall see more of this later, but the point here is this: a masculine sex role represents the constellation of qualities an individual understands to characterize males in his or her culture, and a feminine sex role represents the constellation understood to characterize females in the culture. Physical attributes account for only a small portion of the constellation while social or culturally determined attributes account for a great deal.

Besides the biological and cultural factors involved in sex-role acquisition, there are the psychological factors. While we attempt to provide a global account of sex-role acquisition, as psychologists we naturally gravitate toward and give our central attention to the psychological factors. At each developmental period, we discuss (1) the psychological sex differences, summoning anecdotal and empirical evidence to support or refute them, (2) mediators of sex role, that is, contributors to the socialization of sex role such as parents, school, television, books, and peers, and (3) the child's changing perceptions of sex roles. Because children are active agents in their own sex-role development, we try to see things from their perspective and to surmise how their perceptions will affect their acquisition of sex-typed behaviors. For example, put yourself in a baby's place:

> Early one midsummer's night, Daddy Sam settled upon the plush gold carpet in the nursery to play with Baby while the evening bath was being prepared. Reaching for Baby's teddy bear, he slowly and rhythmically bounced it towards Baby, softly saying, "Here comes Teddy! Teddy's coming to see you! Look, look at Teddy. He's coming to play with Baby." Giggling in delight, Baby opens her arms to hug the oncoming teddy bear.

Next door, a different Daddy and different Baby played on the nursery floor. Holding Baby's teddy bear, Daddy John marched the bear resolutely towards Baby in a series of quick, controlled movements, mockgrowling, "Here comes Teddy! Teddy's coming to *get* you! Better get Teddy, before *he* gets *you!*" Screeching at the challenge, Baby reaches out and tumbles upon his now captive teddy.

What is a baby to do? In the first case, it would look to Baby as if the teddy bear were "coming to call" and all *she* (for you have probably surmised that the baby in the first example is a girl) has to do is wait for Teddy to approach and to welcome it to her loving, trusting arms. It does not take long for the second baby, by contrast, to realize that he had better act and attack Teddy before Teddy attacks him. The message the parent gives the girl is that she will gain the teddy bear by just "being" her smiling self; the message the parent gives the boy is that he will gain the teddy by his actions, that is, by "doing" what needs to be done. This distinction between little girls "being" and little boys "doing" is part of feminine and masculine sex-role differentiation, an aspect to which we shall return in later chapters. Through interactions such as those described above, sometimes subtle, sometimes blatant, occurring at all times and in all places in the children's world, from their first day to their first decade and beyond, children pick up the cues and use them to understand their society's sex roles in general and their own sex-role identity in particular.

SEX-ROLE IDENTITY

An individual's gender, body image, self-esteem, self-concept, skills, weaknesses, and sex role combine to provide him or her with an identity, a sense of the self as unique and separate from others. An individual's sex-role identity is but one aspect of his or her total self-identity. The sex roles of the culture to which a child belongs form a basis for his or her own developing sex-role identity, as do the socialization practices to which he or she is exposed and the personal beliefs and attitudes he or she has acquired along the way.

Sex-role identity is not the same as gender identity. Gender identity refers to an individual's biological sex or sex of rearing. One is born male or female, or, as we shall see in cases where one's sex is unclear, one is labeled male or female by a medical staff and reared accordingly. As early as 2 years of age, children know their gender identity. They are either a boy or a girl, and they are not likely to forget it, ever! Gender identity and sex-role identity differ from each other in the same way that "male" differs from "masculine," or "female" from "feminine." One set of terms, "male" and "female," refers to an individual's sex; the other set, "masculine" and "feminine," refers to an individual's sex role. A boy, having a male gender identity, does not necessarily have a masculine sex-role identity; he can be either "masculine," "feminine," or "androgynous" (i.e., a combination of both). A woman, having a female gender identity, does not necessarily have a feminine sex-role identity.

Another type of identity is sexual identity. Sexual identity refers to one's sexual preference. A person may prefer to have sexual relations with men, with women, with both, or with neither. If one prefers an opposite-sex partner, one is a heterosexual. If one prefers a same-sex partner, one is a homosexual. If one has no preference, one is bisexual. And if one would prefer to do without, one is asexual. Sexual identity is usually acquired in late adolescence, when sexual activity begins. Childhood sex play seems to be unrelated to adult sexual preferences. At least one-third of all children engage in sex play, half the time with a same-sex peer, half the time with an opposite-sex peer; it is simply considered part of the growing-up process, an expression of the child's curiosity about the genitals and their function.

Gender identity is unrelated to sexual identity. A male homosexual can be as sure of the fact that he is a male as a male heterosexual is, but knowing that he is a male, i.e., having a male gender identity, does not stop him from preferring male sex partners.

And sex-role identity does not seem to be related to sexual identity either. Women who are masculine are not necessarily lesbians, just as men who are feminine are not necessarily homosexuals. Among homosexual males, some are positively "macho" and epitomize our culture's stereotypic male, some are feminine, and some possess both masculine and feminine traits. Among homosexual females, some are ultra-feminine, others are more masculine or a combination of the two. Just like men and women with heterosexual preferences, men and women with homosexual preferences show the whole range of sex-role behaviors. This point is crucial if we are to encourage the development of the best of our culture's masculine *and* feminine traits in both boys and girls. Encouraging our boys to be sensitive and nurturant will not turn them into homosexuals, although it may make them more sensitive husbands, more caring fathers, and more valued human beings. Encouraging our girls to compete in sports, to achieve in school, and to strive for careers will not turn them into lesbians, although it may make them more independent, strong, and capable. We need not worry that our active, assertive, and inquisitive girls or our sensitive, expressive, and nurturant boys will necessarily become homosexuals. What *would* happen is that our children, both boys and girls, would develop to their fullest potential as individuals, whether that involves masculine or feminine traits.

Convincing parents and educators of this is sometimes not easy, as, in our society, we have associated being a masculine male with being heterosexual, a feminine male with being homosexual. In fact, when one woman wrote to a newspaper columnist saying that her 6-year-old son was playing with the doll she bought for her daughter and her 7-year-old daughter was playing with the truck bought for the son, the columnist responded forcefully, advising the woman to hurry them off to a psychologist if she failed to convince the children to switch toys. The woman would have wasted thirty-five dollars, as there is no relation between early sex-role behaviors and adult sexual identity.

PERSONAL PERSPECTIVE

With regard to our personal perspective on the subject of sex roles (sometimes known as "authors' bias"), our position is quite simple. First, we see as a goal of sex-role socialization that children grow up to be happy with themselves and their own gender identity. Second, we believe that the wide range of potential options available to one should be available to all and should not be denied to a child on the basis of what sex he or she happens to have been born. Third, it is our contention that equal treatment will enhance rather than hinder human diversity by providing opportunities for individuals to explore options on the basis of their own unique characteristics and abilities, rather than on the constellation of characteristics or abilities they are believed on the basis of their sex to share with every other member of the same sex. Fourth, we need to address some nagging questions which still remain: Is society's view of "appropriate" sex-role behavior truly appropriate? Has it kept pace with the demands being made upon individuals in these modern times? For example, if it is true (and it is) that 90 percent of the female population will be employed at least part of their adult lives, and at least 50 percent will be employed at the same time that they are rearing their children, does it make sense to perpetuate the belief that housewifery and motherhood are the only occupations of women? Is the channelization process that goes on adequately preparing our children for the world in which they will eventually have to cope and survive? Or is it molding them into obsolescence, ill-preparing them for the roles they will one day be called upon to assume?

The development of sex roles is a fascinating, fearsome process. But sensitizing ourselves to it, understanding how it operates in our daily lives, can spur us into seeing how profound the implications are for the child-become-adult in surviving in his or her world. And this realization in turn can make us want to do something about it.

SEX ROLES IN CONTEXT

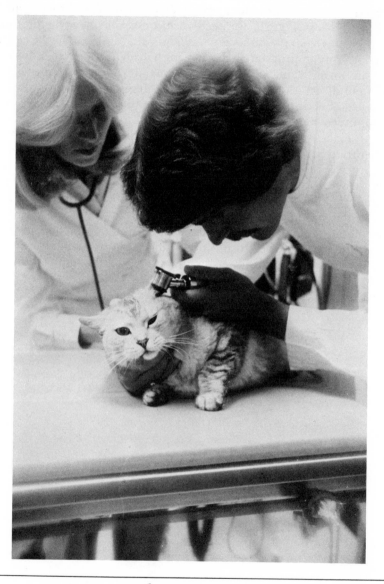

chapter two

A. "She's Acting Just Like a Woman."

She ranted and raved. She complained, pleaded, and threatened divorce. "You'd think I treated you like a dog," the husband remarked.

"No!" she screamed. "A dog *has* a fur coat."

(Reader's Digest, March 1978, p. 134)

B. "Santa and the Plastic Steam Shovel."

When the girl in the green knitted dress's turn came, she walked up to Santa and climbed on his lap. His eyes sparkled and his voice bellowed: "Ho, ho! What a pretty little girl. What would you like Santa to bring you for Christmas?" "A Fisher-Price durable plastic steam shovel with adjustable parts," she replied. "Now what would a pretty little girl like you do with a steam shovel?" Santa asked politely. She looked at him puzzled. "Have you seen the new Chatty Cathy doll? Wouldn't you like one of them?" he inquired. "Well, sure, I guess so." "Good girl. Be very good and Santa will bring you one for Christmas." Slipping off his lap, she scurried to her mother and together they disappeared into the crowd of holiday shoppers.

C. "So You Believe You're a Cowgirl?"

So they let you dress up like a cowgirl, and when you say, "I'm gonna be a cowgirl when I grow up," they laugh and say, "Ain't she cute." Then one day they tell you, "Look, honey, cowgirls are only play. You can't *really* be one." And that's when I holler, "Wait a minute! Hold on! Santa and the Easter Bunny, I understand; they were nice Joes and I don't blame you for them. But now you're screwing around with my personal identity, with my plans for the future. What do you mean I can't be a cowgirl?" When I got the answer, I began to realize there was a lot bigger difference between me and my brother than what I could see in the bathtub.

(Even Cowgirls get the Blues, Robbins, 1976, pp. 129-130)

D. "It Seems She Was Guilty of Being Raped."

Judge Archie Simonson provoked an uproar in Madison [Wisconsin] last May [1977] with his off-the-cuff remarks during a juvenile court hearing when he suggested that a 15-year-old high school youth who raped a 16-year-old girl should not be punished too severely for merely "reacting normally" to Madison's sexually permissive climate and to the seductiveness of women's clothing. Judge Simonson, a 52-year-old former university fencing coach, sentenced the boy to one year in parental custody under court supervision.

The young man's "normal reaction" occurred in a public high-school stairwell last November. The school band, practicing nearby, drowned out the victim's cries for help as her assailant tore her clothing off. Was she scantily and provocatively clad? Hardly. The girl was in fact wearing a turtleneck sweater with a shirt over it, blue jeans and tennis shoes.

The more the judge tried to clarify his remarks, the more incensed some Madisonites became. "I've struck a raw nerve," he acknowledged. "But women are sex objects. . . . I'm trying to say to women, 'Stop teasing.' There should be a restoration of modesty in dress."

(The Christian Century, October 1977, pp. 868–869)

E. "Rich Man, Poor Man, Beggarman, Thief?"

That girls learn very early the societal expectation for them was perhaps captured most poignantly by the expression of that single girl [in a study of six-to-eight-year-old boys' and girls' vocational aspirations] who initially said she wished to be a doctor when she grew up; when asked what occupation she *really* expected to hold in adulthood, she resignedly replied, "I'll probably have to be something else, maybe a store lady."

(Looft, 1971, p. 366)

Sex role is like a corpse sprawled across the floor of the Orient Express. A cast of heavily implicated characters surrounds it, and the question that looms over the investigator's head is "Who dunnit?"

Using a model developed by Jacquelynne Parsons, Irene Frieze, and Diane Ruble (1976) and presented in Figure 2-1, we can identify some of the prime suspects in the development and maintenance of sex role. Let us look at each of the suspects in the five examples with which we introduced this chapter.

A. Cultural norms, or the ideas, the beliefs, and expectations people in a particular time and place hold. The first example, "She's Acting Just Like a Woman," illustrates how our cultural norms stereotype an individual's behavior. Finding the joke funny would confirm that most of

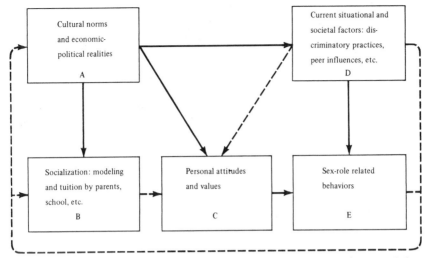

Figure 2-1. Development and expression of sex-role related behavior. (Reprinted from Jacquelynne E. Parsons, Irene H. Frieze, and Diane N. Ruble, "Introduction," The Journal of Social Issues, 32, no. 3 (1976), 2. Used by courtesy of the publisher.)

us, at this time and in this culture, share a strong enough belief in the notion of feminine wiles, willfulness, and vanity to respond to its humor.

B. Socialization, or the direct example and teaching of the child by parents, teachers, and friends and the indirect example of school and media sources which lead the child to adapt the sex role of his or her cultural group. The second example above shows how a socialization agent might provide cues of varying degrees of subtlety to a child, the effect of which is to edge the child a bit closer to a "masculine" or "feminine" sex role.

C. Personal attitudes, beliefs, values, and expectations. The third example, "So You Believe You're a Cowgirl," reveals the protagonist's confusion in *Even Cowgirls Get The Blues* when her personal beliefs and wishes run counter to cultural norms; she believes herself to be a cowgirl, although people laugh, telling her that cowgirls are okay for play, not for real.

D. Current situational factors and societal practices, involving the use of cultural norms, existing laws and institutions, available opportunities, peer influences, and so on. The fourth example, "It Seems She Was Guilty of Being Raped," illustrates how a reactionary and prejudicial judge condoned a young rapist's behavior as an understandable response to a widespread violation of the "modesty" element in the feminine sex-role stereotype, even though the individual girl in the case was clearly not immodestly dressed. The judge's ruling exemplifies the power of the law to perpetuate sex-role stereotypes and to discriminate against individuals on the basis of prejudices.

E. All four forces—cultural norms, socialization, personal beliefs and attitudes, and situational and societal practices—conspire to develop and maintain sex roles (E in Figure 2-1). Sex roles, as we saw in Chapter 1, include activities, personality characteristics, role relations, social positions, abilities, and behaviors—all thought to differentiate the sexes. Our example, "Rich Man, Poor Man, Beggarman, Thief?" illustrates just one tiny aspect of sex roles—early sex differences in vocational aspirations, which ultimately translate into occupational differences.

Having separately introduced the cast of characters, we can now look to the arrows in Figure 2-1 to see how they interact with one another. Cultural norms (A), for example, have a widespread influence, bearing on socialization practices (B), so that parents and teachers, having incorporated the cultural norm into their personal belief system, convey these norms and beliefs, through actions and words, to their children. Norms bear on personal attitudes (C), too, so that individuals believe that men and women are different and believe that they do or do not possess certain sex-related traits. Cultural norms also bear on situational factors and societal practices (D), so that equal opportunities regardless of sex do not exist in most societies. Cultural norms are in turn reinforced by the attitudes (C) and behavior (B, E) of individuals within the culture. Through socialization (B), the message provided by the culture (A) is incorporated into one's personal belief system (C), which in turn affects how an individual thinks, acts, and feels (E). How an individual acts (E) is further affected by situational factors and societal practices (D) as well as the other three forces.

The plot thickens. Realizing how circular the system is, how enmeshed one element is with all the others, we come to the same conclusion that Inspector Poirot did in Agatha Christie's *Murder on the Orient Express* (1940), namely, "They all dunnit!" Poirot, in describing a murder in which twelve passengers on the Orient Express plotted to murder a man who had adversely affected each of their lives related that he saw the murder plot as a jigsaw puzzle and each of the suspects as a piece of it. Their motives and their alibis were such that if one of them was either singled out as the culprit or scratched from the list of suspects, the remaining pieces would no longer fit together to provide a plausible account of the treacherous act.

Poirot's description of the case may very well be applied to the maintenance of sex roles. Since everything fits together, it is difficult to know where to lay the blame or how to effect change. Consider the case of Amanda, who is trying to break out of the mosaic. Amanda, aged 26, is the mother of two children aged 2 and 5, wife of John, aged 28. After being out of the labor force for six years, Amanda decided that she would like to go back to work. Her mother was appalled at the idea and informed Amanda that a mother should under no circumstances work while her children were young. Her husband John encouraged her to do whatever she wanted—as long as her plans did not interfere with his career: he expected the house to stay clean, the children to be duly delivered to a care-giver and tended to while at home, and dinner to be on the table each evening at six o'clock. Amanda's own worries revolved around her ability to succeed in the work place; since she had not worked or been in school for years, she had little confidence in herself. Nevertheless, she set out to the world of work—and she discovered that she was not a prime job candidate. She had been in the work force only three years before her first child was born and was therefore considered inexperienced. Having spent the past six years at home, she was unfamiliar with advances in her field. In addition, she found a shortage of quality day care for her children and discovered how expensive housekeepers could be. In the face of societal, familial, and personal opposition, Amanda abandoned her work plans, at least temporarily.

Ironically, her decision helped perpetuate the sex roles she wished to escape. Her 5-year-old observed a family, like many others in the neighborhood, comprised of a father who works outside the home and a mother who does not. Regardless of Amanda's beliefs, her sex-typed behavior provided the 5-year-old with much information about sex roles. In addition, Amanda became classified, in terms of labor force statistics, as a housewife, not an unemployed member of the work force, further affecting societal practices. Finally, Amanda was perceived as a contented homemaker, an exemplar of the existing cultural beliefs. As a female and, according to sex roles, a "feminine" being, Amanda found herself constrained in particular ways by all the elements in the model. As a male, and therefore a "masculine" being, her husband John would suffer too, though from a set of constraints different from hers. His preoccupation with his career grew not out of the attractiveness of his job but out of a realization of the responsibility society had placed on his shoulders.

While all the elements play a role in the development and maintenance of sex roles, the role of socialization dominates our account of sex-role acquisition, given our interest in the growth of the child's sex role, and it serves as the focus of most of the chapters to follow. For now, however, we would like to touch briefly on the other factors that influence the development of sex-role identity in order to place socialization in its proper context, specifically as an outgrowth of the larger culture, a by-product of situational and societal practices, and the outcome of the behavior and attitudes of those who are responsible for the child's socialization.

THE CULTURE CAST: SEX-ROLE STEREOTYPES

Originally, stereotypes were a boon to humankind, revolutionizing the printing industry by enabling one solid metal plate to print copy over and over again. Now, stereotypes just seem to get in the way. For no longer do they refer to "set type" in the printing sense; instead they serve to "type set" in the psychological sense, placing individuals in groups according to traits which they might not possess.

The current use of the term "stereotype" refers to a culturally determined and relatively inflexible manner of viewing individuals such that one perceives them as if they had been "cast from a mold," as if they shared traits with members of a group to which they belong simply because they are members. Walter Lippman cleverly termed stereotypes "pictures in our heads," to stress the fact that there is no rational basis for stereotypes, they are all in our mind. Gordon Allport, in his definitive work on stereotyping and prejudice, *The Nature of Prejudice* (1954), defined a stereotype as "an exaggerated belief associated with a category. Its function is to justify (rationalize) our conduct in relation to that category." (p. 187) Note that stereotype is not a category, it is a belief associated with a category: the category "black" may be neutral; only when blacks are believed to be lazy or superstitious does a stereotype exist. A stereotype is also not a generalization: a generalization is based on a certain definable *probability* that an individual will be a certain way, rather than an exaggerated belief. Stereotypes are tenacious: they can be held in defiance of all evidence as well as in the face of contradictory evidence. Let's look at an example given by Allport p. 185.

> In Fresno County, California, at one time the prevailing stereotype of Armenians held them to be "dishonest, lying, deceitful." La Pierre made a study to determine whether there was objective evidence to justify this belief. He found that the records of the Merchant's Association gave Armenians as good credit ratings as those received by the other groups. Moreover, Armenians applied less often for charity and appeared less frequently in legal cases.

> *(La Pierre, 1936, p. 234).*

Stereotypes may even interfere with rational, logical reasoning. Again, let us turn to Allport p. 186, who reports a study in which children were given the following test item.

> Aladdin was the son of a poor tailor. He lived in Peking, the capital city of China. He was always idle and lazy and liked to play better than to work. What kind of a boy was he: Indian; Negro; Chinese; French; or Dutch?

> *(Lasker, 1929, p. 237).*

Most of the children ignored the obvious cue—that Aladdin lived in China—and answered "Negro." The "picture in their minds" of Negroes as lazy resulted in their not reading the story objectively and even disregarding the available information!

By employing a stereotype, the perceiver tends to discount the perceived one's *individuality;* this tendency in turn paves the way for discrimination and prejudice. To perpetuate a stereotype is, as we shall see, to perpetuate a tale that recounts how little boys are independent and adventuresome, and little girls submissive and shy. Our purpose in this section is to provide an overview of the stereotypical aspects of our society's sex roles.

The Snare of the Sex-Role Stereotype

All of us have heard countless times the common, everyday nursery rhyme by which this book was introduced. All of us know its meaning: that boys and girls are different and will remain as different from one another in adulthood as they are in childhood. But the unique features being attributed to young boys and men versus those being attributed to young girls and women in the poem extend very much beyond the biologically given sex differences of anatomy and gender, encompassing personality traits as well. Sugar and spice connote sweetness, fragrance, and pleasure giving; frogs and snails and puppy dog tails connote a combination of lively leaping, activity, and insolent youthfulness. The poem is simple in its artlessness. Yet it manages to convey quite powerfully our society's sex-role stereotype as it was then. And now? Does the poem continue to reflect current sex-role stereotypes?

Since the early 1800's, little girls and boys, snuggled in their beds for the night, have listened to parents read, "What are little boys made of? . . ." Its endurance attests to the fact that at least some of the stereotypes upon which the poem was based still exist. From the time it was written to the present, women have tried to get beyond the sugar and spice into what was *really* nice: admission to higher education, which had been closed to them until the 1830's (on the grounds that women lacked the intellectual capacity to pursue knowledge seriously); eligibility for loans and home mortgages, which until the 1970's they had not been entitled to without the consent of a husband or father (on the grounds that they were poor money managers and unstable wage earners); jobs in construction and industry, from which they had been excluded until the 1970's (on the grounds that they were too delicate); the vote, which had been denied them until 1920 (on the grounds that they were too irrational); and equal pay for equal work (an ongoing struggle). And men have tried to get beyond the "sneers and leers" and relax in forthright relationships with others, admitting that sometimes their tears aren't just "crocodile." These examples represent efforts of women and men to alter the artificial limitations that sex-role stereotyping and societal discrimination impose upon them. Many of the struggles continue.

Current Sex-Role Stereotypes

"Well," you might be saying, "the belief that men and women are really quite different was much more prevalent earlier this century than today." How are men and women perceived *today?* Surprisingly, the stereotypes have not changed much since the early 1800's when the poem "What are little boys made of?" first appeared. As psychologists, we are interested in how men and women might be stereotyped in terms of temperament, personality traits, abilities, and aspirations. For simplicity's sake, we shall focus on personality characteristics that are frequently thought to differentiate the sexes. We commonly describe ourselves and others in terms of personality traits (e.g., "I'm pretty brazen when I want to be"; "Isn't he the rudest person you ever met?"). Many (but not all) of these traits are thought to be sex-linked; that is, some are thought to be more prevalent in men, some in women. Those we associate with the male sex role are labeled masculine; those we associate with the female sex role are labeled feminine. The designation of a trait as masculine or feminine is typically agreed upon by a large segment of the society. To give you a concrete illustration of the consensus with which certain traits are linked to either the adult male or female sex role, we invite the reader to "picture" a male and female. With this image in mind, rate as either masculine or feminine the following twelve traits:

- Self-reliant
- Yielding
- Athletic
- Affectionate
- Assertive
- Flatterable
- Tender
- Dominant
- Childlike
- Aggressive

□ Sympathetic

□ Analytical

You probably found the task quite easy. Most adults will rate self-reliant, athletic, assertive, dominant, aggressive, and analytical as masculine; yielding, affectionate, flatterable, tender, childlike, and sympathetic as feminine. These particular traits were taken from a Sex-Role Inventory developed in 1974 by Sandra Bem. She had asked college students to rate 200 personality traits according to whether they were masculine, feminine, or neutral. Only those traits for which there had been a high consensus among raters were included in her Inventory, comprised of 20 masculine traits, 20 feminine traits, and 20 non-sex-typed traits.

What do psychologists learn from studies such as this? First, we learn that many personality traits are considered neither masculine *nor* feminine. Of the 200 traits sampled in the Bem study, the majority of raters considered only 40 traits to be sex-typed. Most were viewed as neutral with respect to sex roles. (Examples of neutral traits are truthfulness, theatricality, friendliness, and adaptivity.) Second, for those traits labeled masculine or feminine, there is a great deal of agreement among raters, suggesting that the sex-role expectations reflected in the sex-typed traits are fairly consistent within a society. Third, not only does there appear to be congruence within our society at this time, there seems too to be a consistency across time periods. The first studies of masculine and feminine personality traits were conducted in the 1930's. Their findings about masculine and feminine personality traits correspond quite closely to those being reported in the 1970's. So it looks as if sex-role stereotypes have not changed appreciably in the last 30 to 40 years!

Finally, most of the traits that have been classified as masculine or feminine seem to express a complementarity in male-female role relations ("he" is dominant; "she" is submissive; "he" is self-reliant; "she" is childlike and tender). The masculine domain is often characterized as *instrumental* in orientation, representative of competence, and oriented toward the self. The feminine domain is often characterized as *expressive* and oriented toward relationships with others (Carlson, 1972). Because society needs both instrumental and expressive characteristics, the complementarity of the two domains has been considered essential; and to assure the perpetuation of the complementarity, society has conveniently apportioned each of the two societal roles on the basis of sex. The man was given charge of the instrumental domain: he was to be independent, analytic, and the breadwinner. The woman was to take care of the expressive domain: she was to be nurturing, dependent, and the homemaker. Few questioned the need that these domains be kept separate nor the rationale behind their assignment by sex alone. Yet, as we have seen, stereotypes are not a true reflection of the world. Not all (and probably few) individuals possess the traits that the stereotype dictates. Armenians are not necessarily "dishonest, lying, deceitful," just as men are not necessarily brave, aggressive, and independent. As everyone knows, not *all* women conform to their sex-role stereotype by being yielding and understanding. We all know men who defy sex-role stereotypes by possessing a minimum of leadership skills, being incapable of throwing a curve ball 25 feet, and unabashedly loving the closeness of a child curled up on his lap for a bedtime story. We all know women whose assertiveness and independence collide with the stereotype of what a woman should be.

Yet, stereotypes still persist, in the face of all of the contradictory evidence, just as Allport showed in 1954. Even though individuals are not cast from the same mold, the existence of stereotypes affects the way others perceive them. Amanda, whom we met earlier, was affected by sex-role stereotypes, as others believed that she could not enter the marketplace: she was a wife and mother, nurturing but not assertive, affectionate but not competent. And sex-role stereotypes, as we shall see shortly, also influence societal practices and discrimination (B in Figure 2-1), individual beliefs (C in Figure 2-1), and ultimately, sex-related behavior itself (E in Figure 2-1).

Reasons We Stereotype

You might wonder why we persist so steadfastly in using stereotypes every day of every week of every year. One answer is that stereotypes seem to be functional even though, as we have seen, they are not. We have seen that a stereotype is an exaggerated belief, a "picture in our head." Since a person is considered to possess certain traits or habits or a certain life style or anything else simply by virtue of membership in a particular group (in this case the "male" group or the "female" group), we as perceivers need to know no more than the individual's sex. Life becomes so simple. No need to bother about the uniqueness of the individual, his or her family background, hobbies, diplomas and degrees, allergies, traumatic experiences, choice of mate, decorating preferences, favorite recipes or restaurants, pet peeves, occupation, or skills. Because we know such things about our friends and relations, it is easy to view *them* as not being defined by the stereotypes, that is, as "exceptions to the rule," while everyone else in the world may be fitted neatly and conveniently into an appropriate stereotype.

Let's ask once again then: Why do we stereotype others? First, stereotypes allow us to act toward others on the basis of minimal knowledge (group membership is all we need to know). Expect an individual to act in a certain way and, sure enough, that is what you will see (even if the truth is distorted). Then one can lie back, breathe a sigh of relief, and exclaim, "See, just as I expected, a woman [or man] 'll do it every time!" A second reason we stereotype others is to fit the unfamiliar into a known framework (never having had a "lady boss" before, we might find that the easiest path toward reaching an understanding of the unfamiliar role relation is to stereotype and deal with her accordingly). People have a need to organize and make sense of their world; if there is too much information, too little predictability, or too many unknowns, chaos reigns. Therefore, we make inferences with relative assurance in the absence of or in defiance of actual information by retreating to the use of stereotypes.

Yet another reason we stereotype is that there *may* be, or may have been, an element of truth to the stereotypes. As a result of the self-fulfilling prophecy, males and females might actually conform to the stereotypes just enough to perpetuate it by making it look true! Appropriately enough, psychologists have called this the "kernel of truth" phenomenon. And the vicious circle spins on: the stereotypes affect the behavior, and the behavior confirms the stereotypes.

A fourth reason that we continue to use stereotypes is that we ignore disconfirmatory evidence. Even with plenty of evidence around that an individual is more than just a caricature or that members of a group are more than walking and talking stereotypes of what a member of that group should be, people have a way of selectively attending to information on the environment, giving more attention to confirmatory evidence and skipping over or dismissing disconfirmatory evidence. So, if a commuter doesn't believe the trains ever arrive on time, he or she will note each and every delay and attribute any prompt arrivals as flukes.

Finally, even if we do manage to notice traits beyond the sex-role stereotype, like Mr. X's reknowned soufflés or Ms. T's political genius, we can tamper with the stereotypes in such a way that all conflict is resolved. We simply say, "Oh, he's secure enough in his masculinity (or she is secure enough in her femininity) that he (or she) doesn't have to worry about adhering to the stereotype."

Stereotypes and Perceptions of Others

Let's look at how sex-role stereotypes affect perceptions of others. One effect has to do with feminine traits being viewed as socially undesirable. When people are asked to rate traits according to their social desirability, the feminine traits are almost invariably rated as less desirable then the masculine traits. In the Bem Sex-Role Inventory, among the feminine traits are gullible, childlike, and shy. In other inventories, sneaky, conceited about appearance, cries easily, and has difficulty making decisions, all undesirable traits, are accorded to women. The sex-role inventories include far fewer undesirable masculine traits, sloppy, loud, and rough being the most common. The fact is that feminine traits come to be viewed generally as less socially desirable than masculine traits. The use of undesirable traits to define a group (any group!) leads to that group's being thought of as generally undesirable, and vice versa.

A related finding has to do with the perception of women as emotionally immature and socially incompetent. In a study by Inge Broverman, Donald Broverman, Frank Clarkson, Paul Rosenkrantz, and Susan Vogel (1970), mental health workers (psychiatrists, psychologists, social workers), who we would hope treat their clients and patients according to their individual needs, were asked to describe a mentally healthy, socially competent female, a mentally healthy male, and a mentally healthy adult (sex unspecified). The descriptions of each revealed that, instead of applying a single standard of mental health to both males and females, these mental health practitioners rated males and females very differently. Males were rated higher on emotional maturity and social competence, while the mentally healthy women were characterized as less independent, more submissive, more emotional, more conceited about their appearance, and so on. Do dependence, submissiveness, emotionality, and conceit describe a mentally healthy person? Most of us would think not. When the raters described the mentally healthy person (sex unspecified), the description that they gave was just like the one given for males, and very different from that given for females. Their responses suggest that women are seen as less healthy by adult standards than are men! One can only speculate on how these different perceptions affect the practitioner's treatment, but it is troublesome to consider that immature and incompetent women may be given a stamp of approval.

Similar perceptions of mental health are held by others not in the mental health field. Jeanne Brooks-Gunn and Melanie Fisch (1979) asked college students to describe a mentally healthy woman, man, or adult (sex unspecified), and found that college students too rate the man and adult similarly and, the woman differently, with more of the undesirable feminine traits ascribed to the woman. College men's and women's descriptions, however, differed somewhat. College women perceived the mentally healthy woman as androgynous, possessing desirable masculine and feminine traits. The college men, on the other hand, described the mentally healthy woman as immature and incompetent, just as the mental health practitioners did. This study, conducted in the mid-1970's, suggests that negative perception of females is slowly changing, at least in women's eyes. We can hope that a similar change will soon be evident in men's perceptions of women.

A well-known study by Philip Goldberg (1968) illustrates that sex-role stereotypes affect our perceptions of academic competence as well. Goldberg asked women students to rate the quality of various scholarly articles. Each student had received the *same* articles; but Goldberg had manipulated the experiment so that some of the students thought the articles were by a female author (e.g., Joan T. McKay), while others thought the identical articles were by a male author (e.g., John T. McKay). He found that those students who thought they had read articles by a woman rated the articles as less well-written and less informative than did the students who thought they had read articles by a man. In addition, the students judged the author as less knowledgeable when a woman's name had been given than when a man's name appeared on the *same* article. This was true not only when the subject matter involved traditionally masculine fields (law and city planning), but when it involved traditionally feminine fields as well (dietetics and education).

Other studies also suggest that women are devalued regardless of their abilities. In 1970, Linda Fidell asked the chairpersons (who were primarily men) of 147 psychology departments throughout the country to rate a number of candidates for a hypothetical faculty position in their department. Identical "candidates" were given male names for some chairpersons, female names for others. Examples of the "candidates" are as follows:

Dr. Eugene (Edith) Wilson, a man (woman) of powerful intellect, received his (her) degree in clinical psychology from the U. C. Berkeley. Although his (her) primary professional interest is in teaching, he and his wife (she and her husband) spend considerable time and effort in recreational sailing and fishing. He (She) has published two papers since he (she) completed his (her) dissertation, neither of which received much acclaim. He (She) does not expend much effort in maintaining affable relations with his (her) colleagues. (p. 1,097)

Dr. Joan (Jonathan) Norton is an experimental psychologist dedicated to her (his) research and to her (his) career. She (He) has published twelve papers, some of major significance, since her (his) graduation from the University of Arizona. She and her husband (He and his wife) are quite friendly and get along well with her (his) colleagues. (p. 1,098)

Fidell's findings show that, like Goldberg's students, the chairpersons rated the female candidates less favorably than the male candidates, offering the women less prestigious jobs.

Still another example of sex-role stereotypes affecting our perceptions is provided by Kay Deaux (1974; Deaux and Emswiller, 1974), who asked men and women to speculate on the success of others in various tasks. When men and women witnessed a man do well on a task, they attributed his success to skill; when they saw a woman do well, they attributed her success to luck. Same performance, different attributions!

Together, the Goldberg, Fidell, and Deaux studies provide us with some powerful evidence of the devaluation of women and of women's work. A final example involves the different adjectives used to describe men and women who exhibit similar behavior. These "conversational clichés" are presented in Figure 2-2. This tendency

Figure 2-2. Conversational clichés. (Reprinted with permission from Colloquy Magazine, 6, *no. 9 (November 1973). Copyright © 1973 by United Church Press.)*

to deprecate females represents a gross injustice to women and is a potent example of the undesirable effects of stereotyping.

Is the negative always associated with the female and the positive with the male? For women, is the grass greener on the other side? In an article by that title, Barbara Polk and Robert Stein (1972) tried to find an answer. They asked male and female students (students again, because they're so handy to ask) to look "on the other side" for a moment and tell what they perceive to be the advantages and disadvantages of their opposite-sex counterparts. Their findings are summarized in Table 2-1. Question: Who has all the rights? Answer: Males. Question: Who has all the proscriptions (i.e., pressures *not* to conform in a certain way)? Answer: Females. Question: Is the grass greener on the other side? Answer: [If female] You bet! [If male] Not very much. Sex-role stereotyping results in many disadvantages for both men and women, although the situation is more disadvantageous for women.

Stereotypes and Expectations of Others

In the play *Pygmalion* by George Bernard Shaw, which was made into the popular musical *My Fair Lady,* Eliza Doolittle, the little flower girl, is transformed into an elegant lady as Henry Higgins's protégée. This tale illustrates the self-fulfilling prophecy often described by psychologists. According to the self-fulfilling prophecy, people, if believed by others to possess a certain characteristic, come to believe it themselves and to act in accordance with the belief. Thus, Eliza Doolittle became beautiful and elegant only after someone convinced her that beauty and elegance were within her grasp.

Robert Rosenthal (1966) demonstrated the self-fulfilling prophecy scientifically, first in studies using rats. College student "experimenters" were told that some of the rats in their learning experiment were "smarter" and therefore could be expected to perform better than other rats in the experiment. All of the rats were littermates, however. Rosenthal had labeled half of them "smart" randomly; so both groups were really equally smart but the students believed that the groups were different. After a time, the rats labeled "smart" did indeed begin to perform better than the other rats on the learning task. The student experimenters, *expecting* them to be smarter, had *treated* them as if they were smarter, encouraging them

TABLE 2-1
Disadvantages and Advantages of Sex Roles
as Perceived by Males and Females

MALE PERCEPTIONS OF MALE SEX ROLE	
Male Disadvantages	Female Advantages
Can't show emotions (P)	Freedom to express emotions (R)
Must be provider (O)	Fewer financial obligations; parents support longer (S)
Pressure to succeed, be competitive (O)	Less pressure to succeed (P)
Alimony and child support (O)	Alimony and insurance benefits (S)
Must take initiative, made decisions (O)	Protected (S)
Limit on acceptable careers (P)	
Expected to be mechanical, fix things (O)	
	More leisure (S)
	Placed on pedestal; object of courtesy (S)

FEMALE PERCEPTIONS OF FEMALE SEX ROLE	
Female Disadvantages	Male Advantages
Job opportunities limited; discrimination; poor pay (P)	Job opportunities greater (S)
Legal and financial discrimination (P)	Financial and legal opportunity (S)
Educational opportunities limited; judged mentally inferior; opinon devalued; intellectual life stifled (P)	Better educational and training opportunities; opinions valued (S)
Single status stigmatized; stigma for divorce and unwed pregnancy (P)	Bachelorhood glamorized (R)
Socially and sexually restricted; double standard (P)	More freedom sexually and socially (R)
Must bear and rear children; no abortions (in many places); responsible for birth control (O)	No babies (S)
Must maintain good outward appearance; dress, makeup (O)	Less fashion demand and emphasis on appearance (R)
Domestic work (O)	No domestic work (R)
Must be patient; give in; subordinate self; be unaggressive; wait to be asked out on dates (P)	Can be aggressive, dating and otherwise (O)
Inhibited motor control; not allowed to be athletic (P)	More escapism allowed (R)

P = Proscription; O = Obligation; R = Right; S = Structural benefit
From Polk and Stein (1972) and J. S. Chafetz (1978).

to do better, reinforcing their successful, task-oriented behaviors and discouraging their meanderings, causing them, in the end, to *act* smarter. Wondering how this phenomenon would work with humans, Rosenthal along with Lenore Jacobson reran the study using elementary school teachers instead of college student experimenters and children instead of rats. The study, aptly titled *Pygmalion in the Classroom* (1968), involved telling teachers that some of their pupils were "late bloomers" with potential to make great academic gains during the school year. In truth, these pupils were no different, in terms of academic potential, from their classmates and, like the rats of the former study, should have performed no differently. But, by the year's end, the "bloomers" were progressing well, showing strides greater than their undistinguished (i.e., unlabeled) classmates. The teachers expected the bloomers to bloom, and bloom they did!

Unfortunately, the self-fulfilling prophecy is often negative rather than positive, and this is nowhere more true than in sex-role stereotyping. If society expects women to be socially incompetent and emotionally immature, its prophecy will be fulfilled and women will begin to *act* and/or *feel* incompetent and dependent. For example, women are expected to do poorly in mathematics, a "masculine" field. Not surprisingly, given the self-fulfilling prophecy, by the time they are in junior high school, girls do perform less well on math tests than boys do. So, one of the prices of negative sex-related expectations of others is a devaluation of individuals' and groups' self-esteem and feelings of worth.

SOCIETY DIRECTS THE SCENE

Society not only sets the scene through the development and maintenance of sex-role stereotypes, but directs the scene by dictating certain practices. Being denied the vote, bank credit, pregnancy benefits, access to higher education, entrance into shop courses are all examples of societal practices that have adversely affected women. Being denied child custody rights is a similar example for men. Other practices may be more subtle—putting boys or girls in different physical education classes, having men use first names to refer to female employees while women are not allowed to do so in reference to men. Such societal practices have several negative consequences—prejudice, discrimination, and the actual development of differences.

Differential treatment of persons based on their membership in a group rather than on individual characteristics is a result of stereotyping and prejudice.

Gordon Allport, whom we mentioned in our discussion of stereotypes, also addressed the concept of prejudice. He defined it as "an antipathy based upon a faulty and inflexible generalization. It may be directed toward a group as a whole or toward an individual because he is a member of that group." (1954, p 10) Like stereotypes, prejudices are inflexible and based on faulty or only partially correct information.

Prejudices persist in spite of contrary evidence for a variety of reasons. First, prejudiced people listen only to evidence that serves to confirm their already held beliefs. If one believes that all women are incapable of performing executive jobs, encounters with competent women executives will soon be forgotten, while those with incompetent women executives will long be remembered. If one believes that all Jews are stingy, selective attention will be given to encounters that tend to confirm that belief. Second, prejudiced people tend to associate with those who hold the same beliefs as themselves. Third, people's prejudices are frequently reinforced; when they are the targets of prejudice, people often act in accord with expectations others hold for them.

All of us acknowledge that racial prejudice exists: the history of slavery, emancipation, and unequal rights cannot be denied. But people balk at the notion that prejudice exists against women in our society. Are our stereotypes of women so negative that we might characterize them as antipathies? The answer, unfortunately, seems to be yes. To prove our point, let's look at the table that Helen Mayer Hacker (1951) once prepared (Table 2-2). On one side of the chart Hacker listed the common negative, prejudicial statements about Negroes. On the other side she listed the corresponding characteristics of women. Look closely at the two columns and you will see that many of the characteristics ascribed to Negroes have also been applied to women: both groups are believed to possess inferior intellectual skills, to have smaller brains, to know their place and be satisfied with it, to be more childlike and emotional, and to use all sorts of wiles to outwit "white folks" or "menfolks."

If you remain unconvinced that prejudice exists against women

TABLE 2-2

Castelike Status of Women and Negroes

Negroes	Women

1. High Social Visibility

a. Skin color, other "racial" characteristics.

a. Secondary sex characteristics.

b. (Sometimes) distinctive dress—bandana, flashy clothes.

b. Distinctive dress, skirts, etc.

2. Ascribed Attributes

a. Inferior intelligence, smaller brain, less convoluted, scarcity of geniuses.

a. Ditto.

b. More free in instinctual gratifications. More emotional, "primitive," and childlike. Imagined sexual prowess envied.

b. Irresponsible, inconsistent, emotionally unstable. Lack strong super-ego. Women as "temptresses."

c. Common stereotype "inferior."

c. "Weaker."

3. Rationalizations of Status

a. Thought all right in his place.

a. Woman's place is in the home.

b. Myth of contented Negro.

b. Myth of contented woman— "feminine" woman is happy in subordinate role.

4. Accommodation Attitudes

a. Supplicatory, whining intonation of voice.

a. Rising inflection, smiles, laughs, downward glances.

b. Deferential manner.

b. Flattering manner.

c. Concealment of real feelings.

c. "Feminine wiles."

d. Outwit "white folks."

d. Outwit "menfolk."

e. Careful study of points at which dominant group is susceptible to influence.

e. Ditto.

f. Fake appeals for directives; show of ignorance.

f. Appearance of helplessness.

5. Discriminations

a. Limitations on education—should fit "place" in society.

a. Ditto.

b. Confined to traditional jobs—barred from supervisory positions. Their competition feared. No family precedents for new aspirations.

b. Ditto.

c. Deprived of political importance.

c. Ditto.

d. Social and professional segregation.

d. Ditto.

e. More vulnerable to criticism.

e. E.g. conduct in bars.

TABLE 2-2 *continued*

Negroes	*Women*
	6. Similar Problems

a. Roles not clearly defined, but in flux as
result of social change. Conflict between
achieved status and ascribed status.

From Hacker (1951).

just as it does toward blacks, scan the following hypothetical situations as described by Sandra and Darryl Bem. You might find little fault in the first. But what about the second? Wouldn't we all label that as prejudiced?

> Suppose that a white male college student decided to room or set up a bachelor apartment with a black male friend. Surely the typical white student would not blithely assume that this black roommate was to handle all the domestic chores. Nor would his conscience allow him to do so even in the unlikely event that his roommate would say: "No, it's okay. I like doing housework. I'd be happy to do it." We suspect that the typical white student would still not be comfortable if he took advantage of this offer because he and America have finally realized that he would be taking advantage of the fact that such a roommate had been socialized by our society to be "happy" with such obvious inequity. But change this hypothetical black roommate to a female marriage partner, and somehow the student's conscience goes to sleep. At most it is quickly tranquilized by the comforting thought that "she is happiest when she is ironing for her loved one." (1970, p. 99)

Prejudice is sometimes difficult to identify, once society has made it commonplace. Some whites acted genuinely surprised at blacks' feelings of hostility and servitude, believing them happy with their lot. However, if the whites had just put themselves in the blacks' place, their misconceptions would soon have been dispelled. The same is true of sex roles. If you believe that women's lot in life is as good or better than men's, just turn the tables, as Jennifer MacLeod did in her satire on how men could please their bride-to-be after the wedding.

> Oh lucky you! You are finally bridegroom to the woman of your dreams! But don't think for a minute that you can now relax and be assured automatically of marital happiness forever. You will have to *work at it*. While

she may only have eyes for you *now*, remember that she is surrounded every day by attractive young men who are all too willing to tempt her away from you. And as the years go by, you will lose some of the handsome masculinity of your youth: you will have to make up in skill and understanding what you will lack in the bloom of youth. . . .

Now men's passion, of course, often does not equal that of women. But you have a wonderful surprise in store for you, if you concentrate your efforts on your wife's pleasure and don't worry selfishly about your own. For sooner or later you will discover the ecstasy of truly mature male coital orgasm that can be induced only by total surrender to the exquisite sensations of a woman's orgasmic contractions. . . .

Remember that your first duty is to your wife. So if you fail to satisfy her (and yourself, too) in the above described natural way, you should talk to a good psychiatrist who specializes in this kind of problem. She will help you if, for instance, you have not yet fully accepted the natural masculine role that will bring you joy or selfless service to others instead of the futile envy of women's natural leadership role.

If you do your job well—for husbandhood is the true career for all manly men, worthy of all your talents—you will keep your wife happy and hold her for the rest of her days. Remember that marriage, for a man, should be Life's Great Adventure. So relax—relax—relax—and enjoy. (1975, p. 5)

The absurdity of the satire serves to illustrate how ingrained prejudices actually are.

The most unfortunate consequence of prejudice is that it leads to discrimination, or differential and unfair treatment of persons on the basis of group membership. Prejudice involves negative and inflexible *attitudes,* discrimination involves behavioral *outcomes* based on prejudicial attitudes. Discrimination, then, is often (but not always) the outcome of prejudice. Women not having access to higher education, to loans and mortgages, and to certain jobs is the result of discrimination, as is unequal pay for men and women, or for blacks and whites in identical jobs. Thus, prejudice, derived out of stereotypes, is inexorably linked to discrimination.

A product of discrimination and societal practices, in addition to the lack of equal opportunity, is a negative view of oneself. Amanda, after not being able to obtain a job because of discrimination, believed herself to be unworthy of a job, incompetent. So, let's move next to personal beliefs and expectations to see how they fit into the total picture.

THE INDIVIDUAL TAKES OVER

Thus far we have discussed society's role in the development and maintenance of sex roles. But what about the individual? Doesn't he or she play a part? The individual, being a member of society, is certainly influenced by societal beliefs and practices, by stereotypes and discrimination. Societal information is incorporated in an individual's self-concept and own belief system. If sex-role stereotypes indicate that women are incompetent, individual women may believe that they are incompetent, even in the face of contradictory evidence. And if societal practices dictate that girls not be allowed to take shop courses, then individual girls will believe that they do not have the ability to rebuild car engines or construct a table. If societal practices and stereotypes join together to deny women the vote or the opportunity to run for office because women are irrational and subject to raging hormonal influences monthly, then individual women will believe that they are subject to crying fits for no apparent reasons or incapacitated during their menstrual period. Or as Eliza Doolittle discovered, when others thought her beautiful, she not only acted beautiful, but felt great as well!

So, when the individual enters, he or she finds the stage set up, altering beliefs to fit the scene. In this section, we shall examine individuals' feelings of worth and self-esteem, individuals' beliefs about sex-role stereotypes as they pertain to themselves, and individuals' expectations for themselves.

Societal beliefs and practices take a toll on self-esteem. Sadly, one of the consequences of attributing to women those traits that society deems undesirable or unhealthy, and expecting women to express those traits, is that they are likely to devalue themselves as individuals as well as women as a group. In Philip Goldberg's study on rating scholarly articles, we saw that women tend to devalue other women's competence. Feelings of worth and self-esteem may also be undermined by sex-role stereotyping. Women tend to blame themselves more for not succeeding than men do. If a woman fails at a task, she is likely to think, "I must have done something wrong," or "I really am not very good at that." A man, on the other hand, is more likely to think, "Well, that was a bad break," or "I really am good at that, but lady luck was against me today."

Women tend not only to blame themselves for their failures, but to denigrate themselves. In instances where women are in no way responsible for the outcome, they *still* see themselves as responsible: "If I had just tried harder or acted differently, things would have turned out all right!" The following anecdote related by Elaine Walster and Mary Ann Pate (1976) illustrates this unfortunate point. A woman applied for an academic position as an assistant professor; internationally known, she had published more and received more acclaim than many of the full professors in the department. Her excellence was acknowledged by the department (one department member stated, "She wouldn't really fit in here—she is too smart"). But, the department decided not to make her an offer.

2058624

When the decision was criticized, one man countered angrily, "Discrimination is an old Wisconsin tradition." To everyone within the department, the reason for her exclusion was clear. She was talented, but she made the department members uncomfortable.

Within one year, however, the [woman] had reinterpreted her rejection. She had convinced herself that she had behaved stupidly and thus destroyed her chances for a job. "I had some personal problems at the time," she confided, "and that prevented me from being sensitive to what was going on. . . . I came on too strong. . . . Probably I was too aggressive. . . . I should have been more enthusiastic (about the Chairman's research interest, a project he has since abandoned). . . . They say they don't hire women, but if I had been convincing enough, I could have changed their minds. At some time everyone reaches a test point. They have to say if I succeed here I'm good. Otherwise I should give up. . . . That was my test and I failed; I'm second rate, and I've accepted it." (p. 398)

The woman had reinterpreted the situation, believing she had failed, rather than realistically assessing her "failure" as an example of discrimination.

Societal stereotypes influence individuals' perceptions of their own possession of sex-role stereotypic characteristics. Although most people agree as to what characteristics are sex-stereotypic—which are masculine and which are feminine—they do not always believe that they possess all of the feminine or all of the masculine traits. Remember the Bem Sex-Role Inventory discussed earlier? By asking people to rate themselves in terms of their possession of each of the traits in the Inventory, Sandra Bem (1975) was able to compute a masculinity and femininity score for each of the individuals. She discovered that about one-half of her Stanford University students characterized themselves as traditionally masculine or feminine. A small number (15 percent) said they possessed opposite-sex characteristics—feminine characteristics for men and masculine characteristics for women. About one-third of the students characterized themselves as possessing *both* masculine and feminine traits, perceiving themselves as instrumental as well as expressive. This group she classified as androgynous.

Because people do differ in how they perceive themselves, we are able to examine the effects of their beliefs upon their behavior. Bem went on in further experiments to do just that. From their individual responses on the Bem Sex-Role Inventory, each student was classified as masculine, feminine, or androgynous. Then, these college students were observed in a series of situations that were chosen to elicit either "masculine" or "feminine" behaviors. In the feminine situation, subjects were left alone in a room with a kitten: those who had rated themselves as feminine were expected to direct more playful and affectionate attention toward the kitten than those who rated themselves as masculine. Sure enough, the women classified as feminine on the Sex-Role Inventory played with and cuddled the kitten, while the masculine men did not. However men and women who were classified as androgynous also delighted in playing with the kitten, and, in fact, seemed to enjoy it more than even the feminine women. The findings for the masculine situation, which involved resisting conformity under group pressure, were similar: masculine men engaged in it while feminine women did not, and androgynous individuals of both sexes performed well on the task. Thus, individuals who described themselves as possessing only masculine or feminine characteristics tended to behave in sex-stereotyped ways—masculine men did not conform to group pressure and did not play with the kitten, while feminine women did just the opposite. The androgynous individuals both acted playfully and affectionately toward the kitten and resisted conforming to group pressure.

Even when Sandra Bem and Ellen Lenney (1976) set up situations in which men and women would gain more money by participating in a cross-sex activity (e.g., women would be offered twice as much money for oiling a squeaky hinge than for preparing a baby bottle), subjects who were strongly sex-typed adhered rigidly to the stereotype. They seemed unable to adapt to the demands of the situations even when it was clearly to their advantage to do so. Perhaps their beliefs were so strong that even money may have been no incentive to change! Though their avoidance of opposite-sex activities was dysfunctional and maladaptive, they continued to adhere to the stereotype. Non-sex-typed subjects (those who possessed both masculine and feminine characteristics), on the other hand, exhibited situation-specific rather than sex-stereotyped behavior, demonstrating a flexible and adaptable approach to new events and dilemmas and a freedom from stereotypical constraints. This research suggests that possessing one set of traits to the exclusion of the other set of traits may not be best for optimal functioning in the world. It seems that it is best to possess some degree of *both* masculine and feminine traits.

Finally, let us turn to individuals' expectations for themselves. Just as others have expectations for us, so do we have expectations for our own behavior. To illustrate, let's look at self-expectancies and sex roles on achievement tasks. In studies comparable to ones discussed earlier, adults and children were asked to estimate their ability on a certain task, then to perform the task, and finally to explain their success or failure at the task. Girls and women tend to have lower expectations for success than boys and men, and this sex difference appears right after children's entrance into school. In conjunction with these lower expectancies, women, as we saw earlier, when they *do* fail a task, blame themselves for the failure while men attribute their failure to bad luck. Alternatively, women attribute a success to luck, men to their own efforts and abilities. Thus, women's expectancies fall even lower than men's: they do not take credit for their successes and blame *themselves* for their failures. In this fashion, negative expectancies may be perpetuated and expanded (Crandall, 1969; Parsons, Ruble, Hodges, and Small, 1976).

LIVING THE PART

All of these forces—societal beliefs, societal practices, socialization, and personal beliefs—converge upon the individual to dictate what behaviors are actually expressed. Just as Monsieur Poirot, the Inspector on the Orient Express murder case discovered, everybody has a hand in the development and maintenance of sex roles. Like the planning of the murder, our social–psychological system that perpetuates sex roles is pretty intricate.

In this chapter we have examined the effects of cultural beliefs and expectations, societal practices, and personal beliefs and expectations on sex-related behaviors. Socialization, too, influences sex-related behavior. We must keep in mind, however, that socialization is affected by and affects the other factors. Through the socialization agents, the child absorbs the message provided by the culture into his or her own personal belief system. More directly, the child is affected by the societal practices (such as discrimination or affirmative action in the work place) which facilitate or inhibit his or her role choices. Finally, all of these factors in combination act to affect one's sex-related behaviors, which, in turn, circle back to affect societal practices, cultural norms, and socialization.

Our notions of sex role are developed and maintained through the circuitous route just described. It is our task to break this cycle, at any or all of the points available to us.

THE PRENATAL PERIOD
Biological Foundations of Sex Roles

chapter three

Before the moment of birth, while environmental forces stand attendant, biology plays the leading role. Biology directs a sequence of events that begins with conception and continues throughout the prenatal period, presenting at its denouement a boy or girl infant. While biology determines whether the individual is a male or female, socialization accounts for the acquisition of masculine or feminine behaviors.

In this chapter, we shall examine the drama of the biological unfolding of a male or female within the womb, the impact of these prenatal events upon the behavior of the neonate immediately after birth, the role of biology in the development of gender identity, the nature of the debate concerning biology's contribution to sex role, and the relationship of biology and behavior.

BIOLOGICAL BEGINNINGS

The processes underlying early sexual differentiation, though complicated, are well understood. Five events predominate in the complex biological sequence leading to sex differentiation. John Money and Anke Ehrhardt (1972) have likened the process of sex differentiation to a relay race. At each relay station, the runner must be in place for the race to continue. If a runner is off-schedule and not in position, then the course of sexual differentiation will be thwarted.

The first and major event involves an individual's genetic inheritance. Even before conception, nature has set the stage for the as yet sex-unspecified individual to appear: it has provided potential mothers with eggs, each of which can contribute an X chromosome to their offspring; and it has provided potential fathers with sperm cells, some of which can contribute an X chromosome and others of which can contribute a Y chromosome to the still-to-be-conceived organism. When an egg and a sperm unite, if the resulting combination is XX (i.e., two X chromosomes, one from each parent), a female is conceived; if the resulting combination is XY (i.e., an X chromosome from the mother and a Y chromosome from the father), a male is conceived. Chromosomal sex is determined by the father, who can contribute either an X or Y chromosome, not by the mother, who can contribute only an X chromosome. Thus, at the moment of conception, one's chromosomal sex is determined by which of the father's sperm cells fertilized the egg. The resulting organism is either male or female; any ambiguities are rare.

The second event centers upon the formation of the gonads, or sex glands. The early weeks of prenatal development proceed similarly for all the newly formed organisms, whether they are to be male or female. Settling into the uterine area, the organisms grow and develop a basic structure which includes arm and leg buds, a primitive heart, precursors to the brain and spinal cord, and a ridge of tissue out of which will grow the main internal organs of urination and reproduction. The beginnings of the gonads are discernible, as two different structures, one that has the potential of becoming the male gonad, the other the female gonad. After six weeks or so of prenatal existence, the gonadal structure of the male differentiates, resulting in the formation of the testes and the disappearance of the female structure; and after twelve weeks, the gonadal structure of the female transforms into the ovaries and the male structure disappears. By the sixth month of gestation, the male and female gonads have entirely formed. The female ovaries, whose task will eventually be the secretion of female hormones, do not function prenatally, though they do at this time possess their entire complement of ova (or eggs)—approximately 400,000 of them. No more eggs will be produced; those a female is born with, except for the ones her body releases monthly between menarche and menopause, are those with which she will die. Unlike the ovaries, the male testes, whose task is the secretion of male hormones, do function prenatally, producing and releasing the male hormone androgen.

The third and fourth events involve the development of the internal and external genitalia in males and in females. The presence of the male hormone androgen promotes the development of a male internal structure (*vas deferens* and prostate) and male external genitalia (the penis). The absence of this hormone leads to the development of a female internal structure (uterus and vagina) and female external genitalia (the clitoris). Thus, each of the sexes' sex organs develop from the *same* original structure, depending on the presence or absence of androgen. The differentiation process of the male and female genitalia from a common structure is illustrated in Figure 3-1.

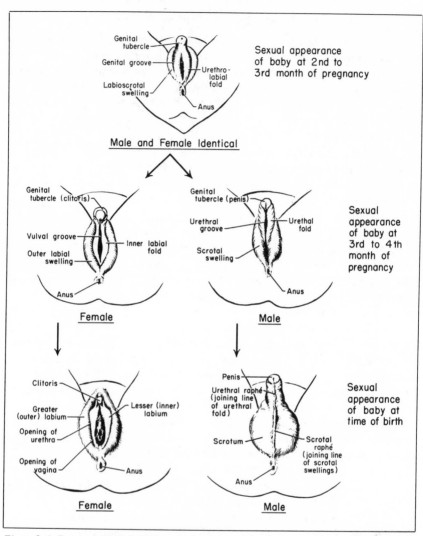

Figure 3-1. External Genital Differentiation in the Human Fetus. Three stages in the differentiation of the external genital organs. The male and the female organs have the same beginnings and are homologous with one another. (Reprinted from Man and Woman, Boy and Girl, *John Money and Anke A. Ehrhardt. Copyright © 1972. Used by permission of The Johns Hopkins University Press.)*

To provide for the secretion of the appropriate sex hormones throughout life, the presence of androgen in the fetal environment affects not only the immediately developing sexual apparatus, but a part of the structure of the fetal brain as well. The portion of the brain that becomes sex-differentiated controls the lifetime release of sex hormones in such a way that, for the male, a predominantly *continuous* (i.e., acyclic) sex hormone release is assured in adulthood permitting him to produce sperm. For the female, the brain operates a predominantly *cyclic* sex hormone release after puberty, permitting her to release an egg, estrogens, and progestins on a monthly basis throughout much of adulthood. The effects of cyclic changes in sex hormones on patterns of behavior will be discussed in Chapter 8 with regard to sexual maturation at puberty.

So, before birth, four of the five major events that determine gender have occurred and have begun to influence the course of sex development: (1) the chromosomal makeup (XX for females, XY for males), (2) the internal gonads (ovaries for females, testes for males), (3) internal structures and reproductive tracts (uterus and vagina for females, *vas deferens* and prostate for males), and (4) external genitalia (clitoris for females, penis for males). The fifth event to determine gender involves the assigned sex of rearing. The newborn baby's sex is determined at a glance, and, coupled with all the elements discussed in Chapter 2, determine how he or she will be treated throughout life. As Money and Ehrhardt point out:

> . . . as soon as the shape of the external genitals is perceived, it sets in motion a chain of communication: It is a daughter! It is a son! This communication itself sets in motion a chain of sexually dimorphic responses, beginning with pink and blue, pronominal use and name choice, that will be transmitted from person to person to encompass all persons the baby ever encounters, day by day, year in and year out, from birth to death. (1972, p. 12)

It is this chain of communication, and its effect on an individual's behavior, that will be the main concern of our account of children's sex-role development.

BIOLOGY AND GENDER IDENTITY

As we just saw, the fifth event to determine gender involves the assigned sex of rearing. Throughout the first two years, the gender-linked chain of communication leads the child to the realization that he is a male, or that she is a female. Gender identity is simply this knowledge: that one is, inevitably, the member of one of the two sexes and that one's membership is based on primary and secondary sexual characteristics.

Once in a very great while, mishaps in one of the five events that determine one's gender occur. These mishaps, due to developmental accidents of various sorts, allow us to study the relative influence of the biological events, (chromosomal makeup, internal gonads, internal reproductive tracts, and external genitalia), and the social events (social labeling as a boy or a girl) in determining one's gender identity. Investigators manipulate neither chromosomes nor hormones, but merely examine the effects of accidental chromosomal or hormonal variations.

John Money and his associates at the Gender Identity Clinic at Johns Hopkins University have been responsible for the bulk of this work, based upon clinical cases of children who have suffered from such accidents. Their case histories, while tragic, provide us with a facsimile of a scientific experiment on the effects of biological variation upon subsequent sex-role related behaviors in children.

Perhaps the most common cases utilized in describing the effect of prenatal androgens on human behavior and gender identity are those termed "adrenogenital syndrome." This condition results either from a pregnant woman's being administered a hormone which acts upon the developing fetus like androgen (administered in order to prevent a spontaneous abortion or premature birth),* from a malfunction of the mother's adrenal glands, or from a malfunction of the female fetus's adrenal glands. Whatever the cause, babies with adrenogenital syndrome (i.e., female infants exposed prenatally to androgen) are born with ambiguous looking genitals. Their external genitalia could be described either as an enlarged clitoris or a small penis, so that it would not be immediately clear at birth whether the arrival of a boy or a girl should be announced. Though their chromosomal sex (XX), their gonadal sex, and their internal genital sex are female, their external genital sex is unclear. Usually, they are assigned as females at birth and are reared as such ever after.

To determine the effects of the prenatal androgenization of these girls, John Money, Anke Ehrhardt, and their colleagues conducted extensive interviews with 25 of the girls and their mothers as well as with a control group of 25 normal girls and their mothers

*The hormones, synthetic progestins, were used during the 1950's and are no longer administered to pregnant women.

(Ehrhardt, Epstein, and Money, 1969; Ehrhardt and Money, 1967). Questioning their attitudes about themselves, these investigators found that the adrenogenital girls (ranging in age from 4 to 16) thought of themselves as tomboys, as did their mothers. Behaviorally, they were very active physically, preferred wearing pants and shorts to dresses, liked masculine-associated toys best, and were more interested in careers than were normal girls. Each of them, however, wished for "romance, marriage, and motherhood" (Ehrhardt, *et al.*, 1969, p. 166). Medical treatment, by the way, enables this wish to become a reality: all received corrective surgery and cortisone treatments, followed by the administration of female hormones in adolescence to promote the development of secondary sex characteristics such as breasts and pubic hair. Since the girls already have female gonads (ovaries) and internal structures (uterus and vagina), they are usually able to conceive and bear children. In another Johns Hopkins study of 23 adult women who were exposed to androgen prenatally, 13 of them were known to have married and 5 to have had at least one baby (Ehrhardt, Evers, and Money, 1968; Money and Raiti, 1967).

Thus, in spite of a dramatic introduction of male hormones in their fetal environment, these girls do not grow up to be the equivalent of their male counterparts, although they exhibit a few of the global characteristics most commonly associated with masculinity. Other researchers have noted, however, that the girls, being fully acquainted with their condition as well as with their interviewers' knowledge of their condition, would feel free to admit to many cross-sex interests and might even feel expected to express such interests. In addition, the interviewers, who knew which girls had the syndrome and which did not, may have been predisposed to *focus* on specific behaviors in the adrenogenital group. Finally, the nonsyndrome girls may have been atypical: more of them reported never wearing slacks and only playing with dolls than in other studies of girls' interests and activities (Frieze, Parsons, Johnson, Ruble, & Zellman, 1978). These problems, along with the fact that the gender and sex-role identities of the adrenogenital girls were appropriate, suggest that socialization overrides the presence of prenatal androgen.

That the adrenogenital girls were not more physically aggressive, although they seemed to be more physically active, is of special interest. As is discussed in Chapter 6, androgen is believed to play a role in aggression. Since these girls were not particularly aggressive, perhaps androgen really enhances activity level, which is then channeled via socialization into sex-typed behaviors. Since physical aggression is thought to be inappropriate for girls, the adrenogenital girls became active tomboys, not aggressive ones.

In the case of genetic males exposed to a female prenatal environment, that is, to an environment free of or insensitive to androgens, female genitals are present at birth. Most commonly, these infants, too, are given a female sex assignment and raised as females. When interviewed by the Johns Hopkins group, they were described as feminine both in interest and behavior. Despite being genetic males, the children, labeled and reared as females, developed a female gender identity. Of the ten patients in the Johns Hopkins Clinic with this syndrome, almost all enjoyed housewifery, preferred having no outside occupation, dreamed of having a family, and, as children, played primarily with girls' toys (Money, Ehrhardt, and Masica, 1968; Masica, Money, and Ehrhardt, 1971; Masica and Lewis, 1969).

The most clear-cut evidence that one's sex-role identity is not preordained by the biological factors operating before birth involves gender reassignment. The case referred to by John Money and Anke Ehrhardt (1972) is unique, but serves to demonstrate the power that socialization can exert over biology. Due to a highly unlikely and unfortunate accident, a seven-month-old male who was an identical twin suffered irreparable injury to his penis during circumcision. The electrical current used in the cauterization was simply too powerful; the penis was destroyed. The child's parents, on the advice of the medical staff, decided that rather than raise the child as a boy, they would reassign his sex as female and raise him accordingly. When the child was seventeen months old, name, clothing, toys, and treatment changed. Via corrective surgery, his external genitalia changed as well. From then on the child was raised as a girl. The parents maintained contact with the medical staff, informing them of the twins' development. As Money and Ehrhardt relate, the parents made a determined and successful effort to socialize each of the twins according to their assigned sex. By the time the twins were over 4 years of age, the mother was describing them as follows: "She (referring to the reassigned twin) doesn't like to be dirty, and yet my son (referring to the unreassigned twin) is quite different. I can't wash his face for anything. . . . She seems to be daintier. Maybe it is because I encourage it. . . . One thing that really amazes me is that she is so feminine. I've never seen a little girl so neat and tidy as she can be when she wants to be. . . . She is very proud of herself, when she puts on a new dress or I set her hair. She loves to have her hair set. . . ." (pp. 119–120)

The twins copied the "same-sex" parent's role behaviors. The daughter helped with the household chores such as cleaning up the kitchen, while the son, like his father, preferred to work with cars and tools. The female twin, in other words, was behaving in sex-appropriate ways, even though she was genetically and hormonally male. Her assigned sex and concomitant socialization history overrode the biological factors of gender in terms of the effects upon her behavior and interests.

As a last example involving accidents of nature and gender identity, let us look at the parental reaction to a daughter with Turner's Syndrome. In this condition, only one X chromosome is present (known as an XO condition). Although the external genitalia are female, the lack of a second X chromosome results in no internal genitalia or gonads being formed. Robert Stoller (1968), in presenting this particular case, described the girl, who had come to him because she had not begun to menstruate, as unremarkably feminine. When the lack of internal organs was discovered, the girl's parents were told that their daughter could never have children but, with the surgical construction of a vagina, could enjoy intercourse. The parents opposed the surgery fearing that it would lead to promiscuity, as though their daughter would be "safe" without a vagina. Stoller's case history illustrates the strength of sex-role behavior: the fear of promiscuity, a sex-inappropriate behavior for girls, led the patient's parents to deny her the operation.

BIOLOGY AND NEONATAL SEX DIFFERENCES

Considering the neonate as an individual still free from the effects of the contextual elements described in Chapter 2, investigators are willing to assume that behavioral differences among individuals or between males and females in the first two weeks of life are biologically determined. It is an assumption that they would be unwilling to make for children even as early as three months of age, since enough socialization has occurred by then to render a demonstration of purely biological effects untenable.

We shall present the early sex differences and speculate on their possible antecedents and consequences.

Physiological Differences

Boy and girl newborns differ from one another in terms of vulnerability and mortality. Males are definitely more vulnerable from conception through at least the first year of life: they are more often spontaneously aborted, they are more likely to die of birth trauma, birth injuries, congenital malformations, and infectious diseases in the first year of life, and their mothers are more prone to birth complications. Several biological explanations for the greater vulnerability of males have been offered. For example, the fact that the male is somewhat heavier and longer than the female at birth may account for their higher incidence of birth injury. Genetics may explain their greater susceptibility to infectious diseases, since susceptibility is controlled by a gene carried on the X chromosome. If a mutant gene with no susceptibility control develops, it would be more likely to be expressed in the male who, with only one X chromosome, would not have a healthy (i.e., nonmutant) gene on the other chromosome to counteract the mutant gene (Garai and Scheinfeld, 1968; Waldron, 1977).

The higher mortality rate of males is partially offset by the higher incidence of males conceived and born. Between 120 to 150 boys are conceived for every 100 girls, even though equal numbers of X and Y sperms are produced by the adult male. Nature somehow manages partially to offset the greater vulnerability of the male fetus and newborn by arranging for more males to be conceived.

Males and females also have different maturational rates, although controversy continues over the issue of how long females maintain their maturational advantage over males and in what specific developmental areas these advantages occur. Females tend to be from one to six weeks more mature skeletally than males at birth. However, there are no differences in other areas of physical development such as the maturation of the parts of the brain that control vision. Since the different areas of the brain mature at different rates, sex differences could easily be found in one area but not another, or might appear but be transitory.

A related finding by Howard Moss (1967) and others involves the greater irritability of boy babies. Irritability, as inferred through more frequent crying and less frequent sleeping, is more characteristic of boys than girls. These are behaviors that certainly influence a mother's perception and handling of her baby and that have implications for the differential socialization of the sexes; but we will be discussing this more fully in the next chapter. For our present purposes, the male's greater irritability has been related to physiological differences, specifically the relative immaturity of and the higher incidence of birth complications in the male (Tanner, 1970).

For the obstetrician, nursing staff, and parents alike, the first concern upon a woman's entrance to the delivery room is, will the baby be all right? Will it be healthy and free of all medical problems? So, when the first wails of a brand-new human being are heard, he or she is checked from head to toe for medical and neurological problems. In 1952, Virginia Apgar (1953) developed one of the first "instant physicals." This physical, rightly called the Apgar Scale, is given by the obstetrician at the instant the infant enters the world and again after five minutes of post-uterine life. The obstetrician examines five crucial physical signs, rating each as absent, below par but at least present, and good (Apgar and James, 1962). The first sign involves heart rate: is the child's heart beating at all, is it beating slowly (below 100 beats per minute), or is it beating at a normal rate for a newborn (over 100 beats per minute)? The second sign involves breathing. Normally, the infant takes his or her first gasp of air and begins to cry; slow or irregular breathing and no accompanying wail are signs that all is not well. Third, babies arrive in a variety of hues, ranging from blue to pink. Blue is not the color of boys, but of all infants at the time of birth, turning pinker and pinker as the baby begins to breathe and the blood begins to circulate freely. Within 90 seconds after birth, a healthy baby's color should have changed to pink. Babies whose color does not change have a medical problem.

The last two signs involve muscle tone—healthy babies are active and moving about—and reflex irritability—healthy babies will cough or sneeze when a catheter is inserted into their noses. An infant who has a perfect score for all five signs gets a score of 10, those below par in all but one sign a 9, and so on. Children who have very low scores due to the absence of the signs (0 to 2) are in trouble medically, and about 10 to 15 percent of them are likely to die (Apgar *et al.*, 1958).

What interests us, however, is whether or not girl and boy babies have different Apgar scores. No one has reported any differences, so we can presume that boy and girl newborns score about the same on the "instant physical."

Activity Level

To date, no conclusive evidence for early sex-related differences in activity level have been demonstrated. But neonatal activity levels do seem to be related to later behavior. In a longitudinal study by Robert Bell, George Weller, and Mary Waldrop (1971), newborn boys who had rapid breathing, both during sleep and when awake, were more lethargic and passive in free play and uninterested in peers during the preschool period than were newborn boys who had lower respiration rates. And newborn boys who responded quickly and intensively when a bottle was removed from their mouths were less likely to engage in peer play and teachers' games at 2½ years of age. The girls' relationship between early and later activity was less straightforward, although high activity in the newborn period (during an episode where a blanket was removed) related to low body movements at 2½ years of age. These findings suggest that high activity level at birth may translate into low activity level at preschool and suggest that the role of neonatal activity level may be quite different for boys and girls.

Perceptual Differences

In the past, the newborn infant was believed to be unaware of the surroundings because of the immaturity of the senses. The infant's world was described as a "buzzing blooming confusion" by William James, as the infant supposedly could not see, hear, smell, or feel, or at least could not do these things very well. However, in the past decade the infant's perceptual system has been extensively investigated and, to the surprise of many, was discovered to be very well developed. Even before birth, the fetus responds to touch and to sound. What expectant mother has not felt her unborn baby squirm and turn at the presentation of a loud noise, an unexpected sound, or sometimes even music? Researchers have studied this phenomenon more scientifically, their results concurring with mothers' reports. At birth, the neonate is able to smell, hear, see, and taste. For example, neonates can quite clearly see objects or people who are approximately 17 centimeters from them; significantly, that is the distance from an infant cradled in a care-giver's arms to the care-giver's face. And neonates can hear quite well, often responding to a loud noise by startling and to a soothing sound by quieting. In addition, preferences for certain types of information are seen very early (Fantz and Nevis, 1967; Kessen, Haith, and Salapatek, 1970).

Are the sensory abilities of boy and girl neonates the same? In general, the answer is yes. No early sex differences in seeing or hearing have been discovered, nor in preferences for visual or auditory information. Likewise, boy and girl neonates have the same sense of smell. As an aside, adult women seem to be more sensitive to odors than adult men, with this sex difference believed to be related to the presence of the female hormone estrogen. Estrogen is present in miniscule amounts in both male and female children prior to puberty. Only after puberty does estrogen production in girls increase, at which time differences in smell acuity appear (Money and Ehrhardt, 1972).

Although boy and girl neonates are similar with respect to sight, smell, taste, and sound, they may differ with respect to touch. Researchers study sensitivity to touch by brushing the newborn on the mouth, by directing a jet of air toward the baby's abdomen, or by pressing different sized strings or filaments on the heel while the infant sleeps. Some researchers, notably Robert Bell and his colleagues (Bell and Castello, 1964; Weller and Bell, 1965; Bell, Weller, and Waldrop, 1971) have found sex differences in touch; others have not. All those who have found differences report girls to be more sensitive to touch than boys.

Summary

The major, and most obvious, difference between boy and girl neonates is the genital difference. In addition, newborn boys are somewhat larger, though less advanced skeletally, than newborn girls. And, they may be less sensitive to touch and more irritable than girls. So, apart from anatomy, sex differences among neonates are scant and have no apparent bearing on the stereotypic beliefs about boys and girls, men and women.

Given the similarity of boy and girl newborns, we might expect parents and medical personnel to treat them the same, at least in the first few days of life. But from the moment of birth, the environment begins to exert its influence. Transcribing every word uttered in a delivery room during childbirth, Aidan Macfarlane (1977) found a preoccupation with gender and the ascription of a host of sex stereotypes on the part of parents and medical staff alike.

One doctor, while bringing a baby girl into the world, said, "Come on, junior. Only a lady could cause so much trouble." Upon seeing that the baby was a girl, the mother said, "Oh I'm sorry darling." The doctor: "What are you sorry about?" Mother: "He (the father) wanted a boy."

Another mother: "I wanted a boy. It can't play rugby. Everyone said it was going to be a boy. What are we going to put her in?"

Yet a third mother: "Oh. Oh, it's a boy" (father kisses and hugs wife). (pp. 61, 90, 109) It is difficult to imagine that these daily vignettes do not set the stage for later parental behavior and expectations, nor that childhood sex differences are not related to such situations.

Another example of differential treatment of boys and girls in the neonatal period is given by Jeffrey Rubin, Frank Provenzano, and Zella Luria (1974). Thirty parents were interviewed 24 hours after the birth of their first baby. The parents of girls rated their babies as softer and smaller and described them as more beautiful, pretty, and cute than parents of boys, even though the babies themselves did not differ in any respect. Interestingly, the fathers were more likely than the mothers to sex-stereotype their babies, describing their sons as stronger, firmer, and hardier than their wives did; their daughters as more weak and delicate.

THE GREAT DEBATE

The question of the relative contribution of biological and social events to sex roles has taken the form of a great debate. This debate goes on, and on, and on. Scientists argue over whether mental illness is caused by social or biological forces, whether or not innate differences in intelligence between people of different colors and creeds exist, whether physical illnesses such as cancer and heart disease can be best understood in terms of environment or heredity, as well as whether psychological differences between men and women are due to nature or nurture.

A classic point in the debate involves whether or not men are innately predisposed to having their major role outside the home and women to having theirs in the home. In psychology, Sigmund Freud (1933; 1965) was one of the first biology proponents, coining the famous, although somewhat simplified phrase, "anatomy is destiny." Women and men, he believed, occupied different places in society because of their biological and reproductive differences. Because women bear children and provide milk for them. they are most satisfied in the home, while men, who are not equipped for these activities, are the builders of society, not the raisers of children. While most of Freud's contemporaries agreed with his notions, a few did not. Karen Horney (1926/1967) another psychoanalyst of the time and one of Freud's followers, believed that the men's and women's roles were shaped by societal practices and cultural beliefs, not anatomical differences. Women stayed in the home dependent upon their husbands because Victorian society offered no other choices (in terms of obtaining outside employment, remaining single, or having no children). Social sanctions against inappropriate role choices (which Horney herself must have felt) proved so effective in keeping women "in their place" that many came to believe that women were most contented at home. Even though most of Freud's patients were women who were discontent staying home, Freud himself never entertained the notion that their dissatisfaction was due to the structure of the society rather than to the structure of their genitals. Horney's beliefs often met with disfavor in the male-dominated psychoanalytic circle, and Freud's theory prevailed through the 1960's, as we shall see in Chapter 5.

Sociology stressed the notion of roles and the necessity for complementarity, without which the biological order of life would be destroyed. For society to function, men and women had to play distinct and different parts. Talcott Parsons, one of the main proponents of this view, wrote:

> Absolute equality of opportunity is clearly incompatible with any positive solidarity of the family. . . . where married women are employed outside the home, it is, for the great majority, in occupations which are not in

direct competition for status of those men of their own class. Women's interests and the standard of judgment applied to them, run, in our society, far more in the direction of personal adornment. (1949, p. 174)

As we saw in Chapter 2, complementary roles and characteristics can actually be dysfunctional. People who rigidly embrace one role or the other are less likely to adjust their behavior to situational necessities. In any case, there is no evidence that a relationship between a man and a woman is better when the woman stays home.

Popular books and advice columnists often perpetuate outmoded views. For example, Marabel Morgan has received a great deal of attention with her book entitled *The Total Woman* (1973). Joining the ranks of thousands of women who have met with success outside the home (by publishing this book, conducting Total Woman classes, and appearing on talk shows), Morgan suggests that a woman's place is in the home beside her husband and children, and that to be elsewhere is against the nature of things.

Morgan likens the marriage relationship to a monarchy, where the husband is king, the wife the queen. In this kingdom, the king has the final word, the decision-making power, even when *she* knows he is wrong! To bolster his ego, Morgan advises women to follow the four A's: accept, admire, adapt, and appreciate their husbands. Accept your husband as he is; admire one of his more masculine traits every day (and if he has lost many of them by becoming paunchy and bald, find something—a muscular bicep or a scratchy beard); adapt to his life style, his schedule, his friends, his food preferences; and appreciate and be attentive to all he does (don't make phone calls after he is home and thank him for everything). Following the four A's will bring you joy and happiness and maybe, if you are lucky, a Caribbean cruise, a new wardrobe, a redecorated living room. Don't be afraid to use your seductive wiles on him: meet him at the door in a sheer nightie or, in the most well-known example from the book, in pink baby doll pajamas and white boots. Such tactics, along with having a well-run home and well-cared for children, ensure a good marriage.

These examples, taken from scientific and popular writings, demonstrate that many believe biology is responsible for the development of different roles, that differences in roles are the natural (either biological or divine) order of things, and that society will break down if the natural order is violated.

The belief that "society will break down" is probably the underlying reason that such theories originally developed. People often have vested interests in maintaining societal procedures and cultural beliefs, even though they are not always aware of this position, and scientists are no exception. If one wishes to maintain the status quo, it makes sense to state that the status quo is best, is natural, and is biologically determined. In an interesting study, Nicholas Pastore (1949) examined the research findings and political beliefs of 24 scientists studying sex differences. Scientists who found sex differences were those who were likely to support the status quo, while those who reported few sex differences in their studies preferred to change the status quo. Thus, evidence for biological determinism seems to be related to one's desire to maintain sex roles and the cultural beliefs and societal practices underlying these roles just as the lack of evidence is related to one's desire to change existing sex roles.

The contribution of biology and socialization to sex differences is not an all-or-none phenomenon, as the preceding discussion implies. The great debate tends to obscure the fact that neither biology nor sociology alone accounts for all the reported sex differences. Instead, the contribution of each must be assessed for specific behaviors. As we shall see in later chapters, certain sex differences, especially spatial ability and aggression, are heavily influenced by biology, while others such as problem-solving and nurturance, are not. In addition, some behaviors are affected by both biological and social factors. For example, infant girls may become attuned to others' voices earlier than infant boys because of girls' greater maturity. During this time, mothers of girls may vocalize back to their daughters' babbling, while mothers of boys vocalize less to their sons' babbling, thereby amplifying the original sex difference. Thus, sex-related behaviors, when they are found, must be examined in terms of biological *and* social contributions.

BIOLOGY AND BEHAVIOR

To examine the interaction of biology and behavior, we typically study the impact of biology upon behavior. Of interest to us is how differential biological foundations, the formation of a biological male or female, might affect later behavior. To do this, one would have to devise a means of experimentally controlling such biological factors as genetic makeup and sex hormone levels and of scientifically observing the behavioral factors that would potentially be influenced by the biological manipulations, factors such as aggressivity, submissiveness, activity level, and so forth. Clearly, however, the biological manipulation of human fetuses is unacceptable: science cannot tamper with the chromosomes or hormone levels of our unborn children just to assuage our curiosity about the effects of biology on behavior. For this reason, we typically use three types of scientifically less satisfactory evidence and from them struggle to make appropriate inferences about the impact of biology on sex differences. We have already reviewed two types of evidence—ambiguous sex and gender identity, and neonatal sex differences. The last type of evidence involves the prenatal biological contribution to certain psychological sex differences established later on—aggression, sexual behavior, and spatial ability. Biological contributions to aggression are discussed in Chapter 6, to sexual behavior in Chapter 8, and to spatial ability in Chapter 9.

To make matters more difficult, biology and behavior interact in complex and not completely understood ways. Previously, we believed that biology affected behavior in a relatively straightforward and unidirectional manner: that is, a high level of a specific hormone resulted in a high level of a certain behavior. However, behavior also affects biology! For example, being in a stressful situation alters chemical substances in the body, and these alterations have been directly linked to ulcers. Stressful situations can cause the cessation of menstruation (called amenorrhea); adolescent girls who go away to camp or to college may find that they do not menstruate for a few months (Sherman, 1971). Presumably the stress causes an alteration in the hormone balance, which in turn suppresses ovulation and menstruation. Likewise, certain personality types are more prone to certain disease states, as has been demonstrated for heart attack victims (Wolff, 1968; Jenkins, 1971). Very little research has been done on the effect of behavior upon biology, so we do not as yet know the full impact of this phenomenon on people's lives. However, it is clear that the interaction of biology and behavior plays an important part in our lives and probably in the development of the sex-related behaviors.

BIOLOGY AND SEX-ROLE IDENTITY

The biological differences between the sexes are relatively straight-forward. Boys and girls do enter the world with different "equipment." Of interest to us here, in our endeavor to understand children's sex-role development, is how their different biological foundations might affect behavior. We find that biology makes some contribution to sex-role identity, but in no way determines it.

INFANCY
The Origins of Sex Roles

chapter four

"It's a boy!" "It's a girl!"

As soon as a baby is born, the news travels from obstetrician and nurse to parents, as we saw in the transcripts of dialogues from the delivery room in Chapter 3, and then on to family members and friends. Just what is the news? Not just that a baby was born, but that a boy baby or girl baby was born. Later, other information, such as the weight and height of the newborn is added. The vital facts concerning the newborn's health and vigor or the parents' emotional state (parents experience a complex combination of excitement, joy, exhaustion, and emotional letdown) are frequently omitted. Thus, the first message transmitted to the mother and the world is the sex of the newborn child. Clearly, gender is perceived by our society as one of the most relevant bits of information about the newly arrived individual.

This early preoccupation with gender is reflected in two inevitable societal customs that follow the infant's arrival into the world. First, birth announcements and congratulation cards are exchanged among friends and family. Greeting card companies offer a wide selection of such cards, usually strongly sex-stereotyped by color (pink for girls, blue for boys), by play material (dolls and cuddly animals for girls, trucks and blocks for boys), by the activity depicted in the drawings (boys are envisioned growing into runners; girls into tea-sippers). Even the cards' rhymes indicate a rough and tumble quality for little boys and a sweet and cuddly quality for little girls:

> So you have a son!
> Baseball and football lie just around the corner
> Bicycles and pogo sticks
> and pockets full of tricks
> Life will be lively around your house now
> 'Cause boys will be boys—
> excitement and joy!

> Smiles and enchantment
> await you lucky ones
> For a daughter has arrived
> to bring happiness by the tons!

She'll charm the world that greets her
with her winning ways and smile
And papa and mama will burst with pride
as she works her feminine wile.

Such cards announce more than the birth of a child and even more than the gender; they announce our society's beliefs about sex roles.

After the cards come the gifts. The articles of clothing and blankets given to the child are often sex-specific with regard to color and detail: baseball and race car decals emblazon boys' sleepers, while napping bears or springtime flowers decorate the girls'. Oddly enough, toys appropriate to the newborn stage are mostly what we might now describe as "unisex." Defying classification according to sex, they serve the needs of what we learned in the previous chapter are the psychological and sensorimotor equivalence of newborn boys and girls. So, it is not surprising that available toys, meant to tap the skills of individuals in that early age range, are not sex-specific. And finally comes the decoration of the room. Parents decorate their sons' rooms boldly in blues and greens, their girls' rooms demurely in pinks and yellows. The use of pink for a baby boy's clothing or room is unthinkable. Surprisingly, the prohibition against pink is relatively recent phenomenon; according to Elena Belotti· (1976), in 1929 a Bolognese midwife initiated the custom of using colored ribbons to announce the birth of the baby—with a pink ribbon signifying that a girl had been born. The buying of different colored and types of clothes and the decorating of rooms differently for boy and girl infants illustrate how our sex-role beliefs begin to separate the young child's world into pink and blue, male and female.

Not only do babies arrive into a world that is of a different hue depending upon their gender, but they enter a society that arranges very different destinies for them. Nowhere are these differences more clearly illustrated than in the birth rituals followed in Lucania, Italy.

In Lucania, when a boy is born, a pitcher of water is poured into the road to symbolise that the newborn baby's destiny is to travel the roads of the world. When a girl is born, water is thrown on to the hearth to show that she will lead her life within the walls of the home.

(*Belotti, 1976, p. 29*)

All of these examples suggest that a baby is born into a world that takes his or her gender very seriously, a world that treats boys and girl babies somewhat differently, regardless of whether or not they behave differently, and a world that has differing expectations for boys and girls. In this chapter, we will raise several issues central to early sex-role development: whether or not early sex differences exist, how early socialization affects sex roles, and how infants learn that the world is divided into two genders and that the infant, like everyone else, is a male or a female. We are interested not only in the "how," but in the "when"—when sex differences occur, when parents (and others) begin sex-role socialization, and when gender identity is learned. Before turning to this task, examining the how and when of sex-role development in the first two or three years of life, we will look at the new world of infancy.

THE INFANT'S WORLD

Our knowledge about how infants develop has increased dramatically in the last few years. We are now aware of the cognitive and social capacities with which they enter the world, the forces of socialization that act upon them from the start, and their own role in the process.

The first years of life represent a time of extraordinary change, a rapid unfolding of an organism who enters the world with little knowledge but with a huge capacity to observe, to learn, and to adapt. By the end of the second year, infants can verbally communicate their wants and needs, control many aspects of their behavior, understand a bewildering number of concepts, and interact effectively as members of a family and, increasingly often today, as members of a day care school and a peer group.

We stated in Chapter 3 that the infant's world was thought to be a "buzzing blooming confusion" until very recently. Today, we know a great deal about infants' cognitive capabilities. Not only do we know that they can see, hear, smell, and vocalize in the first weeks of life, but we understand how they use their senses to learn about their world. For example, young infants can see and visually scan objects in their visual field and enjoy gazing at complex objects more than simple ones. Using sophisticated testing procedures, researchers have discovered how actively and intently an infant will work to focus a fuzzy picture, to change its brightness, or to turn on a melody. Since infants can't talk and tell us when a picture is focused or fuzzy and cannot reach out and physically turn a switch, some ingenious techniques have had to be devised, using whatever capabilities infants have. For example, Arnold Sameroff (1968, 1970) recognized one skill all infants have—sucking. He has shown that infants can easily control their amount of sucking when a nipple is placed in their mouth. An experimenter can relate the number of sucks performed to an outcome, such as music being turned on or a picture changing its focus. Using such a method, infants quickly learn that their action (sucking rapidly) controls an outcome (music coming on). Such action-outcome pairings are extremely important not only for helping us explore the nonverbal child's abilities, but for helping us to see that pairings which occur naturally in the world constitute one of the primary ways that infants learn about their ability to control their world and to see how the world operates. When a baby cries, the mother usually comes running with a bottle or a caress. Infants learn, via such interactions, that their behavior has an effect on others, that others are responsive to their needs, and that certain behaviors (like crying) are more likely to produce desired results (like mother).

A second important discovery concerns the infant's social capacities and shows that much if not all of what the infant learns is embedded in the social world. In fact, infants seem to be biologically prepared to be interested in their social world. Neonates' sensory abilities and preferences seem to compel them toward other persons. They would rather look at a face than almost anything. Why is this so? The three characteristics of the world that hold the infant's attention most closely are sound, movement, and contrast (Bond, 1972). Every parent has noticed his or her infant's attention to a slamming door, a moving hand, or a printed curtain. A human face has all these characteristics, and more. A nodding face and a human voice paired together is the first "object" in which the infant is interested. The fact that newborns can focus best upon objects 17 centimeters away, which happens to be just about the distance between a mother's and infant's face when the mother is nursing her baby, supports the idea that the infant's attraction to people is biological. The infant is born with a sensory apparatus that is especially sensitive to people, and this early sensitivity helps move the infant toward examination of and interaction with other humans rather than other objects, a process that proves extremely adaptive, since the infant is entirely dependent on other people for survival and nurturance (Brooks-Gunn and Lewis, 1979).

As interaction with the social world and as cognitive capacities increase, individuals in the infant's world begin to be treated differently, and a concept of "person" begins to develop. Research from Educational Testing Service's Infant Laboratory illustrates this development. Laurie Waite and Michael Lewis (1977) have demonstrated that infants start learning that a certain face and a certain voice "go" together in the first month of life. One-month-olds respond differently to having their mother's face paired with a stranger's voice, or a stranger's face paired with the mother's voice, than to having their mother's face and voice paired together. Other fairly complex relationships are learned in rapid succession. In a study by Jeanne Brooks-Gunn and Michael Lewis (1976), infants as young as seven months knew about the relationship between face and body size. When presented with a midget whose facial configuration and height, according to a child's experience, don't go together, infants tend to be quite surprised; presumably, they expect that 3-foot people would have the rounded facial features of a child, not an adult, as all of their experience is with 3-foot children and 5- to 6-foot adults.

A third development has to do with the socialization of the infant. People used to think that the infant's social world was small and restricted, centering on the family and almost exclusively on the mother. Other persons were thought to be unimportant and almost nonexistent in the first year of life. In fact, the infant is born into an extensive social network, one that is rich and varied. Infants do not have an exclusive relationship with their mothers, but interact with their fathers, brothers and sisters, grandparents, family friends, other young children, and teachers. Although all these relationships differ in intensity of feeling and in importance, they all affect the infants' perception of and introduction to the world (Weinraub, Brooks and Lewis, 1977; Lewis and Rosenblum, 1979). Although many of us are currently studying the infant's relationships with persons other than the parents, these relationships have not yet been studied in terms of early sex-role development, even though they probably do exert a considerable influence on sex roles.

A fourth discovery has to do with the reciprocal nature of early interactions. The infant is not only affected by the parents but affects them as well. The infant's contribution to the infant-parent relationship, as well as the parent's contribution, has been recognized. After intensive observation of infants and their parents, the interaction has been described as a symphony, a delicate interchange, where rhythms between initiating and responding, attending and not attending develop (Lewis and Rosenblum, 1974).

Let's look at an interaction sequence between a mother and her three-month-old baby, who is sitting in her infant seat in the kitchen watching her mother clean up the breakfast dishes. This sequence was observed by Michael Lewis and Roy Freedle (1973) in a study of the early communication between parent and child. The sequence, although very complex, is only 50 seconds long.

> F is sitting in her seat holding a rubber toy which is tied to the side of the chair. Mother has her back to F as she reaches for dish. F squeaks rubber toy making noise. As a "consequence" F kicks her feet and squeals with apparent delight. Mother turns toward F smiling. F looks at mother and vocalizes. Mother walks toward F smiling, and vocalizing. F quiets, eyes fixed on mother. Mother touches F's face. F vocalizes and moves her hands toward mother. Mother sits in front of F and vocalizes to her. (Talking about the toy which mother now holds.) F watches mother and listens. Mother pauses, F vocalizes. Mother touches F and vocalizes to her. F vocalizes. (1973, p. 127)

It can be seen that much of this early interaction is controlled by visual regard. Early interactions have several functions. First, such interaction helps bond the mother to the infant. Mother of blind babies often report troubles with the bonding process: they don't feel attracted to their infants, they feel that their infants don't belong to them, presumably because early eye-to-eye contact has not been established. Second, such interactions teach infants a sense of mastery and competence, since they can exert some control over their life, even by something as simple as eye-to-eye contact with the parent. Third, such interactions facilitate cognitive and linguistic development, as mothers who are very responsive to their infants' behaviors have babies who are cognitively advanced. Fourth, infants learn what behaviors are most appropriate, since parents selectively respond to the behaviors they wish to encourage in the child.

The explosion of information about the infant has not always been applied to sex-role development. Early studies did not examine sex differences, and parent–infant interactions were not examined in terms of the parent's and infant's gender. Recent work is remedying these deficiencies.

SEX DIFFERENCES IN INFANCY

An examination of behavioral differences between male and female infants is a gargantuan task, beyond the scope of this book, given the number of different behaviors that have been studied. We will concentrate on psychological differences that may be precursors to later differences thought to exist between men and women. A more extensive listing of studies and a summary of the findings may be found in Eleanor Maccoby and Carol Jacklin's thorough review of the sex difference literature (1974).

Exploration, Activity, and Aggression

A common sex-role stereotype holds that boys are more active than girls. Try to picture an eight-month-old sitting on the floor of her living room, not eagerly reaching for the magazines on the table, the cuffs of her mother's pants, the buckles on her father's shoes, and not rushing off on all fours after a ball, the lamp wire, or the record on the stereo. No such healthy eight-month-old, boy or girl, exists. All infants are curious and inquisitive and, unless restrained, drowsy, or asleep, will explore their environs. The enchantment with exploration characterizes the entire infancy period for both sexes.

We are especially interested in possible differences in activity and exploration for several reasons. As we shall see in Chapter 6, boys are more active than girls in the preschool period. Further, activity level is thought to be a precursor to aggression, and sex differences in aggression in older children and adults are widely acknowledged. Differences in aggression have been linked to differences in hormone levels, with high levels of activity and aggression believed to be related to higher levels of the male hormone androgen.

So it is with some surprise that researchers have found little evidence for early sex differences in activity level or amount of exploration. This suggests that later sex differences in activity level and aggression are not likely to be determined solely by biology; the socialization process is extremely important. As discussed in Chapter 6, hormones and socialization probably work together to push preschool boys to be more active and aggressive, although this is not the case in infancy.

Play Behavior

Although boy and girl infants may be equally active, they may differ with respect to the types of play in which they engage. We can easily conjure up an image of the stereotype: girls sit daintily at the sandbox making cupcakes, while the boys scurry around the yard. This picture is not an accurate one in the infancy period. In the first year of life, boys and girls play with the same toys and do the same amount of banging and cuddling. In the second year, differences begin to appear in some but not all studies. By the beginning of the third year, boys spend more time with guns, blocks, and trucks, girls with stuffed animals, dolls, puzzles, and pegboards. And by the end of the third year, sex differences in toy play are firmly established (Maccoby and Jacklin, 1974).

Sociability

One sex-role stereotype involves sociability, holding that women are more sociable than men. Are young girls enchanted with other people from an early age, preparing for their roles as friend, seductress, mother, and hostess? Does Janie rush to the door to greet visitors or climb into uncle's lap while Jeremy barely looks up when visitors arrive and ignores uncle's repeated offers to be held?

The answer to these questions is, as it so often is in psychology, "it depends." A few, but certainly not all or even the majority of studies have found girls to be somewhat more sociable to strangers. Girls sometimes exhibit wariness toward strangers earlier than boys, perhaps because of their earlier maturation (Beckwith, 1972; Robson, Pederson, and Moss, 1969). However, these differences disappear, as boys "catch up" to girls.

Infants' responsivity to others may develop quite early. Investigators such as Martin Hoffman have studied the newborn's response to another baby's cry and have found that newborn girls cry longer than newborn boys when hearing a tape of another crying baby (Hoffman and Levine, 1976; Sagi and Hoffman, 1976). While this finding might suggest that girls are initially more responsive to others, and may even be biologically prepared to be more responsive, studies of babies' interest in faces in the first months of life have found no sex differences and suggest that none exist. At this point, then, the issue of early differences in responses to others is unresolved.

Dependency and Attachment

"My Nicholas is such a clinging vine. He becomes so upset when I leave, he cries and cries."

"Anika is such a big girl. Why, she doesn't even blink an eye when I leave the house."

Mothers are unlikely to say such things. They would more likely characterize Anika as a clinging vine, Nicholas as a big boy. Is there any evidence for these sex-role stereotypes? Researchers have termed such phenomena either dependency (a word which has a slightly negative connotation, as in clinging vine) or attachment or love (obviously a positive attribute). In both cases, the infant's responses to the mother during free play, during the mother's absence, and upon her return have been scrutinized for evidence of attachment and dependency.

Whether or not boys and girls behave differently in such settings is an ongoing debate. Our reading of the literature suggests that boy infants tend to become more upset by separation from the mother than do girl babies. Some studies have shown boys to be more likely to cry when a parent leaves the room, to follow the mother when she leaves, and to play close to the mother upon her return, whereas other studies have not. In a recent study conducted by Michael Lewis and Valerie Kreitzberg (1979), 250 infants and their mothers were followed over the first two years of life. This study, unlike earlier ones, included equal numbers of infants who were from different socioeconomic backgrounds and had different birth orders, since both of these factors have been found to influence infant and parent behavior. Initial findings from this study verify some but not all of the earlier findings. Lewis and Kreitzberg found that twelve-month-old boys were more upset by their mother's preparation for departure, crying twice as often as the girls and staying closer to their mothers. As though the mothers anticipated their sons's distress, they tended to prepare their sons for the departure, often giving them instructions as to what to do while mother was gone. However, while the mothers were gone, the girls began to cry sooner than the boys, perhaps because of the paucity of instruction given or perhaps for some other reason. When the mother reappeared, the boys again cried more than the girls, with the mothers responding by holding their sons more.

In free-play situations where the mother is present, boys and girls engage in similar activities. In early Educational Testing Service Infant Laboratory studies, girls spent more time near their mothers and looked at and babbled to their mothers more often than did boys (Goldberg and Lewis, 1969; Brooks and Lewis, 1975). Other investigators, however, have not always found such differences (Maccoby and Jacklin, 1974). In Lewis and Kreitzberg's large study, girls again talked to, looked at, and smiled at the mother more than the boys did, while the boys fretted and cried more than the girls. Girls tended to sit right beside the mother, while boys played a few feet away, but not across the room.

In summary, the most consistent sex difference in this controversial area is that when boys are in the presence of their mothers in a stressful situation, they become more upset than girls. This difference may mean that boys are more affected by stressful situations in general rather than by the maternal separation situation in particular. To test this hypothesis, stressful situations *not* involving the mother need to be observed and possible sex differences investigated. Or this difference may reflect the fact that mothers treat boys and girls differently (such as "preparing" boys more for departure) and that the result is differential infant behavior.

Perception

"Girls talk while boys watch." It has commonly been thought that boys are more attuned to the visual world, girls to the auditory world. From this assumption, researchers have inferred that girls receive more information through sound, boys through sight; that girls are more responsive to people (who provide sight and sound), boys to objects (which usually provide more sight than sound); and that girls talk earlier because of their interest in sound.

However, recent studies suggest that there are fewer sex differences in perception than previously thought. In terms of sound, the only difference is that girls are somewhat more likely to vocalize when they hear another sound (especially voices), and to cry when they hear another baby crying, than are boys. In terms of sight, it is sometimes reported that boys process visual information more quickly than girls, but this is not a universal finding. In terms of infants' responses to sight and sound studied together, a study by John Watson (1969) found that fourteen-week-old boys were more responsive to visual information presented alone, girls to auditory and visual information presented together. This finding has been cited as support for the belief that boys are attuned to sight, girls to sound. An alternative explanation is that girls mature more quickly than boys and since the auditory system develops later than the visual one, girls, with their greater maturity, have auditory capabilities earlier than boys. Thus, girls may have a slight advantage for understanding sounds, but this advantage would diminish as the boys' auditory systems developed. Not all studies support this hypothesis, however.

Language

Females—all they do is talk. Given this common stereotype, we might expect girls to talk more and earlier than boys. And, in fact, our expectation is confirmed. But it looks as though girls are also talked *to* more than are boys. Let's look at the vocalization of infants which, appropriately enough, is called babbling, and at early mother–infant vocalization patterns. In one study by Michael Lewis and Roy Freedle (1973), mothers vocalized more to their three-month-old daughters than to their three-month-old sons, and daughters vocalized more in response to their mothers' vocalizations than did the sons, even though the boys and girls differed not one whit in their spontaneous babbling! Other studies (but not all) also report mothers talking more to their infants if they are girls, and girl infants cooing and babbling in response. By two years of age, such differences are even more striking. Not only do girls tend to talk earlier and do somewhat better on early verbal tests (Schachter, Shore, Hodapp,

Chalfin, and Bundy, 1978), but Louise Cherry and Michael Lewis (1975) found that when mothers and their 2-year-olds were observed playing together, mothers of girls talked more, used longer sentences, and asked more questions, while mothers of boys used more directive statements. In this setting, girls also tend to talk more than boys. This presents the age-old question—which came first: girls' interest in and responsivity to speech or mothers' more loquacious style with their daughters? Both mother and daughter share the responsibility: girls may respond to sound earlier than boys, and mothers clearly talk to their daughters more, even when the daughters are not talking more.

Summary

The most striking finding when pursuing the infant sex difference literature is that boy and girl infants are much more similar than they are dissimilar (Maccoby and Jacklin, 1974). However, there are a few findings of interest: girl infants may be more responsive to people and talk somewhat earlier than boys, whereas boy infants seem to be more sensitive to stressful situations than girl infants. Each of these differences seems to have been influenced by both biology and socialization. Early language may be due to earlier maturation of the auditory system (biology) and parental attempts to encourage vocalization (socialization). Sensitivity to stressful situations may be related to biological vulnerability (in Chapter 3, boys were shown to be more biologically vulnerable) and parental responses (in the next section, we will see that mothers often handle boys and girls quite differently). Slight biological differences seem to be amplified by socialization practices. However, as we shall see in the next section, sex differences can also be fostered by parental practices even in the absence of any biological differences.

SEX-ROLE SOCIALIZATION

At least three questions are of interest when examining early sex-role socialization. First, just what does the young child's gender mean to adults in our society? Because infants interact not just with their immediate family, but with friends, relatives, health care personnel, and day care workers, the beliefs of parents as well as of an assortment of other care-giving adults are important. And parents themselves are influenced by the beliefs and behavior of others, especially their own parents and friends.

A second important question concerns how gender affects the way in which adults interact with infants. Again, we are concerned with any care-giver's behavior but particularly with the parent's interaction with his or her children. This question involves the effect of both the infant's and the care-giver's gender, since not only do adults interact differently with boy and girl infants, but male care-givers act differently than female care-givers.

A third question that we might ask is: how are boys and girls actually affected by the ways parents and other adults treat them? What is the consequence of parents' encouraging different types of behavior and providing different sorts of environments for their sons and daughters? How do their children react to this differential treatment? In our review of infant sex differences, we found that very few differences appear in the first months or even the first year of life. However, as we shall see in the next chapter, more sex differences begin to emerge in the preschool period. The relatively late emergence of sex differences suggests that differential socialization plays a greater role than the different biological underpinnings in the process of sex-role acquisition. Most sex differences do not occur until infants have had experience with their social world, a world that has definite beliefs about boys and girls.

Society Sets the Stage

Beliefs about the existence of sex differences and the appropriateness of sex roles for infants are quite common in our society. These beliefs have been measured in several ways, including asking about preferences for boy and girl children, inquiring about the appropriateness of certain behaviors for boys and girls, and actually observing adults interacting with infants.

First, little boys are overwhelmingly preferred—whether one has asked adolescents, college students, or parents, whether one has asked in 1970 or in 1950, and whether one has asked Americans, Chinese, or Nigerians. In some societies, daughters are drowned or placed in a rush basket by the river. In our society, such drastic measures are not taken, but preference for a son is clear. For example, in 1954 a group of college students were asked, "If you were going to have only one child, which sex would you prefer?" Ninety percent of the males and 66 percent of the female college students answered "a boy" (Dinitz, Dynes, and Clarke, 1954). In 1970 a similar group of unmarried students were asked the same question. This time, 90 percent of the male and 78 percent of the female students indicated a preference for a boy (Hammer, 1970).

Preferences for boy children affect behaviors that are more direct than just responses to a survey. Examining the length of time between the birth of the first and second child, we find that the interval between children is longer if the first child is a boy, shorter if it is a girl. Parents, preferring a boy child, hurry into extending their family when their first baby is not male, presumably in the hopes of having a boy. In addition, mothers are more likely to report postpartum blues and postpartum depression after the birth of a daughter than a son. And pregnant women have been found to dream more often about boy than girl babies (Sherman, 1971).

In short, the preference for male children is well established. This is true even of people who profess to have no preference. When such people are forced to make a choice, 75 to 90 percent prefer a boy child. If there had really been no preferences, we would have expected one-half of those with "no preference" to choose a boy, one-half to choose a girl. Therefore, we should not be lulled into believing that "no preference" is indicative of equal value being placed upon boy and girl children. Our society still prefers sons. Though recent research suggests a new twist, parents wanting *both* a boy and a girl ("a boy for you and a girl for me"), parents would still like their firstborn to be a boy. This raises an interesting problem. Myriads of research studies have shown firstborn children to be more independent and achievement-oriented than later-born children. In fact, a large proportion of famous people in all fields of endeavor are firstborns, from presidents to Nobel Prize laureates. If parents could choose the sex of their babies, and chose boys as the firstborns, then boys would, just by being born first, be more achievement-oriented. This would have the effect of increasing, not decreasing, sex-role differences!

Second, sex-role stereotypes also appear in adults' perceptions of the appropriateness of certain activities for boys and girls. For example, Beverly Fagot (1973) asked college students to rate a number of activities in terms of their appropriateness for 2-year-old girls and boys. They rated three activities as appropriate only for girls: playing with dolls, looking in the mirror, and dressing up. Roughhousing, playing with cars and trucks, and acting aggressively were considered appropriate only for boys.

Third, adults' sex-role stereotypes influence their behavior toward boy and girl infants. A number of investigators have used a clever technique for observing differential treatment of boy and girl infants; it is called the "Baby X Technique," labeled so by Lois Gould (1972) in a book describing the experience of a family that refused to tell anyone the sex of their infant. In the laboratory, the sex of an infant is kept secret by dressing him or her in neutral clothing. Then, either the adults are told that the infant with whom they are to interact is a boy, or a girl, or they are given no gender information at all. The findings from studies utilizing this method suggest that adults act differently with and hold different views about the baby depending on the sex that they believe it to be. For example, John Condry and Sandra Condry (1976) had adults observe videotapes of infants in various situations. In one segment, an infant was crying in an ambiguous situation; adults who thought the baby was a boy explained that he was probably angry, while adults who thought the baby was a female explained that she was probably frightened, though in both cases the adults were viewing the very same infant in the very same videotaped episode. Carol Seavey, Phyllis Katz, and Sue Zalk (1975) also had adults actually interact with a three-month-old baby. The investigators discovered that those adults who were told the baby was a girl were more likely to choose a doll for the baby to play with than those adults who thought the baby was a boy. Those adults who were given no gender information at all each spontaneously labeled the baby as a boy or a girl. When these adults were asked what led them to believe that the baby was a boy or girl, they said they had used characteristics of the baby to make the judgment. If they thought the baby was male, they cited characteristics such as strength. For a female, they referred to the baby's softness and fragility. Again, remember that the same infant was being characterized as strong or soft, the actual distinction by sex characteristics being only in the minds of the adults. One of the authors has a child who, as an infant, more often than not looked like a Baby X, being typically dressed in overalls and a tee-shirt and having short hair. Depending on the sex Avery was perceived to be, individuals acted very differently toward her. One day the friendly manager of the local supermarket approached mother and child at the baby food counter and chatted amiably. Seeing Avery's sparkling new teeth, he exclaimed: "H-ee-y there fella. Bet ya'll be biting into a big juicy steak this summer!" Those who identified Avery as a girl were more likely to say: "O-o-oh, look at the tiny little teeth. Aren't they cute!" as if their function was strictly ornamental. In short, adults' behavior toward or feelings about babies is often dependent upon their own beliefs about the sex of the child.

Anticipating the Big Event

A pregnant woman is like the mystery prize on a television game show; everyone wonders about the surprise inside! In an effort to guess the contents, some people focus on what's inside by putting their ear to the box and jiggling it while others rely on cues they believe the outside packaging provides. When an acquaintance of ours was pregnant, her husband and her doctor favored the "inside" approach and based their guesses on the fetal heart rate: if over 140 beats per minute, the fetus was a girl; at 124, it was surely a boy. The nurse preferred the "activity" hypothesis: since the baby failed to move before the third month and was not especially active, it had to be a girl. Among those employing the latter strategy and basing their judgments on observable clues, her mother watched for signs of change in her face; when she looked all aglow, according to her mother, a girl was predicted. Her grandmother directed our friend to look at her hand. When she held it spread out in front of her, palms down instead of clenched and up, she was informed that she would have a girl. A laundry attendant's approach was to stand back, examine the pregnant woman's belly, and decree that, since she was carrying high, she would deliver a boy for sure (It was a girl).

Numerous other tests have been developed over the centuries. Elena Belotti (1977) has collected these "recipes," as she calls them. Some of the most common are as follows:

> The man and woman each take hold of one end of a wishbone and pull it apart. If the longest part comes away in the man's hand, the baby will be a boy.

If you suddenly ask a pregnant woman what she has in her hand and she looks at her right hand first, she will have a boy; if she looks at her left hand it will be a girl.

If the mother's belly is bigger on the right-hand side a boy will be born, and also if her right breast is bigger than her left, or if her right foot is more restless.

If a woman is placid during pregnancy she will have a boy, but if she is bad-tempered or cries a lot, she will have a girl.

If her complexion is rosy, she is going to have a son; if she is pale, a daughter.

If her looks improve, she is expecting a boy; if they worsen, a girl.

If the fetal heartbeat is fast, it is a boy; if it is slow, it is a girl.

If the fetus has started to move by the fortieth day it will be a boy and the birth will be easy, but if it doesn't move until the ninetieth day it will be a girl. (1977, pp. 22–23)

Now, rate each of the characteristics above as positive or negative. A woman expecting a girl is pale, her looks deteriorate, she is cross and ill-tempered, and she gets the short end of the wishbone, all negative characteristics. Furthermore, a girl is symbolized by the left —the left hand, the left side of the belly, the left foot, the left breast. Left connotes evil, a bad omen, or sinister. Again, the girls have all the negative characteristics. Sex-role stereotypes about activity also characterize Belotti's recipes: boys are believed to be active from the very beginning and girls have slower heartbeats and begin to move around later. The message, although contradictory (girls cause more trouble even though they are more passive), is clear in that it reflects the sex-role stereotype that boys "do" while girls "are" and the belief that boys are more desirable than girls.

Guessing the sex of the child prior to birth and attributing sex-role stereotypic attributes to the unsuspecting fetus is a common pastime; so is deliberating on possible names. Looking through the birth certificates in New York City for the year 1975, one finds among the most common boys' names for that year all the old standbys: Michael, John, Robert, and David. The list of most common girls' names is much more flexible, changing from year to year. That year, Jennifer ("fair spirit"), Melissa ("honey bee"; "a sweet child"), Nicole ("victory of the people"), Jessica ("rich lady"), and

Erica ("ever powerful") topped the list (McCue, 1977), showing some conformity to as well as some defiance of the sex-role stereotypes associated with "femininity." The greater conservatism of parents in selecting boys' names may have some relationship to the greater attention they give to and the greater concern they express over sex typing for males, a point we shall encounter again and again.

While prospective parents busy themselves with sex guessing and name choosing, they envision what their child will be like, they daydream about the sorts of things they will do together, and they plan for the future. What we would like to suggest is that even their constructions of their as yet unborn offspring are subject to sex-stereotyping. Prospective parents even have sex-stereotypic reasons for wanting a boy or a girl. Lois Hoffman (1977) asked women in a nationwide survey why they wanted a boy or a girl. A boy was desired to please the husband, to carry on the family (husband's) name, to be a buddy to his father. Girls were wanted as a companion and as a play toy. By the time of delivery, the parents have been primed for the reactions exhibited in the Rubin, Provenzano and Luria study cited in Chapter 3, for their expectations about male and female babies have already been formed along sex-stereotyped lines.

After the birth of their child, parents often take great pains to assure that people will correctly identify the sex of their child, even from a distance. While they might stop short of waving pink or blue banners from the carriage hood, they do bundle the baby in sex-typed colors and make sure the boy-baby's bonnet is brimmed and the girl's ruffled. Researchers in Educational Testing Service's Infant Laboratory frequently find that the parents become annoyed if anyone inadvertently mislabels their children's sex. Mothers of opposite-sex twins, who find their babies mislabeled very frequently, find this especially disquieting, as Jeanne Brooks-Gunn and Michael Lewis (1975) found. These mothers have learned to minimize their annoyance by dressing their young children in sex-typed clothing which, of course, prevents mislabeling.

Suppose parents could know or even control the sex of their child. Would they choose to? A spate of books on the subject of choosing your child's sex have recently appeared. Judging by the popularity of such books, many parents or prospective parents would be glad to avail themselves of an opportunity to determine their child's sex. Some, in fact, would go to great lengths to do so, including using amniocentesis, a procedure used to test for chromosomal abnormalities that cause birth defects and handicaps. Because the procedure entails some risks, doctors advise its use only when the parents have some reason to suspect abnormalities in the fetus (e.g., because of the ingestion of certain drugs early in the pregnancy, because of the mother's age or health, or because of a history of genetic defects in the family). Being a male or being a female, when the parents would prefer otherwise, does *not* count as a sufficient "abnormality" to warrant the procedure, nor to warrant the termination of a pregnancy!

Parent–Infant Interaction: Getting Acquainted

The first years of a child's life are a kind of getting acquainted period during which first-time parents try out their new roles and already practiced parents absorb the latest newcomer into the family.

Before reviewing what we know about how parents behave toward their new sons and daughters, let's examine the ways in which the researchers measure and describe the parent–infant exchange. Researchers interested in parent–infant interaction can usually be found in one of two locations: the home of a child under 2 to which they have been invited, or a laboratory into which they have been able to coax a parent and an infant. When observing in homes, they try to be as unobtrusive as possible: they sit off to the side of a room or in a corner somewhere, and they say as little as possible during their visit. Mostly, they watch. Researchers have been known to observe parent–infant pairs in the home for the greater part of the day, in order to catch the pair in a variety of situations, such as feeding, bathing, playing with the mother, or playing alone. Usually, they manage to be so inconspicuous that the families disregard their presence and return to their daily household routine. In the laboratory, investigators are more commonly found in a closet-like room with an assemblage of recording devices. From this room, through a one-way mirror they observe the parent–infant pair interacting in a comfortable playroom outfitted with toys. Often the parent is asked to leave the playroom for a short time while the researchers observe the child's response to separation from and reunion with the parent.

In both the home and laboratory settings, the researchers record four types of measures. First, observers record the *frequency* of be-

haviors, counting the number of times an infant smiles at, moves toward, or looks at the parent, and explores the room and plays with toys, as well as the number of times the parent talks to, picks up, smiles at, or plays with the infant. Second, the observer notes *who is initiating* and *who is responding* in an interaction. When an infant fusses and the mother picks him or her up, the infant has initiated an interaction and the mother has responded to her child's bid for attention. Third, by recording the *speed* with which a parent responds to the child, the observer obtains a measure of the parent's "responsivity." One parent may respond quickly to a child's cry, another may allow the child to cry for a long period of time before responding, and still another may ignore the cry. Fourth, the observer makes note of the *type of behavior* that the parent uses to respond to the infant. For example, one parent may respond to a cry by picking the child up, another by talking to the child. Together, these measures (frequency of behaviors, initiation versus response, speed of response, and type of behavior) can describe how individual parents act. Investigators find that there are a number of different styles of interaction which parents utilize, each having different consequences for the child's later development. For example, having a very responsive mother (mothers who respond to their needs quickly) is related to an infant's being more alert and more inquisitive than infants with less responsive mothers (Lewis and Coates, 1976; Rubenstein, 1967).

Whether parents perpetuate or amplify already existing sex differences or assume sex differences should exist based on their own stereotypes, their interactive style with their infants has an impact on their children's developing sex role. Because we unearthed so few real differences between boy and girl infants, we would be willing to assume that the development of increasingly extensive sex differences depends a great deal on the parents' differential treatment of boy and girl babies.

In the next few pages we shall consider the way in which mothers' and fathers' interactions with their sons and daughters differ and the possible consequences of early differential treatment for the child's later development.

In a study of parents' interaction with their seven-week-old

Figure 4–1.

infants, Howard Moss (1974; Moss and Robson, 1968) watched as parents worked with their seven-week-old infants on a series of tasks. The parents' job was to get their babies to smile, to babble, to follow an object with its eyes, and to grab at a bell. Moss set no time limit for the parents, nor did he give them any hints about how they might encourage their infants to perform. He found that both mothers and fathers spent more time encouraging girl babies than boy babies to smile and to vocalize, even though there are no early infant sex differences in the actual performance of these tasks. But the fact that it is typically as easy to get a boy baby to smile and talk as it is to prompt a girl baby to perform these behaviors counters the commonly held stereotype that girls are more sociable than boys. The fact that the parents behaved more in accordance with the stereotype than with the fact demonstrates, Moss suggests, that differences between the sexes are probably "amplified over time through the stereotyped sex-role attitudes of parents, which evidently are present and functioning when the infant is young" (Moss, 1974, p. 162). To what extent parental behaviors of this kind are precursors and in what way they influence the child are unknown, but as we shall see in Chapter 6, by the age of 4, differences in the sociability of boys and girls do exist.

Parents express their differing views about boys and girls not only in the way they act but in the way they construct the settings within which the child lives and interacts. Just go to your nearest toy store and what do you see? The doll is advertised by a picture of an adorable little girl hugging the equally adorable doll; the truck is advertised by a picture of an industrious little boy pushing the truck through a maze of toys. Although newborn toys are "unisex," infant and toddler toys are not. Now go to your best friend's (or your own!) house and visit the children's bedrooms. As Harriet Rheingold and Kaye Cook (1975) found when they visited the bedrooms of nearly one hundred boys and girls, the typical setting for a daughter was frilly and soft, with lots of floral patterns, ruffles, and lace. Girls' rooms were full of dolls, doll houses, and stuffed animals. Sons' rooms were decorated in an assortment of animal motifs and contained vehicles, sports equipment, and toy animals. The "unisex"

Figure 4–2. Little boys' rooms are equipped with airplanes, tin soldiers, and outdoor toys.

toys of the newborn might have been stashed in a corner somewhere, but from six months of age through the preschool years, the play materials provided for the youngsters were heavily sex-typed. In fact, out of the average 28 toys found in each 1-year-old's bedroom and 91 toys in each six-year-old's bedroom, not a single wagon, bus, boat, kiddie car, motorcycle, snowmobile, or trailer was found in a girl's bedroom, though the boys, on the average, had amassed 36 such objects!

The common parental claim that Santa brought Johnny a truck for Christmas because he adores trucks, or that Suzy longed for a Tiny Tina doll, arouses suspicion. A hefty stock of sex-typed toys finds its way to children's toy shelves, even before they are capable of asking for specific toys, before they have established clear toy preferences, and before they are bombarded with sex-typed media messages. The toy preferences exhibited by toddlers at play in the laboratory or home are probably a reflection of the toys they have had since infancy, rather than of their initial preferences for such toys.

When a boy toddler shows a preference for a truck by playing with it longer than a girl toddler does, the origin of his preference might be his early contact and his experience and familiarity with trucks, combined with a history of encouragement for playing with a truck. In fact, when Jerrie Will, Patricia Self, and Nancy Datan (1974) had parents play in a laboratory setting with an infant whom they were led to believe was a boy, the parents were the ones to initiate contact with the toy train and present it to the baby to play with rather than vice versa. And, when they believed the infant was a girl, they reached for a doll. In the toy preference studies, girl toddlers often show an initial interest in the trucks, but eventually abandon them for a more familiar type of toy.

As children develop, their toy preferences are based less on familiarity and experience than on their own awareness of the toy's sex typing. After about age 5, when, as we shall see in Chapter 6, children have established their sex-role identity, they show clear preferences for any toy that they are led to believe other children of their sex prefer (Liebert, McCall, and Hanratty, 1971).

Figure 4-3. White eyelet and ruffles decorate the bedroom of a typical little girl, where she is likely to be found playing with soft cuddly dolls and tea sets.

In short, parents treat their girl and boy babies differently. In the next paragraphs we shall discuss in detail the ways in which mothers' and fathers' interactions with their male and female infants differ. We suspect that this can affect the infant's behavior and beliefs with respect to sex roles in many ways. We shall discuss the possible consequences of early differential treatment for the child's later development as we go along.

Mothers and Babies

As early as three weeks of age the boy baby enjoys more attention and stimulation from the mother than a girl baby does. As Howard Moss (1967) has found, she holds him and touches him more than she does a girl. This early difference in the way mothers treat their young sons and daughters might be simply a response to the male child's greater fussiness and immaturity which we discussed earlier. In an effort to keep him happy or to soothe him when he is crying, the mother of a son might stay busier with him than she would with a quiet or easily soothable daughter.

Michael Lewis (1972), studying mother–infant interaction, has found two different styles of behavior a mother might use: one involves establishing or maintaining a physical closeness with her child, and the other allows her to "keep in touch" with her baby from a distance. The first he terms "proximal" behaviors, and the latter "distal" behaviors. Lewis found that mothers use the two styles differently depending upon the age and the sex of the child. For example, the mother uses more distal behavior, such as talking, with her three-month-old when the infant is a girl; and she uses a more proximal type of behavior, like touching and holding, with her three-month-old son. Like Moss, Lewis thinks the boys' greater irritability and the girls' greater maturity might account for the mothers' differential responses to their three-month-olds.

Between three and six months, however, something very interesting happens. Susan Goldberg and Michael Lewis (1969) saw that mothers started showing much more proximal behavior toward their daughters, that is, they began to stay in physical touch with them. At the same time, they slacked off on the physical contact with their

Figure 4–4.

sons. So, by the time infants were six months of age, mothers touched their girl babies more than their boy babies. This switch, from boy babies' being held more at three months to girl babies' being touched more at six months, suggests that boys are given more proximal behavior only when they are more irritable. As soon as the boys have matured and have become less fussy, mothers encourage less proximal or feminine, behavior and more exploratory, or masculine, behavior. This is clearly seen by the time infants are twelve months of age. Here are descriptions of how two mothers and their 1-year-olds were interacting in Educational Testing Service's Infant Laboratory:

> Baby walks away from his mother, trips and falls. Baby returns to his mother, fretting. Mother touches baby and baby touches her. Mother takes out plastic ring, shows it to baby, rolls it across the room, saying "See the ring! Bring the ring to mommy! Can you get the ring!" Baby looks, smiles and walks toward the ring.

> Baby walks away from her mother, trips and falls. Baby returns to mother, fretting. Mother picks up and hugs baby. Mother, still holding baby, offers baby a stuffed animal.

In the first behavioral observation, the mother establishes brief physical contact with her son in order to comfort him, but then disengages him from the contact by tossing a ring to the other side of the room. The effect is to lure him away and to encourage him to explore on his own awhile.

In the second observation, the mother prolongs the physical contact initially given to comfort the infant by picking her up, hugging her, and imitating a playful episode in which contact can be maintained. The effect is to encourage the girl to stay close and refrain from exploring on her own.

Such parental practices begin to have an effect upon child behavior. Although studies of 1-year-olds' exploration of unfamiliar rooms and toys show that both sexes explore equally, the exploration and play behavior of boys and girls begins to diverge at age 2. In a study by Marsha Weinraub and Michael Lewis (1973) in the Infant Laboratory at Educational Testing Service, 2-year-old girls played with as many toys as the 2-year-old boys did, but tended to bring the toys back to their mother's chair and play with them there, while the boys played with the toys wherever they found them. While the infants were learning the same sorts of things about the toys, they were experiencing very different situations in terms of the relationship between playing and being with mother. Other infant behaviors associated with the infant's relationship with the parent exhibit sex differences even earlier. In the same study in which Susan Goldberg and Michael Lewis found mothers of six-month-olds to be more proximal with their daughters, these daughters were, at twelve months of age, staying closer to their mothers!

Fathers and Babies

We have seen that mothers treat their sons and daughters differently and treat them in sex-stereotypic ways, encouraging proximal behavior and verbalization in girls and distal behavior and exploration in boys. What about fathers? Until very recently, the father's role in his infant's development was all but ignored by psychologists. It was thought not only that the father was of no importance until the preschool years and the advent of the Oedipal complex (see Chapter 5 for a discussion of the Oedipal complex), but that the father had neither the interest nor the expertise to deal with infants. Interest in babies was thought to be part of the maternal instinct, a biological tendency for mothers to love and protect and care for their young. However, there is now evidence that love comes more from contact than from biology, that the father can play an important role in his young child's well-being, and that he can be as interested in his child as his wife is. One researcher, Harry Harlow (1961; Harlow and Zimmerman, 1959), has shown that baby monkeys prefer to cuddle with a terry cloth surrogate mother rather than with a wire mesh surrogate, in spite of the fact that the wire mesh surrogate provided milk through a nipple and the terry cloth surrogate did not. This study demonstrates that love is not based on nourishment as much as on nurturance.

As part of an ever-growing recognition of the potential role of fathers in a child's development, fathers are taking a more prominent place in the parenting scene. Even before the child is born, the father's involvement has begun through his interest in childbirth preparation classes. And increasingly more fathers are participating in the actual process of childbirth. Figures differ by geographic location, socioeconomic class, and ethnic group, but in middle-class, educated families, paternal participation is the rule. In 1978, fully 75 percent of the childbirths in Princeton, New Jersey, involved the fathers. They had attended childbirth preparation classes, assisted the wives with daily practices in breathing techniques, helped their wives through labor, accompanied them to the delivery room, and witnessed the birth of their child. Many of our friends, after becoming proud fathers, reported that the birth of their child was a peak experience for them, one of the most (if not the most) satisfying events in their lives.

As anecdotal evidence for the responsiveness of fathers to their newborns becomes more accessible, so does research evidence. Observing fathers and mothers interacting with their newborns, Ross Parke and Sandra O'Leary (1976) found that both parents were absorbed, preoccupied, and elated about the birth of their child.

The father's feelings toward his infant are reciprocated: young children do care for their fathers and show a great deal of pleasure interacting with them. How many times have you seen a young child exuberantly greet the father with obvious excitement and joy? This joy comes through to those observing fathers and infants. As Michael Lamb (1977, 1978) has demonstrated, infants enjoy interacting with their fathers, and from the time they are able to form relationships, do not seem to prefer the mother over the father in most situations. In fact, Lamb has found that 2-year-old boys seem to prefer their fathers to their mothers in play situations! In one study in which 2-year-old infants were observed greeting their fathers and their mothers after a brief separation, they would often greet their fathers by engaging them in play, but would not greet their mothers in this way. However, the mother seems to be preferred in somewhat stressful situations; for example, in one study, infants were more likely to turn to their mothers than to their fathers when a stranger entered the room. When only the father is available, of course, an infant turns to him for comfort (Cohen and Campos, 1974). These two sets of observations suggest that infants perceive their parents' functions somewhat differently, with father's function being play and mother's being care-giving and comfort. The infant's perception of his parents' different roles is reflected in his use of the words "Mommy" and "Daddy." The word "Mommy" is often used as a call for help as well

Figure 4–5.

as to refer to a specific person. In her study of 2-year-olds' responses to the departure separation from their father, Marsha Weinraub reports that the majority of the toddlers said "Mommy" as they followed their fathers to the door. All of these toddlers had the word "Daddy" in their vocabulary and used "Daddy" and "Mommy" to refer to the appropriate person. In this case, "Mommy" seemed to mean "don't leave" or "come here," rather than referring to a specific person.

The fact remains that fathers probably do not utilize their competency with babies as often as mothers do. In most families, mothers still do the bulk of the care-giving. When we questioned fathers of infants, only one-quarter of them stated that they had any regular care-giving activities. A most distressing estimate of the amount of time fathers spend with their young offspring is given by Freda Reblesky and Cheryl Hanks (1971). Reblesky placed a tape recorder by the bassinets of several very young infants. In these homes, the father's voice was picked up for about 30 *seconds* per day! Fathers of young infants are not interacting with them, or at least not talking to them. Fortunately, as the infant grows older, the father begins to spend more time with the child, with estimates ranging from 15 minutes to an hour a day for infants under a year of age. Perhaps as paternal participation in childbirth increases, so will paternal involvement after birth. Interestingly, Milton Kotelchuck (1976; Zelazo, Kotelchuck, Burke, and David, 1977) has found that protest over being separated from the father, often used as a measure of attachment, has been shown to be higher when fathers spend time with and take care of their infants. Spending time with the infant is essential for the development of a meaningful relationship.

The activities in which most fathers participate are more limited than those of mothers: the primary activity of fathers is play. Fathers have been observed to engage in more play behavior than mothers. In addition, the type of play mothers and fathers use tends to be different. For example, fathers of eight-month-olds seem to use more physically stimulating, varied, and idiosyncratic forms of play, whereas mothers tend to play with their babies using play materials and conventional games like pat-a-cake and peek-a-boo (Lamb, 1976, 1978). Taken together, these findings suggest that the father does little care-giving and lots of playing while the mother does lots of care-giving and a moderate amount of playing. These differences are reflected in the way infants interact with their mothers and fathers.

In short, fathers usually make an important but different contribution to their infants' lives than mothers do—*not* because fathers are biologically unprepared to care for infants, but because they are socialized to see care-giving as feminine, and playing as masculine.

We have contrasted the father's behavior toward his infant to that of the mother. But what about paternal differences in interacting with their infants depending on whether the infants are boys or girls? While we know that mothers treat boys and girls differently as early as three weeks of age, there is unfortunately less information on fathers in this area. There are indications, however, that fathers are more concerned with sex-appropriate behavior than are mothers. For example, Beverly Fagot (1974) found that parents of 2-year-olds saw different roles for mother and father. They believed that among parents of sons, the father should play with and provide a role model for the son, though among parents of daughters, no such clearly differentiated modeling role seemed necessary. With different attitudes toward their role as fathers of sons versus fathers of daughters, it is not surprising that fathers, in the study by Rubin, Provenzano, and Luria discussed earlier, perceived greater differences between their newborn sons and daughters than mothers did. Not only do fathers perceive their newborn boys and girls differently, but they also treat them differently. They are more likely to touch and talk to their firstborn newborn sons than their later born sons or any of their daughters. These findings suggest that fathers, like mothers (and maybe even more than mothers), treat their boys and girls differently from infancy, even though boy and girl infants are themselves not very different!

INFANTS' PERCEPTIONS OF GENDER IDENTITY AND SEX ROLES

Not only is it important to know how parents encourage sex-role socialization and gender differentiation, but the children's perceptions are also important. Young children, who have limited cognitive abilities, often perceive the world quite differently than adults. Jean Piaget, the famous philosopher and child psychologist, has provided us with fascinating glimpses of the child's understanding of many phenomena. Take, for example, dreams. Young children often believe that dreams are real, that the monsters they experience do live under the bed, only appearing after the lights are out and the eyes are closed. Or shadows. Young children do not understand why they cannot jump into the middle of their shadow, or why it follows them, or why it disappears when the sun hides behind a cloud. Or pain. Young children may think that a stone, when thrown, is hurt or, somewhat paradoxically, that an animal does not mind being kicked or hit. These early beliefs are modified by the interaction of experience, experimentation, cognition, and language. But the young child may construct the world, including beliefs about gender and sex roles, very differently from you or me, despite our best intentions.

Gender Identity

In the late infancy period, we can observe the origins of gender identity. Infants' notions of gender are most rudimentary: they know that there are two sexes in the world and that they belong to one of them. But, for all they know, their sex could change overnight: a boy could become a girl by putting on a dress and a girl could change to a boy by getting a haircut.

We shall be discussing the actual processes underlying their changing notions of gender identity in later chapters; but for now, we will simply report on the status of gender identity in the infancy period. Infants' ideas about gender are tied to their knowledge about categories in general. They know about such categories as age and gender; they know about their own place in these categories, and, as we shall see when we discuss their notions of sex role, they have a fuzzy idea about the relationship between these categories and a number of social functions (such as the link between adulthood and work). We know what infants know because of experiments like those of Jeanne Brooks-Gunn and Michael Lewis. In some of these studies, infants are placed in a baby seat alongside their mothers at one end of a room. At the other end, a stranger appears at the door and proceeds to walk toward the infant. Upon reaching the infant, the stranger bends down, smiles, and touches the infant's hand, after which the stranger leaves the room. The infant is presented with strangers who differ according to a prearranged set of factors—gender, age, height, and so on. From such studies, we have learned that infants, sometimes as early as six months of age, respond differently to adult and child strangers, smiling and reaching to the children, frowning and turning away from the adults. Slightly later, around twelve to eighteen months of age, infants will respond differently to men and women strangers, being more positive to the latter (Brooks and Lewis, 1976; Brooks-Gunn and Lewis, 1979; Lewis and Brooks, 1974).

Other studies by Jeanne Brooks-Gunn and Michael Lewis have examined the labels which toddlers use to classify family members, strangers, and themselves. Infants begin to use gender-related words to refer to themselves as soon as they have the words to do so (Brooks-Gunn and Lewis, 1979). And, gender reassignment (as in the case of the twin in Chapter 3) can be done until about 18 months of age with no difficulty, but children over 18 months have problems adjusting to a "new" gender (Hampson and Hampson, 1961).

Sex Roles

One can learn about an infant's perception of sex role only through indirect means, since infants are unable to tell us what they believe. For example, the fact that they assign different functions to different people suggests that they do have a rudimentary conception of sex role. When both parents are available they approach their mothers for comfort, their fathers for play, because that is how they perceive the initial role differences.

In addition, as we saw earlier, infants are often seen using the word "Mother" when they need help, not just when they want or recognize mother. Such behavior on the infant's part suggests that he or she is beginning to associate certain people with certain functions, laying the groundwork for later sex-role differentiation. Interestingly, such behavior is common even in families in which rigid sex roles do not exist. This is explained by the young child's need to make sense of the world, to understand the relationships among persons, functions, and statuses. Early categorizations may be quite rigid or quite global. With increasing cognitive ability, categorizations become less inflexible, as we shall see in Chapter 5.

Another example of sex-role perception involves the infant's perception of the relationship of certain chores and the persons that do them. Marsha Weinraub and John Leite (1977) have shown that some 2-year-olds have knowledge of sex-role stereotypes. When these researchers gave children pictures of sex-typed items, such as a lawn mower, carpentry tools, a tie, a purse, an iron, and a clothes dryer, and asked them to "give" each picture to a man or a woman, about one-quarter of the 2-year-olds were able to successfully classify the majority of the pictures according to sex-role stereotypes. In addition, those children who had the most clear-cut sex-role stereotypes also exhibited the most sex-typed toy preference, which was measured by having the children build a car garage and a doll house. These findings suggest that knowledge of sex-role stereotypes develop between two and three years of life.

In order to learn about sex roles, the infant must first learn to differentiate between men and women. Infants seem to be able to do this quite early. The first male–female distinction an infant makes is probably the one between mother and father, with infants being capable of this distinction in the first three months. Berry Brazelton, Michael Yogman, Heidi Als, and Edward Tronick (1979) have demonstrated, via intense observation of videotape sequences of mother and infant, and father and infant, that infants even in the first months of life have very definite patterns of interacting with mother and with father. We do not doubt that the infant develops different patterns to use with other persons too, but these have not yet been studied. In terms of general distinctions between male and female, in the first year of life, infants seem to rely on height and voice differences. In a series of studies discussed earlier, Jeanne Brooks-Gunn and Michael Lewis found that young infants do not respond differently to a man and a woman approaching if they are the same height and silent, but do respond differently if they are different heights and talking. Dress and hair style become important by the end of the second year. Genital and reproductive differences do not seem to be noticed until later, between three and four years of age. Much of this information has been gained through an examination of the labels children use for pictures of people. From the beginning of the use of such labels, which is around 18 months through 36 months of age, we have found that "Mommy" is used for adult females, "Daddy" for adult males. "Boy" and "girl" are used correctly as soon as these terms are acquired. Interestingly, gender neutral words, like "child," "adult," and "kid," are acquired much later, again illustrating the importance of gender in our world (Brooks-Gunn and Lewis, 1979).

. . . AND BABY MOVES ON

We have charted the course of the treatment of boy and girl infants by parents and others, demonstrating that boys and girls are perceived and are treated differently from the very beginning of life, even in the absence of infant sex differences.

In addition, the findings discussed in this chapter suggest that differential treatment does not always lead to *immediate* sex differences. Some sex differences may not show up until a later time. The parents' use of more proximal behavior with their daughters than with their sons is a good example. Staying close to mommy is thought to be more appropriate for girls and may lead to later dependency in women. Jerome Kagan and Howard Moss (1962) followed approximately 100 children from childhood to adulthood. Among the many interesting findings is one having to do with dependency. Girls who were very dependent in the preschool and elementary school tended to be very dependent as adult women. Presumably, their early dependency was reinforced, as such dependency is considered appropriate for young girls. Boys, on the other hand, did not show any such stable patterns of dependency. That is, boys who were very dependent as youngsters were not necessarily dependent adults. In all likelihood, the dependent young boys were not rewarded for this behavior and were probably rejected or punished by peers, parents, and teachers when they acted in dependent ways ("Boys don't cry when they fall," "You should be able to do that math problem without help," "If Johnny hits you, don't come to me for sympathy"). Thus, no relationship for dependency in childhood and adulthood existed for boys but did for girls.

Through differential treatment, through the provision of play materials, through the dressing in sex-typed clothing, and through the observation of the role of gender in society, the child at the close of infancy is well-equipped to acquire a sex-role identity, for better or worse. The toddler knows that gender, along with age, are the most important dimensions of the world, that the world is composed of males and famales, that he or she is, along with everyone else, either one or the other, and that certain activities are for males and others for females. Exactly how is this information used to construct a sex-role identity? In our next chapter, we explain this not so mysterious process.

THEORIES OF SEX-ROLE ACQUISITION

chapter five

Morgan identifies himself as the daddy: "I'll work for a while, in my office." "And I'm the mommy, and I'll help you, okay?" asks Jeff. "No," replies Morgan, explaining, "No, you're the mommy. You help David (the baby), okay?"

As Kathy struggles to set up the ironing board, she calls out to Karen, "Hey, Mother, help me!" Karen helps a bit by pulling the iron and the cord out of the way, and says, "We're havin' trouble here, aren't we?" "Yeah, stupid ironing board . . . Mother, come and help me, will ya?" asks Kathy, still struggling. "Oh dear, I got the babies, gotta worry about. . . , probably when Daddy comes home tonight, he'll fix it," replies Karen.

By age 4, the child's store of information about sex roles has expanded: daddies work and fix things; mommies clean the house and take care of babies; boys play with hammers and wrenches, girls with irons and brooms. How does the young child arrive at this view of the sexes? And how does he or she come to acquire sex-related behavior patterns and preferences?

In the first four chapters we saw that adults hold firm beliefs about sex-related behaviors and that sex-role stereotypes pervade our society. We saw that boy and girl newborns enter the world more alike than different, yet meet with differential treatment by parents and care-givers from the start. By later infancy, differences in toy play, vocalization, and sensitivity to stressful situations have begun to appear, all unexplainable by biological factors alone. We saw, too, that toddlers have started to notice that the world is divided into two, that they know they belong to one of these two divisions.

By age 4, the paths of boys and girls diverge still further, as we shall see in this and the following chapter. Before turning to preschoolers' ideas about sex roles and the actual sex differences between boys and girls of this age, we shall discuss the process of sex-role acquisition, summarizing the major developmental theories that have been called upon to account for this process. The three theories that have had the most impact are (1) identification theory, (2) social learning theory, and (3) cognitive developmental theory. All three concentrate on changes occurring in the preschool years, since it is at this time, they all agree, that a sex-role identity becomes established. However, the theories differ considerably in their emphasis on the role of biology, of culture, of family, and of the children themselves in the process of sex-role development.

The three approaches are similar in one very important way, though. All contain a built-in bias stemming from the cultural beliefs and practices of Western society. Almost all of the theorists on the subject of sex-role acquisition were men, who either implicitly or explicitly accepted the societal role divisions and sex-role stereotypes of their day, and who proceeded to construct theories strewn with the assumptions underlying their cultural beliefs. They subscribed with such facility to the existence of many behavioral sex differences that their existence remained both unquestioned and untested empirically (as we shall see in later chapters, when finally tested scientifically, many of the differences turned out not to exist). These social scientists also wrote as if male sex-role development was the norm, while female sex-role development was, if not deviant or diluted, at least different. They never spelled out the processes underlying female development in as great detail as they did for male development. In addition, these theorists presumed that it was unequivocably healthy and correct to conform to the current sex roles. As we saw in Chapter 2, highly sex-typed individuals may not be as healthy, or at least not as flexible, as less sex-typed individuals; and, as we suggested, conformity to current sex roles may prove shortsighted, as sex roles may be inappropriate in today's society.

With these caveats in mind, we turn to the theories themselves.

IDENTIFICATION THEORY

Identification encompasses an entire array of theories, rather than just one. All, however, attempt to explain sex-role acquisition in terms of an identification with the same-sex parent's personality, attitudes, and behavior. The child, through a process to be described in a few moments, literally takes the same-sex parent's personality as his or her own. Once this identification has occurred, the child's newly acquired internal "parent" regulates and motivates his or her behavior. The process is irreversible: the internal "parent," once acquired, cannot be easily disposed of.

Freudian Theory

The first identification theory was developed by Sigmund Freud, the father of psychoanalysis. In Freud's theory, fear motivates the child to identify with the same-sex parent. Freud postulated two kinds of fear-based identification: fear of loss of love (called *anaclitic identification*), and fear of retaliation (called *defensive identification*), with the former underlying a girl's sex-role development and the latter underlying a boy's. The same traumatic event causes fear and thus triggers identification for both boys and girls; namely: the observation of the mysterious fact that males have penises and females do not. How boys and girls interpret this discovery and what they do about it differ, but regardless of their interpretation of this fact of life, they arrive at the same resolution, namely the acquisition of a sex-role identity derived from identification with their same-sex parent.

The story is a complicated one, and is best told through the tale of Oedipus. In the fifth century B.C., Sophocles wrote of a youth in ancient Greece who had conquered a kingdom—killing its king and taking its queen for his wife. Unfortunately for this young man, Oedipus, and for his entire kingdom, his crime was much more heinous than anyone, including himself, could ever have imagined. Unbeknownst to him, the king whose life he had taken was his father and the queen whom he had married was his mother. According to the legend, when the truth emerged after a long, successful reign, nothing but trouble ensued—plague, pestilence, death, and destruction—because Oedipus as a young man had violated the most inviolable law of mortal man by lusting after his mother. At the close of the Greek play, having witnessed the enactment of so unthinkable a theme, the audience was in such a state of excitement and rage that they proceeded to stone the entire cast!

Rewrites of and variations upon the story of Oedipus abound. Bruno Bettleheim, in his book, *The Uses of Enchantment* (1976), tells how the tale appears in safely disguised forms in numerous children's fairy tales such as the Grimm Brothers' "Rapunzel" and similar tales of damsels in distress. He explains that the enjoyment of the young readers derives from their need to savor the forbidden fruits of the Oedipal situation, from the relief that they experience at being able to nurture their Oedipal feelings in the safe confines of an indirect and nonthreatening fantasy story, and from the reassurance that the fairy tales provide that an Oedipal predicament can have a happy outcome (" and they lived happily ever after. . . "). On an adult and contemporary level, in the 1970 film *My Lover, My Son*, the mutual attraction between mother and son leads to uncontrolled passions and murder. The dilemma underlying these popular accounts remains unchanged from the original Greek dramatization: a tragic desire for the opposite-sex parent by the child, who, in wanting to replace the same-sex parent as the object of the other parent's affection, faces what might be the most traumatic crisis of his or her life—a crisis Freud has termed the Oedipal conflict.

According to Freud (1931), desire is part of every child's life. Without its emergence and resolution, the child would be deprived of the core experience required for a strong personality development in general and for sex-role acquisition in particular. The drama unfolds as follows.

Beginning similarly for boys and for girls, the process underlying the development of personality and sex role has its roots in the biological requirements of nourishment and basic comfort common to all infants. Initially, the mother, exclusively, provides nourishment and comfort. Because of her unique ability to meet these needs (by virtue of having breasts to supply milk and, according to Freud, an instinct to provide comfort), the mother becomes the dominant force in her children's life. Regardless of their sex, the children, as a result of the mother's physical and psychological ministrations, grow dependent on her. Out of their dependency on the mother, anaclitic identification develops; the infants fear the loss of her love. This fear, partially because it has some basis (mothers are not always with their children, and brief separations, both physical and psychological, are commonplace), prompts infants to identify with or become like the mother, to acquire her traits, her temperament, and her values in order to please her and to ensure her continued love.

At about 4 years of age the course of sex-role identification for boys and girls diverges. With the discovery of the genitals, boys switch from anaclitic to defensive identification, from the mother to the father. Freud believed that this switch, involving the Oedipal struggle, occurs as follows. The boy's love for his mother continually grows and eventually assumes sexual overtones, which become a source of anxiety when he considers that he has the father to contend with. Realizing that as long as his father is around he can never enjoy the privileged and all-consuming relationship with the mother that he would like, the young boy must somehow relieve himself of the burden of simultaneously loving his father as a parent and hating him as a competitor. Considering the course taken by the young king Oedipus—namely, "doing Daddy in"—only leads to feelings of guilt and fear. He feels guilty because of the filial affection he feels toward the father. He is fearful because of a conviction that father's discovery of his desires would surely lead to retaliation. The retaliation envisioned by the boy as the appropriate punishment for his desire for his mother is castration, the horror of which serves as the motivating force for the eventual resolution of the Oedipal complex and the identification with the father. The child reasons somewhat like this: "If Daddy ever knew what I've got on my mind, he'd do something terrible to me!" This is the famed Freudian notion of castration anxiety, the fear that the father will avenge his son's lustful feelings toward the mother by cutting off his penis. For, having noticed the absence of a penis of his mother and his sister, the boy surmises that whatever fate befell them might soon befall him as well. The anxiety-ridden child figures that he will either lose his penis and become like the mother or that his father will castrate him. In order to escape, the boy resolves to abandon all of his plans and his wishes to eliminate father, and "join the camp." By identifying with the father, becoming as much like the father as possible, the boy can keep his penis. The strategy employed to effect this radical shift in the boy's identification, from the mother to the father, is termed *defensive identification* or *identification with the aggressor.* The boy as potential victim begins, by acquiring the traits of the father, to befriend his potential aggressor. The transition from identifying with the primary love object, the mother, to the secondary love object, the father, marks the beginning of the boy's active acquisition of the masculine sex role.

The girl, not having a penis and not fearing castration, does not shift from mother to father, and her anaclitic identification stays intact. At the same time, a dilemma does develop for the girl. While a fear of losing his penis served as an impetus toward the resolution of the Oedipal conflict for boys, a belief that she has somehow already lost hers serves as a trigger for the onset of the Oedipal conflict for girls. Noticing for the first time the differences between the sexes and her own lack of a penis, the girl suffers from *penis envy* and she holds her mother accountable for her loss. She gradually turns away from her mother as the object of her sexual affection and focuses on her father. Her desire for a penis is gradually replaced with a desire for a baby. This reinforces her original identification with the mother, since she realizes that, in order to get a baby from her father, she must be like her mother. She opts, therefore, to continue to identify with, that is, to become like, the mother. This decision marks the onset of the girl's active acquisition of the mother's personality, especially of those characteristics central to sex-role identity.

Freud believed that the basic Oedipal solution of girls was inferior to that of boys and that defensive identification was superior to anaclitic identification. Without the trauma of the Oedipal conflict and the anxiety of potential castration, girls were not able to develop a strong sense of conscience or competence. As a result, Freud thought women to be morally inferior to men. He wrote:

> I cannot evade the notion (though I hesitate to give it expression) that for women the level of what is ethically normal is different from what it is with men. Their super-ego is never so inexorable, so impersonal, so inde-pendent of its emotional origins as we require it to be of men. (1931/1964, p. 257)

The Oedipal struggle was seen as essential for the development of a normal personality and normal sex-role identity. If an individual failed to resolve the Oedipal situation in the manner described above, he or she would develop irreversible character disorders. In fact, Freud traced most adult neuroses back to the original Oedipal con-flict. He developed his theory not through the examination of chil-dren or healthy adults, but through the treatment of troubled adults who reconstructed their childhood experiences for him during psychoanalysis. So, his method, because it is retrospective and based on "neurotic" individuals, invites some distortion of normal develop-mental processes. In addition, Freud was greatly influenced by the Victorian society in which he lived. Differences between men and women not only were believed to exist, but were supposed to exist. So, when treating women patients who were dissatisfied with the inflexibility of Victorian society and the limitations placed on women's roles (and the vast majority of his patients were women, not men, who could not, by the way, have experienced castration anxiety), Freud attributed their problems to unresolved Oedipal complexes, not to realistic dissatisfactions with their life circumstances. Many of the problems he encountered involved rebellious attitudes and behaviors toward a patriarchal father or husband and desires for more freedom. Women who did not accept the confines of Victorian society or wished to work were considered in the first case hysterical, in the second case masculine, and in both cases deviant.

In addition to reflecting this societal bias, Freud's theory may have grown out of the way a little boy might describe penis envy and fear of castration. In 1926 one of Freud's disciples, Karen Horney, made this startling observation:

> The present analytical picture of feminine development (whether that picture be correct or not) differs in no case by a hair's breadth from the typical ideas that the boy has of the girl. (1926, p. 57)

For example, little boys sometimes believe that little girls also have a penis; the realization that they do not leads to the idea that the penis was taken away because the little girl was bad. The little boy believes he is in an enviable position, given that he has a penis while she has not. From such beliefs could a theory of penis envy be derived! Horney also suggested that Freud ignored the possibility of envy other than penis envy. If little girls realize that they have no penis, might not little boys realize that they have no breasts? The state of pregnancy, certainly seen by young children, might also result in envy on the boys' part.

These distortions and biases did not keep the Freudian theory of identification from having a major impact on later research and beliefs about sex-role identity. No doubt the fact that his theory reinforced existing sex-related societal beliefs and practices contributed to its popularity.

With the popularity of the Freudian identification theory came an almost blind acceptance of it. Not until much later was the theory subjected to empirical test. Even by the 1970's many of Freud's notions had not been adequately tested.

Let us look at the evidence that does exist for the Freudian notions of castration anxiety, penis envy, and women's inferior superegos. Evidence from everyday life does little to support these notions. While many mothers have remarked that their sons and daughters began to show a profound interest in matters of sex at around age 5, many others deny any hint of it. While some young boys have a difficult and competitive relationship with their fathers, others do not. Few mothers report that their daughters blame them for not supplying a penis. And so on.

Evidence from empirical research studies is equally unsupportive. Some researchers begin with the premise that, in order to worry about having and keeping a penis, an individual must first be aware of genitals and of the fact that they differentiate the sexes. After all, if a little boy were unaware of his genitalia and their role in his malehood, penis anxiety and castration could not exist. And if a girl were unaware of genitalia and the role of a penis in differentiating a boy from a girl, a man from a woman, why should she envy the boy that male possession rather than his football shirt or toy tractor? Do young children actually realize the importance of genitals in the proper identification of and distinction between males and females, or don't they? In Chapter 4 we saw that toddlers use body size, voice differences, and dress cues to distinguish between males and females, not genital differences (Brooks-Gunn and Lewis, 1979). Genital differences begin to be noticed in the preschool years. As one little boy sang to his sister, "I've got one and you've got none!" (Belotti, 1976). On a more scientific note, when Allan Katcher (1955) asked children to identify males and females on the basis of genitals, 88 percent of the 3-year-olds, 69 percent of the 4-year-olds, 49 percent of the 5-year-olds, and 30 percent of the 6-year-olds could not tell the difference. When he asked them to identify the sex of a figure on the basis of hair and clothing cues, even the younger children had no such difficulty. These findings do not imply that young children do not notice the genitals, but simply that they cannot use them properly as cues to sex identification (Thompson and Bentler, 1971).

Penis envy in girls, another popular notion, also has little evidence to support it (Sherman, 1971). And the few studies that claim to find penis envy use some very strange measures, like examining how women open a pack of cigarettes (Landy, 1967)! Even many of Freud's disciples, such as Horney, did not believe in penis envy, recognizing the biases discussed earlier. What does appear is a growing awareness of the preferred status of males in our society. This has been termed *status envy*. Little girls who have not yet discovered that their anatomical equipment is different from that of little boys may realize that males are more valued and, therefore, to be envied.

When they do notice that "they" have one and "we" have none, they may make a connection between being valued and having a penis, but the envy originates from the power associated with the male role *not* with the penis!

As we saw in Chapter 2, males do possess more resources in our society and are thought to possess the most desirable traits. Thus, status envy is based on reality. Young children do perceive a differential status of men and women in our society. For example, girls' preferences for the female sex role is weaker than boys' preferences for the male sex role. In a classic study, M. E. Smith (1933) questioned 8- to 15-year-old children on their views of the relative status position of males and females and found that boys, as they grew older, had an increasingly poor opinion of girls while girls had an increasingly improved opinion of boys. We have already seen the extent to which these views are held by adults.

Freudian theory would also predict that as a result of identification with the same-sex parent, the boy child should come to resemble his father quite strongly and the girl her mother. "Like father, like son," "Like mother, like daughter" are the anticipated outcomes of the identification process. In Freud's theory, the child literally incorporates the same-sex parent's personality characteristics and standards into his or her own personality. However, great similarities between children and their same-sex parents have not been found. In fact, both boys and girls tend to be more like their mothers than their fathers on a variety of personality measures (Byrne, 1965). And some studies have even found girls to be no more like their mothers than like other females or idealized female models (Fitzgerald and Roberts, 1966). Presumably a comparison of fathers to other males or idealized male models for sons would yield the same results. Children acquire the characteristics of a wide assortment of individuals with whom they share their world—friends, relatives, and even strangers whom they see in their communities, on television, in books, or in magazines. No one would deny that parents have influence over the child's acquisition of personality, but the influence is not through the literal "taking in" of the parent's personality nor are the parents the only socialization forces in the child's life, as Freudian theory might suggest.

Grounds for believing in inferior superego development for females are also not substantiated. No differences have been found in the level of maturity of children's moral codes nor in their resistance to cheating, though girls appear to confess more readily to transgressions and to be more upset after wrongdoing than boys. In fact, maternal and teacher reports suggest a greater conformity to the rules in girls than in boys. Research on adults verifies these findings with children. Julia Sherman (1971), in reviewing the literature on conscience and moral development, found that few differences exist between the sexes.

With such underwhelming evidence in its behalf, you may be wondering at the vivacity of Freud's theory within the psychological community. As it happens, most researchers do not subscribe to it. And, the advent of many new theories of personality, the training of clinicians in more varied therapeutic techniques, and the continual revisions of Freudian theory by the so-called Neo-Freudians have moved the majority of the clinical community away from the strict interpretation of Freud's theory of identification and sex-role acquisition. Yet, remnants of so powerful a theory are bound to linger; these are seen in beliefs about the biological bases of sex-role identity, the unequivocal acceptance of same-sex parents as the major influence on sex-role identity, and the adherence to innate sex differences in light of little confirmatory evidence.

Positive Identification Theories

Many rallied around identification as the process by which a child acquires sex-role identity; but some disclaimed its foundation of fear and sexuality. They disagreed that identification with the same-sex parent relied upon the perception of genital differences, castration anxiety, and penis envy. Rather than regarding identification as a negative, fear-provoking process, they argued, one should view it as a positive, supportive phenomenon. So, they emphasized identification based on love. One group, exemplified by Robert Sears (1965), developed an identification theory comprised of a combination of love and learning. With the love derived from the continually nurturant interaction between mother and child as an essential precondition, the child comes to value his or her mother's company. Having provided the primary rewards of love and food for so long, mother becomes increasingly associated with the pleasure and gratification accompanying those rewards and begins to take on a reward value of her own. As a secondary reinforcer, she is highly valued, but being human, she cannot sustain an affectionate and approving attitude every minute of every day, nor can she gratify the child's every wish without ceasing. So, the child must figure out a way of reinstating her qualities in her absence. The child achieves this through identification, through imitating her and internalizing her so that, in a sense, she is never far. By the same means, the child can evoke the presence of the father.

But the question remains: how does the child learn to identify in particular with the parent of the same sex rather than with both parents or with only the mother? We have seen that the young child is fully able to categorize people according to their sex, a cognitive skill that becomes refined with maturity. It is this ability, combined with the child's recognition that a similarity exists between the self and the same-sex parent as a function of the gender categorization, that predisposes the child to select the same-sex parent as the identification figure. The boy's switch from mother to father as the object of identification derives from love and the desire to be like the love object rather than from fear and the desire to escape retaliation (Sears, Rau, and Alpert, 1965).

While emphasizing the positive, some theorists admit to some negative underpinnings. Jerome Kagan (1964) has suggested that envy can serve as a motivation for the child to identify with the parent. Having noted the similarities between the self and the same-sex parent, and having started to think of himself as being like daddy, or herself as like mommy, the child wants access to all that the parent has or is perceived to have: power, freedom, and a host of valued resources. Yearning for these goodies, however, does not approach the all-consuming psychological state implied in the Freudian notion of penis envy or castration anxiety. The desperation is gone, and only the ambition to be like mother or father remains.

Research growing out of positive identification theory has attempted, first, to support the notion of identification by demonstrating that a similarity between the child and the same-sex parent who he or she has presumably "introjected" actually exists and, second, to differentiate itself from the identification theories based on fear by focusing on the parental characteristics of warmth, power, and punitiveness to see which figures most prominently in the identification process. As we saw earlier, girls *and* boys are more similar to their mothers than to their fathers, and sometimes are not more similar to a parent than to another adult. Clearly, evidence that children are more similar to the same-sex than to the opposite-sex parent does not exist. The belief that parental characteristics are important in the process of sex-role acquisition, however, does have some support.

Although the research in this area is frought with methodological shortcomings and contradictory findings, a few facts consistently emerge. For example, the degree of warmth and power exhibited by the same-sex parent does seem to be related to sex-typing in boys and girls (Maccoby and Jacklin, 1974). In one study, kindergarten boys who were rated high in masculine sex-role preference perceived their fathers as powerful sources of both reward and punishment. By high school, the strongly masculine boys reported that their fathers were highly rewarding and affectionate and not punitive or restrictive (Mussen and Distler, 1959). The theory that boys with a strong identification with their father portray him as rewarding supports the idea that identification is a positive phenomenon. However, the fact that punitiveness is sometimes related to identification supports the idea of identification as a negative phenomenon also. These contradictions, as well as evidence reviewed later, actually point us away from identification theories in general and toward more cognitively oriented theories of sex-role development.

So, we leave identification theory with no overwhelming support for it, particularly insofar as it is said to grow out of fear, and turn to social learning theory and, later, cognitive developmental theory for their explanations of the acquisition of sex-role identity.

SOCIAL LEARNING THEORY

Sears modified Freud's theory of identification by adding the love and the learning, but social learning theorists went one step further. They omitted identification as a process altogether and instead relied entirely on learning principles to explain the acquisition of sex role. Theorists such as Albert Bandura (1969) and Walter Mischel (1970) denied that sex-role identity needed to be predicated on an intense relationship with the same-sex parent and they questioned the value of saying that a child has internalized parental standards and personality characteristics rather than simply that the child now acts more like his or her same-sex parent. Rather than postulate an internal motive to identify with the same-sex parent, social learning theorists recommend looking for the external forces that might lead the child to imitate some individuals more than others. Rather than think of the identification process driving the child toward the acquisition of a set of personality traits patterned after the parent, social learning theorists view personality characteristics in general and sex-role identity in particular as more flexible, less inevitable, and more situationally dependent phenomena. Sex-role acquisition depends on the imitation of sex-typed behaviors. And imitation depends on differential rewards and punishment—actual or anticipated. It does *not* depend on the perceived similarity between the child and parent, nor on the bond of love between them.

According to social learning theory, the most important learning principles to influence sex-role learning are (1) *reinforcement,* the process by which rewards and punishments are dispensed such that the probability that the child's behavior will occur again is controlled, (2) *observation,* the process by which the child learns how things are done, by whom, and what consequences follow, and (3) *imitation,* the process by which the child actually practices what has been learned and acquires the behavior as his or her own. What behaviors will be observed and imitated depend upon one's previous reinforcement history or one's expectations about the consequences. As we shall see, the process of sex-role acquisition described by the social learning theorists approximates the way we commonly and intuitively view things.

Reinforcement

Socializing agents (such as parents, teachers, baby-sitters, ministers, police officers, dormitory counselors, and sports coaches) either encourage or discourage an individual's behavior through a system of rewards and punishments. The reinforcements they provide can be as subtle as a twinkle of the eye at the sight of a little girl admiring her image in a mirror or as blatant as a promised trip to McDonald's if the child makes first string on the Little League team. By responding with either praise, punishment, or indifference, the parent (or whoever) is said to *shape* the child's future behavior. The child will begin to act according to the outcomes he or she envisions, working hard for the Twinkies and Big Macs, and trying to avoid the scorns and spankings.

It should be obvious that the processes described by the social learning theorists underlie the child's general, not just sex-role, socialization. We use the strategies of reward (praise, gifts, smiles, encouragement) and punishment (scoldings, spankings, withdrawal of love, rejection) to encourage or discourage all sorts of behavior, from a straight A school performance and generosity, to bed wetting and cheating. But our interest here is in how these processes relate to sex-role socialization in particular.

Consider our response to care-giving and help-seeking behaviors in young children. First, imagine the following scene: It is the day after Christmas. The living room overflows with aunts, uncles, grandmothers, children, and a profusion of holiday gifts. Little Nicole pushes her baby carriage proudly around the room, pausing to lean over and arrange her doll more comfortably under its covers. One of the aunts exclaims, "Oh, Helen, your Nicole is such a little mother!" and all beam delightedly at the scene before them. But suppose Nicole's brother Paul were to be observed in exactly the same posture. Adults would be likely to say, "Oh Paul, why aren't you playing with the terrific dump truck Uncle Sal gave you!" or "Paul, little boys don't play with dolls; give that doll back to your sister!"

Next imagine a typical winter weekend with the children playing boisterously in the snow. Pretending to be cleaning the driveway, they flail their snow shovels wildly. Suddenly a scream is heard above the usual din and Joanna runs crying into the house with a sharp cut above her eye. What can Joanna expect when she steps through the storm door? Comfort and condolences and sighs like "My poor little injured darling; everything will be all right. We'll just fix it right now." If the injured party were Johnny, rather than be rewarded, his cries either would be ignored ("It's okay, fella. Let's get you fixed up and back in action!") or punished ("Only girls and sissies cry").

Reviewing the situations, it would seem that little girls are obtaining rewards for showing sensitivity to baby dolls, while little boys are not; little girls are, if not rewarded, at least not punished for showing dependence and weakness under stress, while little boys are more likely to be actively encouraged to show bravery and independence. Social learning theorists contend that it is in just such commonplace, seemingly trivial situations that the differential reinforcement of boys and girls occurs.

Examples from everyday life abound; but empirical evidence for differential reinforcement is less consistent than one might expect. Parents are more likely to offer comfort for a girl's minor injury and withhold comfort from a boy in the same situation, or at least they say that this is what they would do (Lambert, *et al.,* 1971). But in other situations, parents do not seem to treat their sons and daughters differently. We shall deal more fully with the matter of parental reinforcement in the section on the family as a mediator of sex-role development in Chapter 6.

Observation

Parents do not seem to live up to our intuitive belief that they are constantly reinforcing their sons and daughters differently. However, parents are, by just being themselves, exhibiting sex roles. Do children notice sex-related behaviors, and if so, does such observation influence their own sex-role acquisition?

By just being themselves, the individuals to whom the child is exposed (at home, at school, on television, etc.) act as models for the child. They display a whole range of behaviors to fit their roles as men, or women, or gym teachers, or preachers. All of us are models. It is nothing we consciously work at—we just do it. We model; children watch. And by watching, children learn. It is important to realize, however, that children observe everything, regardless of the rewards and punishments that might befall the model or themselves (if they were to behave similarly). Children observe good as well as naughty behavior, cross-sex as well as same-sex models.

In order to prove that observation influences the acquisition of sex-related behaviors, we would have to show that children either are exposed to or pay more attention to same- rather than opposite-sex models. If girls observed mostly women and boys observed mostly men, one could simply conclude that they had learned their sex-typed behavior through the observation of same-sex models. But the facts are that children do not have more exposure to same-sex than opposite-sex models, nor do they attend to them selectively in the preschool years. As long as children are at home, and even after they have entered school, the female model predominates. Between mother and elementary school teacher, male models are few. So, if observation were a fundamental mechanism of sex-role acquisition, we would expect all children to acquire a female sex-role identity, which they don't. Or, to look at it another way, as long as children are reading or watching television, the male model predominates and the female models are few. In this case, we would expect children to acquire a male sex-role identity, which they don't. Young boys and girls are exposed to adult models to the same degree, so the amount of exposure to a same-sex model fails to account for their increasingly sex-typed behavior. How about the possibility of their attending more often and more receptively to the same-sex model? Selective attention to same-sex models might well occur, but not until the child is older, when he or she has already developed sex-typed interests and a stable sex-role identity and seeks out the same-sex model on the basis of his or her similarity to the model.

Imitation

The process of imitation by children is never as clear-cut as a game of "Simon says do this." Children's imitative activities, like our own, are resplendent with complexities: What has Simon done? Do I want to do it too? Just who is Simon, anyway? Is he someone I'd like to resemble? Do I like him? Is he a powerful person or a weak one? Will any goodies come my way if I act like him, or will I be punished? Complicated though the process is, the social learning theorists contend that, with regard to the child's active acquisition of sex-typed behaviors, he or she is guided by the desire for rewards and has figured out that rewards are accrued via the imitation of those behaviors that individuals around the child view as sex-appropriate. The child reasons: In this system of rewards and punishments, I like rewards best. I am rewarded for doing boy-type things. Since I am rewarded for doing boy-type things, I want to be a boy; or I am rewarded for doing girl-type things; therefore, I want to be a girl. (Kohlberg, 1966) By this reasoning, the child adopts a sex-role identity which will serve as a guide for the further acquisition of the sex-typed behaviors, that is, the behaviors leading to the rewards. They acquire a sex role by first observing (and eventually, by selectively watching those they know to share the quality of "boyhood" or "girlhood" with them) and by then imitating what they see, with the intention (conscious or not) of maximizing their rewards.

The distinctions between observation and imitation, and between acquisition and performance, are crucial. A child may observe, and thus acquire, a certain behavior, but will not necessarily imitate or perform that behavior. A host of factors such as who modeled the act, what happened to him or her as a result of the behavior, and what sort of reinforcement the child might receive for imitating the behavior all come into play to determine whether or not the act will be performed. Thus observation must precede imitation, but it does not necessarily guarantee it.

A classic study by Albert Bandura, Dorothea Ross, and Sheila Ross (1961) demonstrated the possibility of observation alone (i.e., without rewards or punishment) leading to imitative behaviors. In this study, one group of children was exposed to an aggressive adult model who abused a poor innocent Bobo doll—punching it, knocking it down, jumping on top of it—and another group of children to a nonaggressive adult model who simply played peacefully with some toys. After the children had observed the model, they were left alone in a playroom while the experimenter noted all their imitative behavior. Those children who had observed an adult playing peacefully did the same; those seeing the aggressive one, however, played aggressively, particularly the boys. In order to find out whether the girls had actually noticed and could remember as much about the model's aggressive behavior as the boys, Bandura conducted a follow-up investigation in which he offered the children a reward for performing as many of the model's acts as possible. In this situation, the girls showed that they knew how to hit a Bobo doll over the head with a hammer as well as the boys. When offered a reward, the girls overcame their initial unwillingness to behave aggressively, either because the reward served to dispel a former fear of punishment or because they realized that, in this particular instance, it was in their interest to aggress.

Bandura and his colleagues' findings have been replicated with a multitude of variations (with same-sex adult models, opposite-sex adult models, same-sex peer models, opposite-sex peer models, live models, ad infinitum). Each of these variations was intended to discover characteristics of the model (sex, power, consequences, control of resources, etc.) that determine whether or not the child would imitate the observed behavior. Each time the experiment was repeated, the body of evidence supporting the power of observation and imitation in the child's acquisition of social behavior grew. Each demonstrated that various characteristics of the model influenced the child's propensity to imitate. Taken cumulatively, they show that reinforcement, observation, and imitation all influence not just sex-role acquisition but socialization in general.

Some specific findings, of interest to our account of sex-role socialization, relate to a child's willingness to imitate sex-typed behavior. In a study by Thomas Wolf (1975), children individually entered a playroom where they watched seven videotapes of other children playing there. In each of the seven televised episodes, the sex of the model and the consequences to him or her for playing with a "sex-appropriate" or sex-inappropriate" toy varied. After each of the subjects had watched one of the episodes on television, he or she was invited to play freely in a playroom while the experimenters observed from behind a one-way mirror. Girls were more willing to touch a sex-inappropriate toy (for girls, a fire engine) than the boys were, especially if the observed model was also a girl, and particularly if the girl model had not been punished for playing with it. The boys were much less likely to play with a sex-inappropriate toy (for boys, a doll), especially when they had seen another boy punished for doing so, and particularly after having seen a girl play with it.

The Wolf study not only lends support to social learning theory and the role of observation and imitation in acquiring a sex role, it also joins with other studies in suggesting that boys adopt a stereotyped sex role more vigorously than girls, for a number of reasons. First, in the preschool years, same-sex role models are much harder to come by for boys than for girls: father is seen pecking mother's cheek and leaving the house with briefcase or lunch box in hand; his work is seldom a visible one for his son. The boy may, in the face of no contradictory evidence, perceive the male sex role as more rigid or strictly defined. Second, boys are exposed to more sanctions for what are deemed sex-inappropriate behaviors, while such behaviors are tolerated for girls: a little boy pushing a doll carriage is more likely to meet with scorn than a little girl playing with trucks. Third, boys may depend on their predominately male peer group for guidance in establishing what is appropriate and what is inappropriate sex-role behavior. And, as we shall see in the next section, preschoolers are avid stereotypers; just by relying on each other, boys may be likely to exhibit sex-typed behavior.

Social learning theory, like identification theory, does not seem to account for the inevitability and complexity of sex-role learning. Although reinforcement and modeling play a role in the process, the empirical evidence suggests that it is not the central one. Therefore, we shall turn to our last theory to investigate the process of sex-role identity.

COGNITIVE DEVELOPMENTAL THEORY

Popping M & M candies into a boy's mouth everytime he puts on a baseball glove won't make him masculine, nor will providing him with only male models. And chocolate kisses for the girl who uses her "Happy Little Housewife" carpet sweeper to clean up the bedroom rug won't make her feminine. Something more is going on than children's tallying the rewards against the punishments or wearing blinders to block out the actions of the opposite sex; and that something has to do with the child as an intellectual being.

Piagetian Theory

After having had three children of his own and having interviewed hundreds of schoolchildren, French epistemologist Jean Piaget (1954, 1969) realized that children have their own ideas about the world. They are not like miniature adults, but perceive and think about the world in qualitatively different ways than adults do. For example, when you ask a child of five or six how the sun began, you might be told that the sun is a fire which was lighted by a match that God had thrown away. By middle childhood, the child might reply that the sun originated from an accumulation of smoke rising from the chimneys of the town. By puberty, the adolescent might finally believe that (1) the sun is not a living thing capable of "knowing" when to rise and set, (2) nobody is up there "directing" its activities, (3) no man-made material such as chimney smoke is responsible for its continued existence, and (4) basically, there is such a thing as a natural phenomenon. After charting children's beliefs concerning several such phenomena, such as the changes in the shape of the moon, the nature of the night, the origin of trees, the working of bicycles, water faucets, and steam engines and, later, the child's conception of space, number, movement, and volume, Piaget concluded that young children progress through various stages of understanding. In infancy, the child knows the world only through his or her actions within or upon it. Infants learn about the roundness of a ball by holding it in their hands, by mouthing it and by rolling it across the floor. By preschool, the child is capable of acting upon the world mentally as well, but the thought of the "preoperational child" (i.e., from about 4 to 7) is still limited. Preschoolers cannot deal with too much information at one time. Their thought is static in the sense that if they watched you pour the same amount of Kool-aid from two identical glasses into two different glasses, one tall and narrow, the other short and wide, they would be more impressed by how different the amount of Kool-aid looked in the two different glasses than by the fact that the same amount of beverage was poured into each. The child with the short, wide glass might point to the two levels and complain bitterly that he or she didn't get as much Kool-aid as the child with the tall, narrow glass. Or, focusing on the width, the child with the narrower, though taller, glass would be the one to feel cheated. Their thought is irreversible in the sense that your pouring the Kool-aid back into the original same-sized glasses would not make the one who felt cheated feel any better. By 9 or 10, children move from the preoperational to the concrete operational stage during which thought is *decentered;* now they are capable of attending to and coordinating multiple aspects of a situation. Now the child can understand that while the glass was shorter, it was also wider. The concrete operational child's thought is also *dynamic* or sensitive to transformation. And it is reversible; the child can recognize that what has been done can be undone.

How do children move from one stage to another? Several factors, which are all thought to be important in this process, have been considered. The first factor of transition is *maturation.* The level of children's cognitive functioning is to a large extent dependent upon the maturity of their physical systems. No matter if you have two legs; if you are only six months old and your legs haven't yet developed strength, you will not be able to walk. And no matter if your IQ is 148; if you're only 6½ and your brain has not developed sufficiently, you will not be composing a symphony. A second factor is *experience* and contact with objects; a third is *social transmission;* and a fourth is a self-regulating process known as *equilibration.* Equilibrium has been called the "backbone of mental growth" since it integrates the effects of the other three factors (Ginsberg and

Opper, 1969). Equilibration is where the mind of the child comes in, where the child actively deals with the world and comes to know it through his or her intellectual efforts.

Kohlberg's Theory

Agreeing with the need to focus upon the role of the child, who, in interaction with his or her environment, passes through the various stages of development, Lawrence Kohlberg (1966, 1969) saw that as intellectual growth goes, so goes the development of a sex-role identity. Children have different ways of perceiving the world, depending upon the stage they are in, and their perception of sex role is related to their current intellectual stage.

Kohlberg postulated the following steps in sex-role acquisition. First, children realize that the world can be divided into two groups, male and female, and that they belong to one and only one of these groups, as do parents, friends, and strangers. After children have acquired the notion of "I am a boy (or a girl)" they use gender to categorize the world, often extending the categorization scheme beyond folks, to include objects, ideas, and behavior, too. Seeing the world in dichotomous terms, they categorize with a vengeance, fabricating a system of rigid gender distinctions. The effect of this categorization is, as we shall see in a moment, children's particular versions of sex-role stereotyping.

The second step in the process of sex-role acquisition involves attaching a *value* to people, attitudes, and behaviors of the same sex. Since a certain object or activity or individual is female (or male) and since I am female (or male), and, since I like myself, I will regard highly those things that are similar to me, the reasoning goes. Children begin to seek out actively same-sex people to emulate, same-sex objects with which to surround themselves, and same-sex activities in which to participate. For Kohlberg, imitation of same-sex individuals is not due to a previous reinforcement history but to the perception of same-sex persons as similar to the self and therefore valued. The different role of reinforcement and reward in social learning and cognitive developmental theories is described by Kohlberg:

> [In the view of social learning theorists] sex-typed behavior and attitudes
> are acquired through social rewards that follow sex-appropriate responses

made by the child or by a relevant model. The social learning theory syllogism is: "I want rewards, I am rewarded for doing boy [girl] things, therefore I want to be a boy [girl]." In contrast, a cognitive theory assumes this sequence: "I am a boy[girl], therefore I want to do boy [girl] things, therefore the opportunity to do boy[girl] things [and to gain approval for doing them] is rewarding." (1966, p. 89, bracketed material added)

In the former, the desire to conform to one's sex role follows reinforcement and in the latter it precedes it.

Finally, the children, valuing same-sex people and activities, *identify* with their same-sex parent. The process of identification derives from their developing a gender identity and consequently valuing those with whom maleness or femaleness is shared, and *not* from a fear of loss of love or retaliation as in Freudian theory. To a cognitive developmentalist, identification represents a positive, internal process motivated by the child's active search for understanding and striving toward mastery in the world.

Examining Kohlberg's theory in the light of research findings, we find that it fares well. The first step, the realization that the world is divided into two genders and that the child belongs to only one of them, is well-documented. For example, Arnold Gesell (1940) demonstrated that children are aware of their gender at an early age. When he asked children, "Are you a little girl or a little boy?" he found that the majority of the 2-year-olds did not know for certain, though about three-quarters of the 3-year-olds did. Jeanne Brooks-Gunn and Michael Lewis (1975) have found that as soon as toddlers have the words "boy" and "girl" in their verbal repertoire, they verbally refer to themselves as a "boy" or "girl" and are remarkably accurate in their use of these terms for themselves. The attainment of gender identity and its impact on the developing child has also been noted by John Money and his colleagues, whose work with gender-reassigned children was mentioned in Chapter 3. His clinical experience and case studies have shown that gender reassignment should be undertaken before the age of 3, and preferably before 2. After this time, the child will have psychological difficulty adopting to a new gender.

Young children also label others with respect to gender. In the Brooks-Gunn and Lewis study mentioned earlier, toddlers between 1½ and 2 years of age could label adults according to their gender, and between 2 and 3 years of age could label other children by sex. By 4, most children can successfully label both adults and other children by sex (Rabban, 1950), primarily on the basis of hair, dress, height, and voice cues.

In addition to the ability to categorize self and others by sex, young children begin to realize the stability of classification systems. Once a red cube has been categorized as a red cube, it can never be categorized a blue cube, or a red circle (unless some drastic alterations occur). Similarly, once one is labeled "boy" or "girl," one can never be classified otherwise (again, unless some drastic alteration occurs). To us as adults, it seems obvious that once a male, always a male, and once a female, always a female. But to very young children, awareness of gender constancy, the technical term for the stability of one's sex designation across time, develops at the time other constancies develop—between 5 and 7 years of age. Researchers such as Walter Emmerich (1977) have proven this by asking children such questions as: "If Janie really wants to be a boy, can she be?" "If Janie played with trucks and did boy things, what would she be?" "If Janie put on boys' clothes, what would she be?" "If Janie cut her hair short, would she be a boy or would she be a girl?" Those children who fell below a certain stage in intellectual development could not seem to grasp the fact that, since Janie is a girl, she will remain a girl, (1) whether she likes it or not, (2) no matter what kinds of activities she engages in, and (3) no matter what she wears or how she chooses to look. When gender constancy is achieved, the questions receive the following responses, "She can't change," "She has to be a girl," "She would just look like a boy, but she wouldn't *be* a boy," etc. In other words, children eventually understand, and can demonstrate their understanding, that sex is a stable characteristic of all individuals. And, as the cognitive developmentalists claim, understanding is achieved at the time when corresponding intellectual skills are achieved.

The second step in sex-role acquisition, according to Kohlberg, is that children come to value same-sex people, objects, and activities. Young children do prefer same-sex activities and toys, suggesting that they do value those things that are like themselves. In a study by Spencer Thompson (1975), preschool children were told that some pictures were boy things and others were girl things. Later on, the same children were asked which objects they liked best. The vast majority of the girls picked objects labeled as girls' things, boys the boys' objects, with these trends being seen as early as 3 years of age. The last step involves identification with same-sex persons. As we have seen in preceding sections, imitation of same-sex persons and identification with the same-sex parent is not clear-cut. However, Kohlberg's belief that children first acquire a gender identity, then categorize others according to gender, then value objects and persons like the self, and finally develop a preference for sex-typed objects and activities seems to be true.

An Extension of Kohlberg's Theory

In his original theory, Kohlberg did not put much emphasis on societal influences, instead relying on the child's cognitive construction of the world. Irene Frieze, Jacquelynne Parsons, Paula Johnson, Diane Ruble, and Gail Zellman in their book *Women and Sex Roles,* (1978) have taken a more social cognitive approach to sex-role acquisition, hypothesizing that cultural stereotypes and role divisions, in conjunction with cognitive abilities, influence how the child actually uses gender to categorize the world. The coupling of the child's desire to categorize by gender and the actual divisions existing in the society result in the preschool child's acquisition of sex-role stereotypes. They believe, like Kohlberg, that the child uses gender to categorize people and things, but unlike Kohlberg, believe that the child is influenced by current sex roles. In Chapter 2 we defined a stereotype as a culturally determined and relatively fixed view of others. Earlier in this chapter we saw that young children hold fairly rigid beliefs about all aspects of the world, not the least of which is sex role. When a child perceives a distinction between the sexes, it tends to be simplistic and rigid, not susceptible to change. Jacqueline Parsons tells of her daughter, who at 2½ thought mommies went to school and daddies went to work; her mother did go to school: she was a college professor. When the daughter was told that mommy worked at a school and that other women worked in other jobs, she did not believe it. This illustrates the preschooler's attempt to categorize her parents' occupations vis-à-vis societal expectations that men work and women do not. The young child also tries to fit behaviors not believed to be sex-related in our society into sex-stereotyped molds. Again, Parson's daughter believed that mommies drank coffee while daddies drank tea, because that is what *her* mommy and daddy did. Individual behaviors which are not related to gender are generalized to a whole class of people and considered gender-relevant, just as we saw for adult stereotypes in Chapter 2.

Why do children use gender to classify and stereotype, rather than other attributes? First, the child's cognitive way of perceiving the world favors gender. The young child's thinking is physical and concrete, so that attributes such as age, race, and sex will be the first on which the child focuses. In addition, the child focuses on one attribute at a time, and if gender is salient, it will be used over and over. Also, the child generalizes from individuals to groups early, as with the coffee-tea example. Finally, the child observes the importance society places on gender, making gender even *more* salient.

As we have just seen, the inflexible way preschoolers see the world predisposes them to stereotype. In fact, we find this age group adhering to sex-role stereotypes even in families that portray less rigid role divisions (as in the examples from Parson's daughter) than society in general portrays. Early sex-role stereotyping will occur, much to some parents' dismay, with its degree being more dependent on societal beliefs and practices than on parental exortations (since the preschooler invariably comes into contact with other families, peers, books, teachers, and television).

However, as the child becomes older, and more flexible, sex-role stereotypes may diminish. Again, what with existing societal beliefs, the diminution may not be as great as we would like. Parents will be relieved to know that their influences and role modeling can affect later sex-related behavior and beliefs, as we shall see in Chapters 7 and 9. For now, we will give just one example: Adolescent girls are more likely to work or want to work outside the home if their mothers were employed. Presumably these young women have a more diverse set of roles at home with which to emulate.

A COMPARISON OF THE THEORIES

The three major theories of sex-role acquisition have all attempted to explain the process underlying this acquisition. The three differ along a variety of dimensions, including the source, age, and permanence of learning, and the roles of motivation and biology underlying the

TABLE 5–1

Comparison of the Three Theoretical Positions
of Sex-Role Development

Freudian-Identification	Social Learning	Cognitive Development
ROLE OF INNATE CHARACTERISTICS		
Large role: anatomy is destiny; body structure determines personality	No role	Small role: cognitive maturation; structuring of experience; development of gender identity
ROLE OF CHILD IN LEARNING PROCESS		
Active	*Passive*	*Active*
Motive		
Internal: reduce fear and anxiety	External: reinforcements Internal: expected reinforcements	Internal: desire for competence
Permanence of Learning		
Very permanent and irreversible	Permanent only if external reinforcements or self-reinforcements maintain behavior; difficulty in changing comes from internalized self-reinforcements and conditioned emotional responses	Semi-permanent once schemata are stabilized; change depends on presentation of discrepant information and on the child's cognitive maturity
Sources of Learning		
Parents or parent surrogates	Parents as well as the larger social system	Parents and the larger social system in interaction with the child's cognitive system
Age of Learning Sex Identity		
By 4 or 5	Throughout life, but early years are very important	Throughout life, but years between 3–20 are most important; years between 6–8 and 16–18 are crucial for change in stereotypic beliefs

From Frieze, Parsons, Johnson, Ruble, and Zellman, eds. (1978).

learning. In their review of sex-role theories, Irene Frieze and her colleagues (1978) tabulated the differences between the theories, which we have presented in Table 5-1. We will briefly discuss two of these dimensions—the role of innate characteristics and the role of the child, as well as the role of identification in this process.

Role of Innate Characteristics

For the Freudians, the origin of sex-role patterning is biological. The identification process by which sex-typing occurs begins with the biological dependency of the infant upon its mother and eventually rests on the child's growing sexuality and the resulting confrontation with the lack of a penis or the fear of losing it. Because biology determines whether one has or has not a penis, biology also determines one's sex-role development (or, as Freud would express it, "anatomy is destiny"). Because of the difference in genitalia, the values and behaviors of the two sexes are believed to diverge predictably.

For the social learning theorists, the source of the patterning is to be found in cultural factors. The way men and women behave in a particular society, that is, the modeling characteristics they convey as they proceed in their day-to-day activities and the manner in which they dispense rewards and punishment, determines the course of their children's sex-role development. The pattern of sex-role characteristics exhibited by the children reflects the sex-typing of the culture at large.

The cognitive developmentalists regard children's sex-role acquisition as reflective of neither innate, biological structures nor culturally imposed patterns. Instead, they view its basic source as stemming from children's intellectual development. To the extent that children are cognitively mature, so will they assume or perceive sex-role differentiation and act upon the newfound assumptions according to what they deem appropriate for their own sex. The cognitive developmental position has been extended to include a greater role for cultural forces. Specifically, the culture provides the raw material from which the child constructs sex-related beliefs and behavior, as the child's categories are a function of the child's culture.

Role of the Child

For social learning theorists, the process of sex-role acquisition is beyond the control of the developing individual. One is passive to the extent that he or she responds to the impinging reinforcements originating from the cultural milieu.

For Freudians, to the extent that anatomy inevitably determines the course of psychosexual development, the individual is passive, but to the extent that each individual must *perceive* the difference between male and female genitalia and must construct a fear of castration and a plan for overcoming it, the individual is active or at least reactive.

Cognitive developmental theorists view children as active rather than reactive, being capable of using the environmental cues selectively to form their own conception of what it is to be male or female.

Role of Identification

Identification, as we have already described, is the process by which the child focuses upon and becomes like the parent of the same sex in Freudian theory. In social learning theory, it is imitation that is the process by which same-sex models are copied. For Freudian and social learning theorists, identification and imitation precede sex-role identity. For the cognitive developmentalist, however, they follow sex-role identity. According to Freud, out of the identification with the same-sex parent grows an identity, an incorporation of that parent's judgments and personality. According to the social learning theorists, imitation of the same-sex parent involves an entire socialization history of rewards for "sex-appropriate" behavior and punishment for "sex-inappropriate" behavior. Once children learn which of the two parents is the more appropriate model (the imitation of whom leads to the greatest rewards), they determine what sex that parent is and accept it as their own. For the cognitive developmental theorists, however, the gender identity comes first. Very early in life (and the evidence supports this) children figure out which sex they are. As a result of this information and of their valuing similar people and activities, they selectively focus on indi-

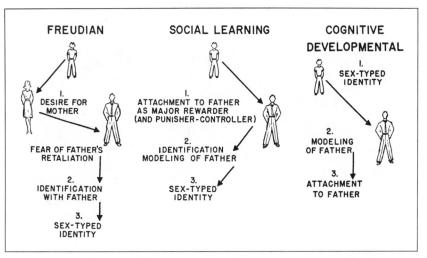

Figure 5–1. Theoretical sequences in psychosexual identification. (Reprinted from "A Cognitive-Developmental Analysis of Children's Sex-Role Concepts and Attitudes," by Lawrence Kohlberg, in THE DEVELOPMENT OF SEX DIFFERENCES, edited by Eleanor E. Maccoby, with the permission of the publishers, Stanford University Press. © 1966 by the Board of Trustees of the Leland Stanford Junior University.)

viduals of the same sex as models, one of the most important of whom is their parent. Before long, they recognize a special link between themselves and their same-sex parent; and out of this awareness grows an attachment for, or an identity with, the same-sex parent. Figure 5–1, taken from Kohlberg's 1966 paper, illustrates the differences between the three theories vis-à-vis a boy's identification with his same-sex parent.

EARLY CHILDHOOD
The Emergence of Sex Roles

chapter six

Christmas morning
Kids: LEGGOS! "From Dad, To Everybody!" Thanks, Dad!
3:00 P.M.
Johnny: Hey, Dad! Let's play Leggos now. Hey, Dad; hey, Dad!
Father: Sure, son. Come on. What do you want to build? Well, go to it!
4:00 P.M.
Suzy: Hey, Daddy, will you play Leggos with me? Please?
Father: Sure, sweetie! What would you like to build? How about a castle? Here, I'll show you. . . .

This scenario is typical of early childhood. The differences between boys and girls which were only hinted at in infancy now become more pronounced, as does the differential treatment parents accord their sons and daughters.

The preschoolers' store of information about sex roles has expanded. They have acquired a gender identity, are able to categorize persons, objects, and values on the basis of gender, and have developed a preference for sex-typed objects and activities.

At the same time, children's ideas about sex role begin to develop. They are aware that daddies carry briefcases and mommies carry purses and that boys make ammunition out of clay and girls make cupcakes. But, unlike the toddler who also knows these things, the preschooler also knows that boys don't necessarily make bullets because they want to, but because they are supposed to, and that boys don't make cupcakes because that is what girls are supposed to do. They can now sex-stereotype whole categories of objects and activities in sometimes startlingly unique ways, like the little girl who stopped playing with her friend Susan because Susan had insisted that girls wore belts, when everyone knows only daddies wear belts! These newly acquired beliefs and behaviors are part of the social and cognitive process of sex-role differentiation.

In this chapter we shall first review the research on early childhood sex differences. Then we shall consider the family's role in sex-role socialization, including the effects of a mother's working, a father's absence, and the presence of brothers and sisters on the child's sex-role development. Finally, we shall take a look at sex role from the child's point of view. We shall see that young children, with their division of the world into two genders and two separate gender-tied roles, mirror in their own immature but ardent way our culture's sex-role beliefs and practices.

SEX DIFFERENCES IN THE PRESCHOOL YEARS

During the early infancy period, observed behavioral differences between the sexes are few and are attributable primarily to biological factors bearing on the type and quality of the physical apparatus with which the infant enters the world. Yet, despite the similarities between boy and girl babies, adults do tend to treat them differently—*systematically* differently depending upon the infant's sex. This we have seen in adults' play strategies, their provision of play materials, their attitudes toward exploratory activity, and their verbal interactions. Sometimes, convincing evidence of the immediate effects of the differential treatment exists; studies demonstrate a relationship between a mother's encouragement of exploratory behavior and the tendency for baby boys to move away from the mother. However, delayed effects may also follow early differential treatment: sometimes, the boy–girl differences that may have been nurtured in the infancy period do not emerge until late in the preschool years. So, sex differences characterizing this period may be due to contemporary differential child-rearing practices (which we shall discuss shortly), to the delayed effect of the parental treatment differences in infancy, to existing biological factors, to the child's own decision about how one of his or her sex should act, or, of course, to a complex interaction of all these factors with the more global influence of culture, as illustrated in the model from Chapter 2, Figure 2-1.

Examining the most predominant of the real or imagined sex differences of the preschool period, we shall, where appropriate, speculate on the possible origins of the differences. But first we need to caution the reader about a nasty habit we all sometimes have of saying what we don't really mean. Take the statement, "boys are taller than girls." Suppose we have just presented you with the finding that the average height for a boy of 4 was 40¾ inches and for a girl of 4, 40½ inches and concluded that "boys are taller [or slightly taller] than girls." One might easily read the statement to mean that

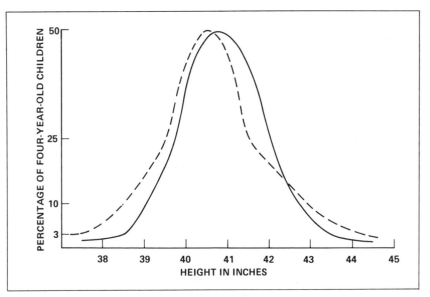

Figure 6-1. The height distribution of 4-year-old girls and boys is indicated by the dashed and solid curves, respectively.

all boys are taller than *all* girls. But we all know some 4-year-old girls who are taller than some 4-year-old boys so the statement should correctly be read as "Some [or most] boys are taller than some [or most] girls." Look at the graph of the height of 4-year-olds (Figure 6-1); the extensive overlap makes it obvious that 4-year-old boys and girls are, in general, very similar in height. On a different dimension, such as aggressivity, the overlap may not be as great. But it should still be recognized that a girl may be more aggressive than some or even most boys and a boy may be as unaggressive as some or most girls. Only when we consciously consider the area of overlap do we duly account for the individuals involved in the group comparison and only then can we guard against blindly dumping all girls into one category (e.g.; "not tall" or "unaggressive") and all boys into the other ("tall" or "aggressive").

With this caveat in mind, let us turn to what sex differences in personality characteristics actually do exist in the preschool years. Aggression, activity level, and dominance, thought to be characteristic of boys, and sociability, empathy, and dependency, thought to be girls' domains, are examined. Also discussed are differences in impulsivity and in play behavior.

Aggression

The most substantiated research findings on sex differences involve aggression. When Helen Dawe (1934) conducted her early observational study of the quarrels of preschool children, no one expressed great surprise over her finding that little boys fought more than little girls. Similar research findings of greater aggressiveness in boys have accumulated vastly since then, employing many different methodologies in many different cultures. No matter how, no matter where one looks, aggression appears more often among boys than among girls.

In Kenya, Okinawa, India, the Philippines, Mexico, and Orchard Town, U.S.A. (in other words everywhere Beatrice Whiting and Carolyn Edwards [1973] and their colleagues' travels took them), boys exhibited more aggression than girls, although neither exhibited much direct assault. On the lookout for three types of aggression—rough-and-tumble play, verbal aggression such as insults and derogations, and physical aggression—the researchers found that boys scored higher than girls in all forms of aggression. Thus their research confirmed the common stereotype that boys are generally more aggressive than girls. At the same time, it countered the popular idea that boys might exhibit their aggressive tendencies by direct physical means but that girls aggress in an indirect verbal way such as through "cattiness" or thwarting behavior; boys were also more verbally aggressive.

The work of Walters, Pearce, and Dahms (1957) in the United States and of Brindley and his colleagues (1973) in Britain substantiates this finding. Observing nursery school children in free play, they found boys to be more physically as well as more verbally aggressive.

Aggression during the preschool years has its advantages. As part of a research group that wondered, along with ethologists such as Konrad Lorenz (1966), whether aggressive behavior might actually have a conducive effect upon the relationship of young children, Wendy Matthews (1972) conducted a study with Bianca Zazzo of the Centre National de Recherche Sociale in Paris on the relationship between aggression and sociability in preschoolers. Matthews hypothesized specifically that the most popular child (as measured by a sociometric test) would be the most sociable as well as the most aggressive. A team of observers watched play groups of six, comprised of a very popular boy and girl, a moderately popular boy and girl, and an unpopular boy and girl and recorded their behavior. The most popular children were found to be the most aggressive in nearly every respect, be it toward an object or another child, be it in a verbal or in a physical manner. The high-status children also proved to be the most social, though in very particular ways: they were most likely to be found in play with other children, were most often observed leading their play partners, and were most likely to initiate a change in play activity. In other words, their social behavior demonstrated a quality of leadership, initiative, and forcefulness, in contrast to the social behavior of the moderately popular children, which was of a more compliant nature. Integration into the group at this age appears to be best achieved, then, through forceful behavior, be it what would be considered "aggressive" or "social." With age, aggression becomes dysfunctional, more likely leading to rejection than to popularity; and more sociable expressions of forcefulness such as "sportsmanship" take over. By the elementary school years, more mature styles of interaction predominate and aggressive behavior is scorned. Seven- or 8-year-old children, having reached a more advanced stage of intellectual development, are capable of taking the perspective of the other. They realize that the other child is like themselves and that they are like the other child. Since they don't like it when the other child hits them, it occurs to them that the other child probably does not like getting hit either. This increased comprehension of social events leads to empathy, which we shall discuss more fully shortly. The point here is that empathy or "the ability to understand the feelings or emotions of others" mediates the child's earlier aggressiveness and before long, only the boys who are low in empathy continue to be high in aggression, while the boys who are high in empathy are seldom aggressive (Feshbach and Feshbach, 1969). The importance of aggressivity and its role in the developing relations among children in the preschool years for this discussion of sex differences is this: given that the quality of forcefulness is a relevant feature underlying both the aggressive and the social behavior of the high-status children, and that it is the boys more than the girls who exhibit this quality, one can speculate that the origins of leadership and dominance might actually reside in these early activities and that they favor the boys. We shall return to this point soon.

Frank Pederson and Richard Bell (1970) wondered if the

greater aggressivity of boys had anything to do with their neurological status at birth. They reasoned that the complications of pregnancy and delivery more commonly associated with males than females might lead to a greater tendency to aggress, just as the birth difficulties of males are suspected to be associated with the greater vulnerability of males to minimal brain dysfunction (MBD) and hyperactivity, and to the greater irritability we saw in infancy. So, they studied a perfectly healthy group of children from which all problematic cases, that is, all with a history of prenatal or delivery difficulties, were eliminated. Despite their precautions in selecting their sample, however, they continued to observe a significantly higher incidence of aggression in boys, causing them to conclude that aggressivity in boys stems from something other than an impaired neurological status at birth.

Many researchers believe that the higher incidence of aggression in males comes from the influence of the male hormone androgen. By injecting androgen into female monkeys prenatally, scientists have found that the presence of this hormone does effect the monkeys' later aggressive behavior: in fact, the androgenized female monkeys' levels of rough-and-tumble play, aggression, physical activity, and threatening behavior were more characteristic of the average male monkey than of the average female monkey (Young, Goy, and Phoenix, 1964). Similar studies involving rats, mice, and hamsters also indicate that the prenatal manipulation of androgen levels effects aggressive behavior. The difficulty, of course, is generalizing these findings to humans.

As one climbs the phylogenetic scale, instincts, drives, and biological predispositions of various sorts exert a lesser and lesser influence upon the organism. In the case of aggression, for example, while a relatively clear association can often be inferred between hormones and behavior insofar as lower animals are concerned, human beings confound the relationship dramatically by socialization practices that discourage the expression of aggression, by an intellectual level sufficient for us to take a multitude of situational factors into consideration before acting aggressively, and by personality factors that determine whether or not we are the sort of an individual to act in an aggressive manner. So it is tricky business to draw any conclusion whatsoever about the relationship between human prenatal hormone levels and later aggression from the animal studies. Eleanor Maccoby (1975) is exploring a more direct approach to the study of the relationship between hormones and behaviors; she is measuring the amount of sex-related hormones that are present in the umbilical cord at a child's birth and following that child through various stages, relating initial hormone levels to behavior at different ages.

Biological factors probably do play the predominant role in the manifestation of aggression. Whatever the precise aspect of biology that we eventually call upon to account for the greater aggressivity of boys, however, we cannot discount the role of situational factors in the determination of whether the aggression will actually be displayed. For example, we have seen from the Bobo doll studies discussed in an earlier chapter that aggression, especially among boys, can be facilitated by the presence of an aggressive model. All kinds of situational factors, such as rewarding or punishing consequences, the presence of others who are aggressive, the size of the group, and the level of activity engaged in, influence the amount of aggression in boys and girls. Considering this, one can wonder to what degree the high levels of aggression in boys is biologically determined and to what degree situational factors account for it. We have a long way to go before we understand the complex interaction between biological and social forces.

Activity Level

After 2 years of age, sex differences in the activity level of boys and girls begin to appear, a fact that parents, teachers, and researchers alike observe.

Four possible hypotheses have been offered to account for the emergence of high activity levels among boys. The first concerns again the possibility of constitutional differences between boys and girls: perhaps boys' birth difficulties lead to high-magnitude behavior. In the Pedersen and Bell study mentioned earlier, the experimenters examined activity level as well as aggressive behavior. As with aggression, they found that despite the fact that they screened the children for birth complications, boys showed the higher incidence of physical activity, engaging in more gross motor activities (like jumping and climbing), as measured mechanically by an activity recording device attached to their backs, and also in more movement from one location to another. Girls, on the other hand, participated more in sedentary activities (such as playing with clay) and in activities with a restricted range of action such as moving passively on a glider or swing.

A second hypothesis centers on the greater likelihood of boys of preschool age to play amidst a group of three or more (primarily composed of other boys) than girls, who are apt to play alone or with one other girl. In most observational studies, boys spend more time in groups than do girls. Different group structure may be sufficient to account for the higher incidence of physical activity in boys. The question can be asked: If girls were observed in similarly composed groups, would they exhibit a higher magnitude of behavior? And if boys were observed alone, would their activity levels fall?

Donald Routh, Carolyn Schroeder, and Lorcan O'Tauma (1972) observed the activity of children who were individually invited to play in a laboratory playroom. The floor of the room was divided into quadrants and the child's movement from one quadrant to another was recorded. Using this procedure, the researchers found no sex differences in activity level, lending support to the suggestion that the larger the group, the more action.

A third hypothesis concerns the effects of hormones on activity levels, but, as with aggression, the relationship has not been adequately tested.

A fourth hypothesis concerns the notion that activity level is just one more reflection of cultural and social sex-role stereotypes and as such is governed by sheer conformity. Accordingly, one asks: Do girls participate in sedentary activities because they implicitly perceive it is appropriate for girls to do so; or less directly, do they do so because conformity to another sort of stereotype, for instance, the wearing of dresses, might necessitate a reduced level of activity? In a film shown at a meeting of the Society For Research in Child Development (Freedman, 1971), a researcher illustrated the phenomenon of boys running in packs and girls sitting sedately by the sandbox; one could not help but observe that the boys were wearing jeans and sneakers, appropriate dress for rough-and-tumble activities, while the girls were daintily dressed in neat, clean little frocks. In contrast, Grace Brody (1975) has reported on the sex-role differentiation in the play activities of preschoolers enrolled in a program which explicitly deemphasizes sex differences. Counter to traditional behavior patterns, the boys and girls at Brody's child care center exhibited equal amounts of activity such as running and jumping, lending further support to the idea that high activity levels in boys is at least partially a manifestation of sex-role stereotyping in action. In environments where stereotypes are minimized or eradicated, the difference disappears, but in environments where sex-role socialization is strong, differences in activity levels are amplified.

Dominance

In our discussion of aggression and its relevance to social relationships among children, we offered the hypothesis that early aggression might serve to establish patterns of dominance, with the boys assuming the higher positions on the dominance hierarchy. Studies of dominance generally suport this idea. Donald Omark and his co-workers (1973) have looked at dominance hierarchies based on which child is the "toughest" among both the boys and girls and have found that boys were generally rated as tougher than girls. To show that more was going on than aggressiveness, he and Edelman asked pairs of children to draw a picture together. Since each member of the pair was given a different color crayon, the dominance of one member of the pair over the other was obvious by the color used in the main outline of their picture. The researcher found that boys dominate girls at nearly every age (4, 6, 7, and 8).

Impulsivity–Reflectivity

If someone were to offer you a Honda Civic now or a Cadillac Seville two years from now, which would you take? If you chose to grab the Honda while it's hot, rather than hold out for the Caddie, you would be considered "impulsive." In studies of impulsivity in children, the choice is usually between a handful of M & M's now or a giant Hershey bar two weeks hence. To snatch at the here-and-now and bolt down the goodies is to behave impulsively, rather than waiting, delaying one's gratification, deliberating on the manifold joys of a giant supply of goodies to come. There is some evidence that preschool boys are more "behaviorally" impulsive, preferring immediate over delayed rewards, or acting in a way that is inconsistent with goal-directed acting, although these differences do not persist.

Researchers can also be interested in reflectivity–impulsivity as a cognitive response strategy differentiating individuals who respond quickly to a problem, that is, impulsively, from those who prefer to deliberate on it awhile, that is, respond to the problem reflectively. To measure "intellectual impulsivity," they might use an instrument called a Matching Familiar Figures Test, developed especially for reflectivity–impulsivity studies by Jerome Kagan, who conceived of the reflectivity–impulsivity dimension in the first place (Kagan, 1965). The test involves presenting the child with seven very similar figures—for example, of a soldier. One of the seven figures is a standard; the remaining six are choice items, only one of which matches the standard. The child must examine the choices in an effort to find the one that exactly matches the standard. The experimenter tabulates the number of errors and the amount of time the child takes to respond and, from these measures, determines whether he or she approaches problems impulsively or reflectively. Researchers find differences neither in the mean number of errors nor in the response times of boys and girls engaged in a matching figures task.

Sociability

If to be sociable is to seek out and enjoy the company of others, boys seem to be more so. By the preschool years, boys demonstrate their gregariousness by taking the initiative to make friends (Baumrud and Black, 1967), by tagging along after other children (Emmerich, 1971), by surrounding themselves with a larger number of peers, and by engaging in more social interaction with their peers (Whiting and Edwards, 1974), possibly as a result of their higher activity levels providing more "countable" acts for researchers to scribble on their observation sheets. By middle childhood, boys also prove their sociability by yielding, for example, to a peer's choice of summer camp over their own, even if the peer's choice failed to provide as attractive an array of activities (Hollander and Marcia, 1970), and by seeking more positive attention from their teachers (Yando, Zigler, and Gates, 1971). By puberty, boys show themselves to be more sociable than girls by addressing a newcomer and by incorporating the newcomer's ideas sooner than do girls; or, if newcomers themselves, by speaking to a group sooner than girl newcomers would (Feshbach and Sones, 1971).

Not that girls are unsociable. Socializing, for girls, however, has a different quality. While Mike might share hours with Ted on the baseball field, even though he does not particularly care for him, Ann would just as soon seek a diversion which did not require that she spend time with a child she did not like. Rather than play together as boys will for the sake of the game (e.g., because Ted, however obnoxious, happens to be the best and only pitcher), a girl will seek out one or sometimes two "best friends" and enjoy an intensive (as opposed to extensive) relationship (Waldrop, cited in Maccoby and Jacklin, 1974, pp. 609-610). Great stock had once been put on the greater sociability of girls; but the belief was founded on the fact that girls more frequently included people in their drawings than boys did (Goodenough, 1957), or, as we shall discuss now, that girls exhibited a greater sensitivity to others than boys. As is so often the case, the existence of sex differences depends on one's definition of a trait. Fellowship and *esprit de corps* might characterize the boys; intimacy and understanding, the girls.

Empathy

Perhaps the belief of a greater sociability among females stems from their greater sensitivity to social cues. We have already seen that as infants, they tend to cry longer and harder at the sound of a compatriot's cries than boys do. By questioning children about their understanding of the feelings and motivations of male and female characters in a televised adaptation of a fairy tale, Aimee Leifer and her colleagues (1971) found the boys and girls to be equally sensitive; however, when Norma Feshbach and K. Roe (1968) investigated the ability of boys and girls to distinguish emotions portrayed in pictures, the boys proved more accurate in identifying the emotion as happiness, sadness, fear, or anger when the character pictured was a boy, while the girls were more accurate when the character was a girl. The children were apparently more empathetic toward those they perceived to be more similar to themselves. As we have seen in earlier discussions, perceived similarity can represent a powerful force in the acquisition of attitudes and behavior.

When Martin Hoffman and Laurie Levine (1976) conducted a study similar to Feshbach and Roe's, they noted that boys gave more active coping responses than girls did. Girls, either because they are more willing to answer an experimenter's request to describe their feelings or because they are less likely to deal pragmatically with the situations depicted by the pictures, showed more of what the experimenters would call empathy than the boys did. Norma Feshbach (1978) suggests that girls are less inhibited in expressing feelings than boys. She notes that in her study of empathy, described above, the largest sex difference occurred in responses to the pictures depicting fear.

Dependency

A common sex-role stereotype for adults holds that females are more dependent than males. As we have seen, parents respond to dependent behavior in boys and girls differentially, encouraging proximal behavior of their daughters and distal behavior of their sons. By thirteen months, girls stay close to the mother, touch her and talk to her more than boys (Goldberg and Lewis, 1969). Does differential treatment lead to increasingly greater dependence among girls as they grow older?

The trouble with looking for sex differences in dependency is that one must tackle not a unit called "dependent behavior" but a host of often very dissimilar behaviors. In infancy, "dependency" usually refers to how close the infant stays to the care-giver, that is, to "proximity seeking." By preschool, the term could involve attention seeking (such as doing a jig or turning a bowl of spaghetti upside down just to let folks know who's around), help seeking (such as approaching an adult or older child for assistance with a particularly troublesome jacket zipper), approval seeking (such as waving both arms gaily in the air to show how well one can balance on a bicycle), or seeking reassurance, consolation, or protection.

When Carolyn Edwards and Beatrice Whiting (1974) looked at dependent behavior in children from the six different cultures they studied, they found that the best predictor of dependency (measured by a cluster of behaviors like those just mentioned) was not the sex of the child, but the culture to which he or she belonged. For example, American children sought help and attention more frequently than children from other cultures, maybe because the small family unit typical of American society can dispense help more freely. Age was the second best predictor of dependency. Not surprisingly, the younger the child, the more dependently he or she behaved, particularly with respect to seeking physical contact (hugs and kisses and just wanting to be held) and seeking interaction with others. One sort of "dependent" behavior for which the child's sex was a good predictor was seeking physical contact: chances are that if someone is looking for a hug, she is a girl. As children grow up and seek contact less, sex differences in dependency nearly disappear.

Within our culture, observational studies of nursery school children show some sex differences on many of the dimensions of dependency, particularly negative attention seeking, which is more characteristic of boys. Boys are more likely to boast, to seek praise or recognition, to annoy and interrupt others, and to act aggressively than girls are. Whether these negative attention-seeking devices indicate a dependent nature among boys or are part and parcel of their aggressivity depends on how the observer prefers to categorize the child's behavior. In the case of girls, dependency is more likely to take the form of seeking help, reassurance, or affection and staying close to home or to the teacher (Speer, Briggs, and Galovas, 1969; Golightly, Nelson, and Johnson, 1970; Munroe and Munroe, 1971; Omark, Omark, and Edelman, 1973).

Play Behavior

In the preschool years, sex differences in play behavior become obvious. Some of the differences stem from a general preference by boys for active, outdoor play—they climb, hide in pipes, and ride tricycles—and some with a general preference by girls for indoor play with toys—they play with clay, work with design boards and puzzles, and draw. Other differences are linked to adult-related sex-typed activities: Maccoby and Jacklin summarize, "girls sew, string beads, play at housekeeping; boys play with guns, toy trucks and tractors, and fire engines, and do carpentry" (p. 278).

A favorite activity of boys and girls alike, one in which they will spend most of their time if given half a chance, is fantasy play. When left to their own devices, what do children of 4 fantasize about? Wendy Matthews (1975) analyzed the thematic content of fantasy play and found the girls' play to be much more constrained and home-bound. Nearly three-quarters of their play time, when they were left alone in a playroom with a peer, involved "playing house." Boys' fantasy play was less quotidian, reaching out over an expanse of theme, locale, and activity.

Top priority for each sex, however, were activities associated with the preparation of meals. Boys and girls alike spent nearly one-third of the fantasy time "fixing dinner." For girls, "playing house" did not mean just cooking as it did for boys; it meant child care (to which they devoted another one-fourth of their fantasy time), as well as dusting, ironing, and sweeping.

Less mundane but nearly as home-bound adult activities engaged in by the children in make-believe were photography, telephoning friends and repairmen, driving and maintaining an automobile, going to church, and dressing up for an evening out. The boys spent a lot of their play time (31 percent) this way, particularly when cars were involved: they raced them around the carpet, drove them to gas stations for fill-ups, and searched high and low for parking spaces. While these sorts of "adult activities" were the second most frequent theme for girls after playing house, the proportion of time spent at them was considerably less (12 percent) than for boys.

The apparent avoidance by boys of activities centering around child care or housekeeping raises the issue of sex-role identity versus sexual preference once again. As we mentioned in Chapter 1, sex-role identity and sexual identity are two separate phenomena. The most "masculine" man in the world, the fellow with the strongest male sex-role identity, might prefer to spend a wintry evening in bed with another guy. And the most "effeminate" man might be happily married and the father of three. In spite of their inequivalence, however, parents, teachers, and J. Doe continue to equate the two. As a result, they become quite anxious when they observe children, particularly boys, engaged in "cross-sex" behavior, that is, doing what the stereotype says that only members of the other sex should be doing. We shall be discussing parents' efforts to sex-type their children shortly. But, for now, we might just take note of the already existing boundaries children are placing on their play activities and suggest that the parental behaviors are taking effect.

A third class of fantasy themes transported the child well out of the immediate family, but kept him or her in the neighborhood. "Community" themes involved garbage collecting, including making the lengthy round of pickups, grinding the garbage, stopping for coffee breaks, and negotiating the traffic, and also waiting on tables, including taking the order, serving the meal, and running for ketchup, for example. They took about 8 percent of both boys' and girls' play time.

Sometimes children at play enact "special events," extraordinary events that they have probably experienced at some time. Marching bands, vacations, parades, boat trips, firework displays, and other activities of this sort comprised nearly 13 percent of the boys' fantasy play. But curiously, they comprised none of the girls'. And, finally, "exotic" themes carry the child totally outside his or her realm of experience: witches and magic, intrigue and adventure, battles, spies, ghosts, and animals. Fantasies of this kind consumed 11 percent of the boys' fantasy time and only 1 percent of the girls'.

These fantasy themes seem to be mirroring a society in which the male role is active and diverse and the female role stationary and confined, a distinction that Nancy Chodrow (1971) has described as males' "doing" and females' "being." More about the child's eye view of sex roles later.

THE FAMILY AS A MEDIATOR OF
SEX-ROLE ACQUISITION

Throughout childhood and perhaps even beyond, the family serves as one of the most influential mediators of an individual's sex-role acquisition. Though we could talk about the role of the family in the socialization of sex role in any one of the chapters, we have chosen to deal with it primarily in relation to the infant and the preschool child for a number of reasons: First, being home, the infant and preschooler are still predominantly under the influence of their parents, though television and picture books probably play a part in early sex-role development as well. Second, the majority of research on the effects and quality of parent–child interaction deals with the child under 6 years of age. However, we recognize and want to point out that the family remains an important socializing agent through all stages of development, and that the role the family plays has a dynamic quality stemming from the parents' recognition of change in the characteristics of their children and in the demands that will be made upon them both within and outside of the home. Where the research evidence permits it, we shall try to foresee how parents of an elementary or high school student will eventually deal with the child, particularly inasmuch as later chapters will bypass family influences to treat other sex-role mediators, such as the school and peer groups.

Parents' Responses to the Characteristics of the Child

Responses to the Child's Sex

To answer the question of whether parents respond to children differently according to the child's sex, Mary Rothbart and Eleanor Maccoby (1966) conducted a study analogous to the Baby X studies we discussed in the infancy chapter. Taking advantage of the fact that a young child's voice can be as ambiguous with respect to sex as a baby's face is, they presented parents with a recording of a child saying things such as "I don't like this game—I'm gonna break it!" or "Daddy, help me," or "Ow! Baby stepped on my hand!" These statements, respectively, reflect aggression, help seeking, and comfort seeking by the child. The parents, who were to imagine being at home reading while little Johnny and Susan played with a puzzle on the floor, responded to the statements by writing down their immediate reactions, as if they were actually interacting with the child. On the basis of common sex-role stereotypes, one might expect parents to be more tolerant of aggression in boys and dependency in girls. But, judging by the parents' responses, mothers and fathers show what researchers call "cross-sex effects": fathers show more tolerance of both aggression and dependency in girls, while mothers are more permissive of these behaviors in boys.

In a study of sex differentiation in socialization behaviors of mothers and fathers, Jeanne Block (1977) summarized the differential treatment accorded to children on the basis of their sex. Sons, for example, receive more encouragement for achievement and competition by both mothers and fathers than daughters do. A light in the workshop window at 3:00 A.M., signifying the laborious preparation for the next day's model train show, is more likely to be shining on the boy than the girl. Parents exert more effort to teach their sons to control their expression of affection than their daughters—now and forevermore (Block, 1977). We see the effectiveness of their efforts with every case of a small boy injured in body or soul, doing his best to stifle his tears.

Parents provide their sons with greater encouragement in the areas of independence and assumption of personal responsibility; also, they act in a more authoritarian manner toward their sons; fathers "lay down the law," as they say.

While the boys are getting trained in achievement and self-reliance, girls are steered in the direction of nurturance, obedience, and responsibility. Block describes the parent–daughter relationship as one characterized by greater warmth and physical closeness, greater confidence on the part of the parents in their daughter's trustworthiness and truthfulness, a greater concern for "ladylike" behavior such as staying clean or avoiding fights, a greater reluctance to punish, and a greater encouragement of curiosity and wonder about life. Mothers, in particular, tend to restrict and to supervise their daughters more than their sons.

Parents clearly treat their sons and daughters differently, perhaps more so as they grow older (though more research is needed to specify how the parents' differential treatment changes as their child grows). It is also clear that mothers treat their sons and daughters differently from the way fathers do. But research on this point is needed, too, because fathers have so infrequently been called upon to participate in investigations of sex-role (or any other kind of) socialization. The importance for more evidence on the role of the father is underscored by the strong belief that fathers play a crucial role in sex differentiation. Being warmer with their daughters and firmer with their sons, sharing more concern for the welfare of and providing more comfort to their daughters, and expecting more aggression and competition from their sons, fathers act to differentiate the two more so than the mother does.

Responses to Aggression in Sons and Daughters

Robert Sears, Eleanor Maccoby, and Harry Levin (1957), on the basis of extensive interviews, rated nearly 400 mothers (fathers were not included in this study) on a variety of dimensions related to child-rearing practices, including how they handled aggression in their sons and daughters. Just as Rothbart and Maccoby found that the same-sex parent is more frequently the disciplinarian, the mothers in Sears's study were less permissive of their daughters' than their sons' aggression in and out of the home. Where the neighborhood children were concerned, the mothers tolerated aggression much more in boys than in girls, to the point of actually encouraging their sons more than their daughters to fight back. The question remains:

Are girls expected to submit to the aggression of others? Or are they trained in alternative responses such as reason or negotiation? The answer is unclear. Girls do seem to submit to the aggressive dominance of others (Goggin, 1975). However, the reason need not be that submission is the response parents have encouraged of them. No one wants their child to be the passive recipient of abuse by other children. When one asks parents what they would tell their child to do if attacked, parents report that they would tell the child, whether a boy or a girl, to hit back (Newson and Newson, 1968).

Another situation no one likes is a child throwing a temper tantrum. Boy or girl, the child is equally likely to suffer the harsh recriminations of an angry parent (Lambert, Yackley, and Hein, 1971).

Yet, some kinds of aggression bring on different consequences than others; some seem to fall into the parents' "boys will be boys" category and are met with tolerance rather than tirade.

Responses to Dependency in Sons and Daughters

We have seen that preschool is still too early to discern any sex differences in dependency. Yet, in terms of parent–child interaction, differential treatment of boys and girls can (1) be having indirect effects on other but related aspects of a child's personality development and (2) be promoting personality characteristics that may make the child prone to dependency later on.

The foundations for the development of an independent individual lie in infancy, when a child who has been given affection, acceptance, and understanding develops a secure base from which to undertake the steps toward independence. But even with a foundation of trust, the infant needs actual encouragement rather than mere tolerance of his or her independence striving. As Baumrind's research (1967) has shown, the child's competence, which is at once a product of and a catalyst for independence striving, grows out of parental guidance and encouragement. Efforts to mask apprehension over the child's first run into the sea or ride on a ferris wheel are often feeble, and the child is the first to sense the parent's fear and misgivings and to receive the ambivalent message that independence is an acceptable but dangerous enterprise. And that mix of tension and delight is more likely to accompany a daughter's independence efforts than a son's. An anecdote told by a professor striving to raise his children with some degree of equality illustrates how conditioned we are to think of girls as fragile and boys as death-defying. One summer afternoon his children were playing on the swings and jungle gym in the backyard. Suddenly, above the usual din of children at play, he heard a hair-curling cry. Glancing out the window, he saw his daughter Jennifer hanging by a heel desperately trying to raise her writhing body to the rail to prevent a fall to the ground. Just as he began to dash heroically through the screen door to rescue her, his wife's calm voice prevailed over the chaos of the moment. "Where are you going, John?" she asked flatly. Breathlessly, he exclaimed that Jennifer was about to break her neck. "John, would you go running out there if it were Ian [their son]?" she questioned. He stopped short. Of course not, he realized. Ian would be expected to wiggle his way out of a jam, so why not Jennifer? Swallowing his anxiety, he resolved to give Jennifer the same opportunity. And by the time he had decided, Jennifer was well out of her dilemma and spared the scene of an overly solicitous father clamoring out the door to reinforce her dependency and to deprive her of the pride of mastering a difficult situation.

Laboratory studies have shown that mothers and fathers may act differently toward their daughters' independent and dependent behavior. Citing evidence from the work of Winterbottom and others, Lois Hoffman (1972) tells us that parents begin independence training earlier for boys than for girls and emphasize it more. Asked at what age parents should let a child use scissors without adult supervision, cross the street, tie one's own shoes, play away from home without first telling the parents, take a bus ride, and so on, parents of girls invariably set a later age than parents of boys (Callard, 1964). In addition, parents allow boys free access to a wider area of the community (Saegert and Hart, 1976).

The effect of the greater achievement demands upon sons than daughters and the greater autonomy granted to sons is to encourage "stick-to" power. The effect of the ambivalence often surrounding girls' achievements and the restriction of autonomy may be to lower the threshold of frustration and make it easier for them to withdraw from difficult situations. This would explain the lamentable "I can't" response of a little girl at the edge of a diving board or on the wrong side of a brook, clearly a dysfunctional response which diminishes her sense of competence and thwarts efforts to gain experience with her world.

When Beverly Fagot (1978) observed parent–child interactions in the home, she found that the parents of toddlers did indeed respond differently to dependency in boys and in girls. When their daughters asked them for help, they were more likely to react positively, but when sons asked for help, they would react negatively. Even so mundane a behavior as manipulating objects is greeted by differential responses by parents, presumably affecting the child's willingness to act independently. When girls manipulated objects, they received a more negative reaction from their parents than boys would. Fagot concludes, then, that boys can explore objects and learn about the world with less chance of criticism than girls.

Independent sons and independent daughters have different sorts of parents. The parents of the least dependent boys discipline them consistently, place high demands for maturity on them, encourage them to make independent contacts, use reason to obtain compliance from them, and are neither overly coercive nor overly restrictive. The parents of the least dependent girls place high socialization demands on their daughters, and are punitive (though not coercive) toward them.

Parental Treatment of Their Children

Punishment

When it comes to spankings, boys get more than their share. As early as infancy, fathers use more physical punishment toward their sons (Tasch, 1952). By preschool, fathers of boys are still more likely to be using corporal punishment than fathers of girls (Baumrind and Black, 1967). Reviewing the findings, the reddened bottoms of little boys stand out as glaring evidence of sex-differentiated behavior by parents.

No only do boys receive more physical punishment than girls do, but they endure many other forms of power assertion as well—coercion, disapproval, prohibition, and the like. Are boys "asking for it," or are parents acting in accordance with the stereotypes they hold for little boys? When parent-child interactions are examined closely, researchers find that a parent's demands escalate as they go unheeded. So girls, who are likely to obey early, avoid the harsher variations of parental discipline, while boys hold out until severity rules (Minton, Kagan, and Levine, 1971).

Not all is castigation; boys also receive more rewards than girls. This pattern of high praise and high punishment shows up at home and, as we shall see in Chapter 7, at school as well. It looks as if boys receive more attention for *everything* they do.

Parental Warmth

How affectionately a parent treats a child is probably related more to the child's age than to the child's sex. In the infancy and preschool years, when cuddling and hugs run high, parents treat young children of both sexes equally warmly. As the children grow, however, a differentiation occurs, with girls usually enjoying a somewhat warmer and more loving relationship with their parents than boys do.

Parents who treat their children warmly reap the benefits of having confident, self-reliant children who tend to imitate their parents more than children of less warm parents. If we assume that children's imitation of their parents leads to a greater similarity to them, then we can understand more fully the mechanisms underlying our common belief that a home characterized by warmth and love has the effect of bringing the family closer together. A daughter of a warm mother is more likely to imitate her than her son is; and a son of a warm father is more likely to imitate him than his daughter is (Hetherington and Frankie, 1967).

If we think of parental warmth in terms of a positive, supportive attitude toward one's children, then further consequences accrue. Lucy Rau Ferguson has conducted several studies in this area. In one study, she and C. L. Winder compared two groups of boys judged high and low on self-sufficiency by their teachers. They found, in a problem-solving task in which both mothers and sons participated, the mothers of the highly self-sufficient boys expressed more positive attitudes toward them and interacted with them in a more positive and supportive manner than the mothers of the low self-sufficient boys did toward their sons. Ferguson (1970) noticed that these highly self-reliant 8- and 9-year-old boys engaged in a lot of self-instruction (e.g., "I've got it now!") as they struggled with the task (in contrast to the less constructive and often aggressive or regressive behavior of the boys low in self-reliance). She speculates that the early attentive, supportive, but noninterfering behaviors of the boy's mother may be serving as a basis of imitation for the boy; for now he is engaged in just the sort of informative and encouraging behavior toward himself as his mother once did toward him. If this interpretation is correct, we can see that parental warmth and the development of a secure and loving attachment with one's parents can have indirect but extremely beneficial effects on the developing child.

Achievement Pressures

When studies focus on young children in interaction with their mothers, few differences emerge in the amount of pressure parents exert on boys and on girls. When older children and their fathers are considered, one can see that boys and girls do actually live under differential demands for achievement. Jeanne Block, Jack M. Block, and D. M. Harrington (1974) arranged a situation in which mothers and fathers each separately taught four cognitive tasks to their child. While the mothers' teaching styles did not differentiate between the sexes, the fathers' did. Fathers showed more concern for their son's achievement than for their daughter's. With the son, they concentrated upon cognitive aspects of the teaching situation and tried to focus the son's attention on his task performance; with daughter, they showed a sensitivity to the interpersonal aspects of the teaching situation and tried to make it fun. They were more protective of and less requiring of their daughters in the achievement tasks.

Different achievement expectations for daughters and sons also become evident when parents consider the qualities or characteristics that they would like to see in their children when they grow up. Parents, but especially fathers, think in terms of career or occupation success for their sons. Also, parents are twice as likely to want their sons to be hard working and ambitious than their daughters. Sons more than daughters should be intelligent, highly educated, responsible, self-reliant, and strong-willed, while daughters should be unselfish, loving, and attractive. Parents' most common wish is that their children be happily married. But the wish for success and respect is more common for their boys than for their girls (Hoffman, 1975). The possible consequences of differential demands and expectations for achievement will be discussed in detail in Chapter 9.

Sex-Typing Sons and Daughters

House-hunting recently, one of the authors had just finished a tour of the house and yard and stopped to discuss with the house owner a few details that the realtor had been unable to answer. "Would the drapes stay?" I asked. "Yes," the woman replied, explaining that she would prefer to spare the new owner the expense and inconvenience of searching for draperies to match the wallpapered and wall-to-wall carpeted rooms. She then added, "The flowered room was originally decorated to be a nursery; but as my son Jeff grew older, it became too feminine, so we moved him to another room." The bright red, yellow, and orange geometric forms of which she spoke were barely recognizable as flora. Yet her conception of masculinity was such that flowers of any sort were taboo for a growing American boy. We have seen how young children organize their world along a dimension of masculinity and femininity. At the moment when Jeff's parents started hauling his games and toys out of the room, they conveyed information to him; and, according to cognitive developmental theory, Jeff would surely make further use of that message. Always reconstructing his notion of sex role, he would now understand (1) that flowers are henceforth to be regarded as feminine and scrupulously avoided, and (2) that he had better keep a sharp eye out for other sex-inappropriate aspects of his environment, for the arbitrariness of sex-typing objects and events can often prove fairly illusive.

By their reactions to their child's behaviors, and by their treatment of the child, parents act as important instructors in the categorization of the world by gender. For example, part of the process of sex-typing sons and daughters, that is, of sending the gender message, depends on the parents' toy-buying practices. We've already seen that by the time children are 2, the surrounding milieu of toys created by parents, grandparents, and friends is very different for boys and girls: the "masculine" toys are moveable, and active, complex, and social, while the "feminine" toys are the most simple, passive, and solitary. Boys receive dump trucks and chemistry sets; girls receive dolls and puzzles. When boys receive gifts for birthdays, Christmas, and holidays, 73 percent are toys; when girls receive gifts, only 57 percent are toys—the rest include clothes, jewelry, cosmetics, and furniture. Levy and Stacey infiltrated a toy department at Christmas and came upon a doctor's bag, marketed for boys. It contained "a stethoscope with amplifying diaphragm, miniature microscope, blood pressure tester, etc. The corresponding nurse's kit, marketed for girls, came equipped with a nurse's apron, cap, plastic silverware, plate, sick tray, and play food." "In these two kits," they remark, "the professional recruitment for boys is straightforward, whereas the homemaker recruitment for girls is more subtle." Any nurse will attest to the fact that there is more responsibility attached to her position than serving breakfast. So the manufacturers are guilty not only of steering children toward one or the other medical career on the basis of sex alone, but also of the inaccurate portrayal of the typical nurse's job function.

In a more comprehensive study, conducted in the early 1970's, members of NOW chapters in the national capitol area and Montgomery County, Maryland, conducted a survey of over 800 toys on the shelves of a large chain of children's toy stores. The 800 toys included in their study were only those generally believed to be appropriate for both sexes. Among the preschool toys, they found almost twice as many boys on the covers of the toys as girls. Those girls who were depicted on the boxes and toy covers were twice as likely to be passively watching than actively playing with the toy. Of the cars, trucks, and trains, only 2 percent of the illustrated packages depicted girls. Though large muscle toys frequently come unpackaged, those that had wrappings showed four times as many boys as girls. Even on game boxes, boys are depicted twelve times more than girls. If the game box shows both boys and girls, chances are 10 to 1 that the girls will be on the sidelines. Perhaps less surprising, on the packages of science and educational toys, illustrations of boys outnumber girls 16 to 1. When boys and girls are shown together, chances are 14 to 1 that the girls will be looking on. However, on the least active and least creative of all toys, namely the paint-by-numbers, females (mostly women rather than girls) outnumbered the males 10 to 1. The group saw that the boys were clearly "center-stage" while the girls had the bit parts.

Parents can easily replicate this study by paying a visit to the local toy store. When their motive is to make a purchase rather than to conduct an informal survey, parents are primarily concerned with selecting an item that will be appropriate for their child. Toy manufacturers often offer explicit notices of the age-ranges for which the toy is appropriate, a practice most parents find extremely helpful. Much more subtle, however, is the implicit message on the cover. Complicated, enriching, creative, and career-serving play materials are

Figure 6-2. In fantasy play, boys practice the daddy role.

for boys; girls get to stay on the side line. The theme of boys "doing" and girls just "being" is a recurring one.

Whether parents buy their children sex-typed toys because they have been swayed by the advertiser's message or because they have as a goal the masculinization of their son or feminization of their daughter, the effect is the same. They further sex-type their children. In an effort to steer their boys toward masculinity and their daughters toward femininity, parents often deliberately limit play materials or discourage certain activities (as we have already suggested with regard to a boy's playing house). In order to determine the extent of a parent's guidance of sons and daughters away from or toward sex-typed activities, Sheila Fling and Martin Manosevitz (1972) asked parents to answer an "It" test for their children. An "It" test is a projective test in which a person (usually a child) can select from among a variety of sex-typed activities, the activity that a cutout doll known as "It" should best like to engage in. Boys are expected to select boy-type activities for "It," and girls, girl-type activities. Fling and Manosevitz found that both mothers and fathers were more likely to choose sex-typed activities for their sons than for their daughters. When they asked parents how strongly they would object to their son's or daughter's involvement in the rejected activities, that is, those they had considered sex-inappropriate, they found that parents would react much more strongly toward sex-inappropriate behaviors in their sons than in their daughters. Research substantiates over and over again the tendency for parents to apply more pressure on sons than daughters for sex-typed behavior. When girls choose boyish activities or act like "tomboys," parents, especially fathers, aren't too concerned. When boys choose girlish activities or act like "sissies," all hell breaks loose. As Robert Sears (1965) put it, "Sex anxiety is essentially heterosexual in females, but is essentially homosexual in males" (p. 159). When concerned parents write to "Dear Abby" about their sons' dress-up or doll play or their daughters' enjoyment of football, she frequently expresses her accord with their anxieties, thinking such "opposite-sex" activities worrisome.

Our own feeling on this matter is that they are only opposite-sex activities if the child perceives them to be. And they are worrisome

Figure 6–3. In fantasy play, girls practice the mommy role.

only to the extent that the child expresses his or her dissatisfaction or unhappiness with his or her gender identity. Boys playing with dolls or dressing up, like the little boy in Figure 6-2, are not necessarily role-playing female roles, the interpretation parents usually jump at, but rather are role-playing the "Daddy" role. As the "Future-Daddies-of-America," this is as it should be. If, however, a boy continually dressed in Mommy's rather than Daddy's clothes and professed that he was a girl or that he wished he were a girl, *then* we too would worry, for his unhappiness with his gender identity is a problem that will only be compounded if not dealt with *early.*

Working Mothers

Maternal employment has been increasing at an amazing rate. Of women with school-aged children and husbands present, the percentage who are employed passed the 50 percent mark in 1975, and it continues to climb steadily. In 1977, more than 40 percent of mothers of preschoolers (children under 6) worked (U.S. Dept. of Labor, 1977). The increased participation of mothers in the labor force is not a transitory phenomenon; there is every reason to believe it will continue.

Before examining how maternal employment might be affecting children's sex-role development, we should consider some of the many factors mediating the effects of maternal employment, including the mother's satisfaction with her employment decision and with her employment situation, the contribution her job or career makes to her self-esteem and her desire to define her self-identity through other than her wife or mother role, her husband's attitude toward her employment and its effect on the extent of his participation in traditionally female household activities, and her satisfaction with and confidence in the child-care arrangements she has made for her children.

Sociological and economic factors also mediate the effects of a mother's employment: inflation and the decrease in buying power have made it a necessity for two members of many families to work in order to maintain the family's standard of living, and the rising rates of separation and divorce have placed many women in the position of head of the household and forced them into the work place.

Demographic changes influence a woman's participation in the labor force, too, and thus affect her child's development. The birthrate has fallen. With the smaller family size, combined with a longer life expectancy, childbearing and child-rearing have come to occupy a small proportion of a woman's adult life and work has come to occupy a larger one.

The decline in birthrate does not mean a decline in parenthood. In 1975 less than 6 percent of the women and less than 5 percent of the men surveyed by Lois Hoffman indicated they wanted no children. In fact, since 1930, actual childlessness in marriage has decreased, thanks to fertility breakthroughs. Men and women will continue to have children, but fewer per family.

It is likely also that societal attitudes toward maternal employment are important in their effect on the mother's feelings about her career decision, her guilt about her employment, her ability to find employment, and the availability of adequate child-care arrangements. The growing presence and acceptance of women in the marketplace and the increased education, prestige, and salaries that have come their way have had the effect of increasing the woman's positive feelings about employment, and increasing society's, or specifically the prospective employer's, positive feelings toward her.

So, you can see that there is a lot more going on than signing a W-2 form. Women who work can be thrilled or dismayed about it, willing or forced, needy or affluent, organized or overwhelmed. Their reactions and the reactions of their husband, friends, and culture, will together mediate the effects their employment will have on their children. Keeping this in mind, let's turn to what those effects might be.

So far as the fast accumulating evidence is concerned, infants of working mothers are in as good physical, emotional, and cognitive shape as infants with mothers at home. Studies comparing day care to home-reared babies indicate that infants in good day care are as free of anxious behavior and as attached to their mothers as home-reared infants, though they might differ from them by being somewhat more assertive (Bell, 1974). School-aged children of working mothers show no detrimental effects either. However, whether a family consists of a working or nonworking mother does affect the child in various ways. Of interest to us here is how it affects boys and girls differently.

Girls whose mothers work are, for instance, more likely to view women as more active and less restricted than are girls whose mothers remain at home. When Ruth Hartley (1960) asked elementary school girls who they thought could do things like use a sewing machine, fire a gun, select home furnishings, or climb a mountain, daughters of working mothers saw a wider range of activities open to both men and women than daughters of nonworking mothers. They held more positive attitudes toward any activity, be it work or play.

A host of studies of elementary school girls, adolescent and college girls, and professional women all tell us that work is something that the daughters of working women *want* to do. After the age of 7, there is some indication that these are the girls with higher achievement and aspirations. A working mother seems to provide a stronger role model for the child than a nonworking mother: when girls are asked what person they would most like to be like, more daughters of working than nonworking mothers name their mothers (Douvan, 1963).

Having a working mother seems to have little or no effect on the child's overall sex-role ideology. The home remains in the domain of the woman, and the finance in the domain of the man, even for the working woman's daughter. But her conceptions of male and female are more likely to permit a more active participation of the father in household responsibilities. She could envision men acting expressively and women competently, without either of them losing their "masculinity" or "femininity."

The working women's daughter is more likely to think of a woman as a more competent individual than the stereotypes suggest. In fact, when Grace Baruch (1972) gave girls of working and nonworking mothers articles attributed to male and female authors as Philip Goldberg (in Chapter 2) had done, she found the daughters of working mothers did not downgrade the articles they supposed had been written by women. Rather it was the daughters of nonworking women who were more likely to assume a lower competence of the female author. Baruch found that the workers' daughters also had a more positive attitude toward the dual role of mother/worker.

Daughters of working mothers differ from daughters of nonworking mothers not just in attitude but in behavior. They are frequently seen as more self-reliant, aggressive, dominant, and disobedient (Siegel and Haas, 1963) and more independent, autonomous, and active (Douvan, 1963).

The effects of a mother's working are less straightforward where her son is concerned. They emerge in his relationship, not with her, but with his father. If he is from a middle-class family, he is more likely to view his father as nurturant than is a son of a non-working mother, probably because the husband of a working wife takes a more active role in the workings of the household including the care of the children. In lower-class families, a son's attitudes toward his father are less approving when his mother works than when she does not (McCord, McCord, and Thurber, 1962), as if the son were perceiving his mother's employment outside the home as an indication of a failure on his father's part to provide for the family economically.

A working woman's son's perceptions of men and women in general differ from those of a nonworking woman's son. Questioning young, male, middle-class university students whose mothers had worked, investigators found that not only did they perceive smaller differences between men and women than the young men whose mothers had not worked, but they had a higher estimation of their own sex as well (Vogel, Broverman, Broverman, Clarkson, and Rosenkrantz, 1970). How a lower-class young man's general perceptions of men and women are affected by his mother's employment has not been a subject of study, but one would expect him to share the views of other children of working mothers with regard to females' competence. His attitude toward males might, however, be less favorable than that of middle-class sons.

Some of the factors associated with working mothers characterize sons and daughters alike. For example, in a study of lower-class families, boys and girls with working mothers showed a better adjustment to school and higher intelligence scores than children of non-working mothers, particularly when the mother's attitude toward her job was a positive one. The mothers' employment could have been having beneficial effects by raising the family's standard of living and enabling them to function above the poverty line. The economic as well as the psychological advantages of the financial security made possible by the mothers' employment could account for the sense of well-being exhibited by the children (Woods, 1972).

Another effect common to sons and daughters alike is their less stereotypic view of men and women when their mother has worked (Vogel, Broverman, Broverman, Clarkson, and Rosenkrantz, 1970).

Absent Fathers

Not a theory exists that does not acknowledge the importance of fathers for their children's (particularly their sons') sex-role acquisition. A review of the research has shown us that fathers play as great as or perhaps even greater role in the establishment of sex-typed behavior in their children than mothers do. So, it is logical to ask about the course of a child's sex-role development in his absence, particularly since 42 percent of all children will probably live without their fathers at some time in their childhood (Burlage, 1976).

Not surprisingly, father absence is associated with a wide range of social, cognitive, and behavioral factors, some of which are related to sex-typing. Some researchers, using projective tests, have studied the masculinity and femininity of children from father-absent homes. Some have looked at specific sex-related abilities like verbal and mathematical aptitude or spatial reasoning. And some have examined sex-typed personality characteristics such as aggression and dependency. Most of the studies show few effects of father absence on children for whom separation occurred *after* 5 years of age, and lesser effects on girls than on boys.

Research on the masculinity and femininity of children from fatherless homes usually looks for sex-role confusion in children, and, in boys, for feminization or compensatory masculinity. Findings are often difficult to interpret, however. If a boy from a father-absent home scores high on masculinity, he is often regarded as just as "disturbed" as a boy who scores high on femininity because his score is taken as an indication of an overcompensation for the absence of the father by acquiring an undue proportion of masculine traits!

Focusing on behavioral indices such as the activities that children prefer to engage in reaps more substantive findings. For example, Hetherington (1966), studying the possible effects of father absence on the sex-typed behaviors of boys reaching preadolescence, found that boys whose fathers had left home before their sons were 5 years old tended to participate in nonphysical, noncompetitive activities more, and in contact sports less, than boys whose fathers were currently present or had been present in their first five years. As long as their fathers had been present in the children's early years, the boys from father-absent homes were as aggressive, as independent, as eager for adult company, and as sex-typed as boys from father-present homes. The later separation from the father seems less disadvantageous for many reasons. First, by 5 years of age, the boy is already well along in establishing his sex-role identity. Second, his world has sufficiently widened to include a broad spectrum of alternative sources of information about the male sex role, such as peers, male teachers, and community figures; that is; he need no longer rely on his mother to convey normative information. And, third, his intellectual development has progressed to the point where he can utilize the alternative sources. Television (as we shall discuss more fully later) may have been available all along, but it is only with maturity that he can use it selectively to pick up the information most relevant to him. Indeed, the only finding in the Hetherington study to differentiate the late-father-absent boy from the father-present boy was a greater dependence on peers. He was more likely to hang around other boys, to seek attention from them, and to accept any form of recognition—be it praise or punishment— from them.

Looking at the effects of father absence on a child's intellectual development, researchers have found a general pattern of under-achievement. Included in the pattern is a deficiency in the cognitive skills considered to be sex-linked, like mathematics. When Karolyn Kuckenberg (1963), for example, compared the Scholastic Aptitude scores of boys whose fathers had been away during World War II to boys whose fathers remained at home, she found that mathematical aptitude, relative to verbal aptitude, was lower among the father-absent boys than the father-present boys, particularly when the period of absence occurred prior to 3 years of age. (See also Carlsmith, 1964.)

Explanations for such findings begin with the conjecture that the presence of a father mediates math learning in particular or the acquisition of sex-typed interests in general. But just when we begin to convince ourselves that rubbing shoulders with Daddy makes math scores soar and dependence wane, along comes a study like Gregory's (1965), which finds that, relative to verbal scores, mathematic and aptitude scores are also lower for *mother*-absent boys.

The fact is that it is not the father absence per se, but the many aspects of day-to-day living accompanying a loved one's or not-so-loved one's absence that can disrupt the child's development. In terms of the economics of the situation, a father's absence can lead to anxiety over the family's financial insecurity without his earnings and the recognition of a new low status associated with the family's

Tuesday, March 27, 1951

Dear Woody,

If your daddy were home to-day he would have to have a talk with you about your report card and your work in school. It seems that you have not been doing your work the way you should and you have not shown proper respect for people who are older and wiser than you.

Now, I don't want you to be a cry baby about this. You must listen to what I have to say and act like a man about it.

I know that you are a good boy. As far as I am concerned you are the best boy in the world. I would fight anybody who said different. But you must learn things as you grow older. Two of those things are: to do your work and to respect other people.

You want to be a fine man when you grow up, don't you? That is one reason why you must learn those things

Figure 6–4. Absent fathers often maintain a presence in the family by writing home.

lower standard of living. It can bring about the necessity for the mother to find employment outside the home and to arrange for alternative child care. Sociological factors such as the community's attitudes toward divorce, illegitimacy, or imprisonment will affect the child. The child's own understanding of the situation matters too: whether he or she is old enough to seek substitutes, what he or she considers the reason for the absence, and so forth. The child who can interpret the father's absence as an act of abandonment will probably develop very different feelings of self-worth than one who can interpret his absence as an extreme sacrifice for the welfare of the family or state. A mother's attitudes toward the father's absence (that is, pride, shame, tolerance) as well as her competence in managing the household alone, also affect the child. Even simple logistics can determine how father absence will affect the child—for example, whether the father has the opportunity or ability to communicate with the family during his absence. Serving in the military or accepting a job as a traveling salesman, many fathers manage to maintain a presence by writing letters home or telephoning every day, commenting on family matters, offering advice, reassuring the family of their continued love, and the like.

In the family of one of the authors this was surely the case. Stationed far from home, my father kept up a steady stream of letters for my brother, my mother, and me. They assured us that he had not abandoned us, that he was away for honorable reasons, that he continued to love us, that he could always be relied upon for help and guidance, and that he could hardly wait to be home. To me, he sent love and kisses, to my brother, he sent love, kisses, encouragement, and a dose of "how to be a man" (see Figure 6-4). Considering all these factors, it becomes clear that any statements regarding the effect of father absence must always be qualified by the reasons he left and the circumstances of the household in which the child remains (Herzog and Sudia, 1973).

Brothers and Sisters

The sex of a child's siblings also has an effect on his or her sex-role development. According to Brian Sutton Smith and B. G. Rosenberg (1970) children reinforce characteristics typical of their own sex in their siblings. For example, in terms of a child's sex-role preferences, in two-child families, having a sibling of the same sex translates into more sex-typed behavior. Boys with brothers more often say they prefer games like darts, baseball, model airplane building, and cops and robbers than do boys with sisters; and girls with sisters more often say they prefer games like jacks, farmer in the dell, and dress-up than do girls with brothers (though boys with sisters were just as likely to avoid the girls' games as boys with brothers, and girls with brothers were as likely to avoid the boys' games as girls with sisters). In three-child families, however, the boys with two sisters were more likely to prefer the "masculine" games than the boys with two brothers, as if they were compensating for and counteracting the effects of being around girls (Rosenberg and Sutton-Smith, 1964).

Other aspects of an individual's interests are affected by the sex of one's siblings. Boys with sisters show less of an interest in athletics and more of an interest in strategy-type games than boys with brothers do. And girls with brothers express a greater interest in recreational activities involving physical skills and strategy than do girls with sisters or no siblings. Even vocational interests depend in part on the presence of brothers or sisters. Boys with brothers are more likely than boys with sisters to choose entrepreneurial occupations, while girls with sisters select more traditional female occupations, such as secretary. Opposite-sex dyads, that is, boys with sisters and girls with brothers, lean toward the creative occupations of artist, music performer, author, and architect (Sutton-Smith, Roberts, and Rosenberg, 1964), especially if the boy's sister is younger than himself and the girl's brother older.

Studying brothers and sisters in an east African community, Carolyn Edwards and Beatrice Whiting (1976) too found that the sex of one's sibling had an important influence on how the children behaved. Older brothers, for example, were more likely to act in an insulting manner toward their younger siblings than older sisters did. And they were the ones to terminate the interactions, especially with their little brothers. Younger brothers were more likely to be the target of scolding by older siblings than younger sisters were. Older sisters received more bids for help and comfort, especially from little sisters, than older brothers did, and more bids for sociable interchange, especially from their little brothers. Since older brothers seem more aggressive (scolding their little brothers more), the younger turn to the older sister for sociable interchange. She does not actually offer any more help and comfort and attention than an older brother would, but, since she becomes the object of the little brothers' and sisters' attention, she unwittingly assumes the nurturant role by being the recipient of their bids for support and assistance.

YOUNG CHILDREN'S SEX-ROLE
PERCEPTIONS

One autumn afternoon, our friend Terrence and his 5-year-old daughter Jennifer were watching the circus on television. The acts included a lively tango, in which the man became increasingly rough with his female partner, spinning her wildly out from his embrace. Gradually, however, the woman began to resist his tyrannical dance style, until finally she had assumed the lead entirely, picking up her partner, flipping him over her back, and causing him to spill upon the floor like a discarded banana peel. "Did you see that!?!" exclaimed Terrence. "Did you see that woman flip that guy over?" "She did not," replied Jennifer demurely. "You mean you didn't see it?" asked Terrence, astounded at her denial. "She *didn't*," asserted Jennifer.

Children of preschool age seem to have a very particular way of regarding male and female roles, and deviations are not to be tolerated, even if it means denying one's very perceptions. So powerful is their tendency to stereotype and overgeneralize, that youngsters often view life and men's and women's roles in a very distorted light. However, these distortions are related to societal beliefs and socialization practices. Sally Smith, a teacher at a child care center corresponded with readers of *Ms.* magazine on the outcome of a program devised by the Women's Action Alliance to acquaint children with career choices open to them without regard for sex. She wrote:

> In a short time . . . we've discovered some interesting things about the way our children think about the world.
>
> One little girl looked at the picture of a woman bus driver and said, "Ladies can't drive." And a child whose mother is a teacher was asked what job her mother had. "She does dishes," she said. "Is that all?" we asked. "Well, she cleans, too."

A boy was doing a puzzle which pictured a young man giving a bottle to an infant in his arms. I asked the boy what the pictures showed. "A mother holding a baby," he said. "A mother?" I questioned. "Oh, no," he laughed. "It's the grandfather." Further discussion revealed he was sure it could not be the father. (Feb. 1974, vol. 2, p. 90).

In the laboratory, researchers have employed a number of different procedures to discover how children view sex roles. In a study of young children's discrimination of parent roles, Walter Emmerich (1959) presented youngsters with cards depicting male-female pairs. By asking each child a series of questions such as "Which one (the male or the female) says, 'You can have it'?" "Who says 'Stop doing that'?" Emmerich was able to determine that, while children perceive parents of both sexes as powerful, they view mothers as more facilitating and fathers as more interfering. When Jerome Kagan and Judith Lemkin (1960) studied differential perceptions of parental attributes, in addition to asking the questions indirectly as Emmerich did, they straightforwardly explained to their subjects, "Now I am going to ask you a few questions about your mommy and daddy. . . . Who gives you the most presents? Your mommy or your daddy? . . . Who spanks the most?" and so on. By this more direct means, they affirmed the strong tendency of children to attribute nurturance to the mother and punitiveness, competence, and power to the father.

In another study (Williams, Bennett, and Best, 1975), researchers translated the Sex-Role Stereotype Inventory described in Chapter 2 into stories that young children could easily understand. After reciting the story to their preschool subjects, they would ask, "Which person is gentle?" or "Which person is a bully?" to which the children would respond by pointing to a drawing of either a male or a female. They too found that by preschool, the children had already acquired stereotyped views of the sexes. They concluded that "the child's earliest learnings regarding sex stereotypes occur during the preschool period, and . . ., these are further refined by experiences occurring during the first year or two of school" (p. 640). What these reinforcing experiences in the elementary school years might be will be discussed in the following chapter.

Another way to explore young children's perceptions of sex roles is watching children play. Robert Sears (1947) referred to children's fantasy play as a kind of psychological X-ray. For investigators interested in the state of the 4-year-old, sometimes an "open sesame" seems to be precisely what is needed. Taking the cue from Sears, it occurred to Wendy Matthews (1977) that a key to answering questions of this kind may well reside *not* in tests or interviews, but in the very everyday fantasy play of young children. In interactive fantasy with friends, children are often observed assuming the roles of others and, in so doing, conveying to us their notions about the characteristics and the status of those roles. So, instead of probing young children's self-conscious thoughts and feelings about sex roles by traditional laboratory means, a naturalistic approach to children's sex-role understanding was adopted. The major question was: What does children's fantasy play reveal about their sex-role perceptions, portrayals, and preferences?

The unelicited fantasy play of same-sex pairs of children was observed and videotaped during one hour play sessions in a room full of pots and pans, trucks, dolls, puzzles, pounding boards, and puppets. Both the boy-pairs and the girl-pairs spent nearly half of their play time in fantasy play.

Observing those activities in which the boys were engaged at the time they explicitly stated that they were the "mommy" or the "wife" yielded the following portrait of mother as perceived by their 4-year-old sons: Mother is the one who cooks, sweeps, makes phone calls (with a telephone which is hooked up to her house), lets daddy pick up dropped objects for her, asks daddy to plug in irons for her, and stays home to watch and help the babies. For example, as Nathan swept the carpet with the broom, Chris chanted, "There, mommy sweeps, mommy sweeps. . . ."

When boys played "daddy" or "husband," they demonstrated that they perceive father as the one who takes photographs, comes in a limited supply (one per house), has a large coffee cup with his name on it, serves ice cream to everyone, cooks breakfast *sometimes,* does not iron (except when mommies are away), tells mommy which car to take, plugs in irons for helpless mommies, tells mommy to sit down when she is clumsy, suggests when bedtime is, holds baby and takes control in emergency situations, works in an office, and has a telephone that is hooked up to his office. For example, as the boat on which Morgan and Jeff had been taking an excursion burned, the boys struggled to extinguish the fire and save the occupants. Morgan came to the rescue; "I'll be the driver, okay? I'll be the daddy; I'll drive, r-r-r-r-."

With respect to the girls' perceptions of mother and father roles, as evidenced by their portrayal of these roles, we find that somewhat different pictures are drawn. Mother is the one who knows where everything is (ovens, refrigerators, etc.); prepares tea, coffee, soup for lunch, chocolate goosecakes from cookbooks, and spaghetti; wears high heels; does not forget to take baby along when mother and father go out for supper; offers tea; holds and hugs babies; does *not* fix ironing boards because "when daddy comes home, he'll fix it"; announces company; tells father when baby is sick; cuts food for baby; speaks gently to baby; sets the table; does dishes; fetches knives, tea, drinks, and food; helps grandmother fix things; throws the garbage away; carries a purse; picks up the children's toys; dresses baby; tells baby to behave nicely; repairs rugs; expresses delight when the doctor comes for dinner; brings baby to the hospital; discusses periods of confinement with the doctor; introduces the family to the doctor; stays home and takes care of babies; delivers babies; and arranges for the baby-sitter. For example, as Karen cleared off the table, Kathy (the father) emerged from her book-reading and said, "Mother, plug the iron in and iron your clothes." "Oh, I can't," replied Karen, "I gotta do the dishes," as she cleared the table and placed the dishes on the counter.

As viewed by girls, father is the one who brings home the ice cream, irons sometimes, dresses the baby, fixes things, is bigger than mommy, assists in setting the table, is noncommittal about company coming, and wakes up the baby when mother asks him to. For example, after finishing dinner, Kathy rose from the table and announced that she was going to the store. "Thank you, wife. That was a good supper. Goodbye," she added as she left.

These behavioral portraits show us that 4-year-old boys' general perceptions of the female in the role of mother are as home-bound and concerned primarily with housekeeping and with child-care duties (for example, as "daddy," Morgan went off to work in his office; when Jeff, as "mommy," offered to help in the office, Morgan replied, "No, no, you're the mommy. You help David [the baby], okay?"). When cast in the role of wife, mother becomes somewhat helpless and inept. For example, as "mommy," Jeff asked helplessly from the ironing board, "Daddy? . . . Would you put the plugger [of the iron] in?" pointing to the outlet. Morgan rose jauntily from the table to perform his manly task.

The male is perceived by the 4-year-old boys as a leader with respect to both his father and husband roles. Unlike the female's, his participation in housekeeping responsibilities is viewed as optional in nature.

From the girls' point of view the mother is generous, nurturant, and highly managerial. Her housekeeping activities are conveyed as mandatory and generally, skillfully executed. As "wife," however, the female role again acquires an element of helplessness, particularly marked in contrast to the frequently manifested competence associated with the mother role. For example, when Kathy struggled to set up the ironing board and called out to Karen the "mommy" for help, Karen replied, "Oh dear, I'll get the babies, gotta worry about . . . , probably when daddy comes home tonight, he'll fix it."

With respect to nurturance, the portrait of the mother as perceived by the sons is somewhat lacking in nurturant qualities, relative to the findings of the other researchers discussed earlier. A number of factors might account for the boys' failure to convey a portrait of the mother as nurturant, however. Fathers of 4-year-olds may have not yet begun to exercise control over their sons, or mothers may have not yet turned over the disciplinary functions to the fathers. It could also be that nurturant behavior among boys at play is, in the context of the mother role, considered unboylike and is therefore inhibited, whereas in the context of the father role, within which all behaviors are ipso facto "masculine," nurturance can be freely expressed. The latter account would be consistent with the cognitive developmental theory of sex-role acquisition of Kohlberg, according to which the boy, having an awareness of his gender identity, is motivated to incorporate into his behavioral repertoire only those behaviors consistent with that identity. The behavior of other males is automatically permissible (even if it does not conform to the adult sex-role stereotype) while the behavior of females is suspect and, particularly in the presence of a same-sex peer, best avoided.

Sometimes disagreements foiled the children's role enactments. For example, after declaring himself "daddy" (I'll be daddy 'cause I'm the Good!"), Jeff began to iron. Seeing this, Morgan, who was playing the "mommy," marched over to Jeff, grasped the toy iron firmly with his hand, bringing Jeff's ironing activity to an abrupt standstill, and insisted, "No, no, daddies don't iron." Caught short, Jeff stared first at Morgan, then down at the iron, considered his dilemma, and explained suddenly, "But when mommies are gone, they [daddies] iron." "When, when mommies are gone, daddies iron?" stuttered Morgan incredulously. "Yeah," assured Jeff. "Oh" said Morgan, releasing his hold on the iron and returning to his position by the stove. Judging by the number of similar debates that arose in the course of role-taking, the children appear to be acutely concerned about portraying the roles accurately. The debates reflect both their general uncertainty about the role content and their willingness to exert considerable effort to resolve the uncertainty and achieve some degree of proficiency in their role portrayals.

Through fantasy play, the children reflect (and can even achieve) greater accuracy, and also greater depth, than we might have imagined. While the more obvious, physical, gender-related cues such as dress (mommies wear high heels and carry purses) and body build (daddies are bigger than mommies) are prominent in the children's role portrayals, the portraits extend into the behavioral realm as well (mommies iron; daddies go to work). Whether focusing on the physical or behavioral aspects of male and female roles, however, the children's enactments are pretty superficial, seldom reaching into the realm of covert, psychological role attributes like anger, caring, or envy.

While children of 4 can recognize that a child's mommy can also be a daddy's wife and a daddy can be a mommy's husband, they stumble at the idea that he or she can be a worker too, or someone's brother or sister. The nieces of one of the authors are forever working out their father's role as their daddy, their aunt's brother, their grandmother's and grandfather's son, their great grandmother's grandson, and their cousin's uncle. They inquire of their aunt, "Is my daddy your brother?" and "Grandma is my daddy's mother, is she your mother too?" The limited breadth of most children's portraits (of parents as spouses but little more) is in part a function of limitations in their intellectual development, as Kohlberg suggests, but it can also be a function of their familiarity with their parents' occupational or extended family roles. Farm children are probably much more aware of what their father does when he leaves for work than city children are; and children in large households are probably more aware of their parents' relationship with grandparents, aunts, or uncles than children in nuclear families.

Though the study focused on children's perceptions of *adult* sex-role differences, we would conclude that the perceived differences surely affect a child's own behavior and, therefore, his or her own developing sex-role identity. As Eleanor Maccoby has remarked, the children, in assuming the role of male or female adults, play at and exercise male and female sex-typed behaviors and come to acquire them as their own.

MIDDLE CHILDHOOD
The Consolidation of Sex Roles

chapter seven

The child's is an ever-expanding world. As it widens, so does the distance between parents and children. Out the front door, past the garden gate, down the road apiece, across the school yard, and into the school, the door closes temporarily each day upon the familiar security of house and family. Now the children's immediate surroundings include the school, teachers, texts, and peers, each of which will serve an important role as socialization agent for the child.

Even at home, mediators other than the parents are at work influencing the child's sex-role development. Television blares its catchy, colorful message about masculine and feminine sex roles, and children's books do the same. Although parents still play a part, their effect is not as far-reaching as it was or will be in the infant, preschool, and adolescent years.

As in the preceding chapters, we shall explore some possible sex differences in behavior, summarizing here differences characteristic of the middle years (spanning roughly 6 to 11 years of age) in particular. Then we shall turn to the three prominent mediators of the elementary school child's sex-role acquisition, namely, schools, media, and peers. Finally, we shall take a look at sex roles from the child's new, somewhat more mature perspective, seeing how it has changed since his or her preschool years.

SEX DIFFERENCES IN ABILITY

Arguing about sex differences in abilities, be it among babies, toddlers, preschoolers, elementary school pupils, teenagers, or adults, is a favorite cultural pastime. In the delivery room we wonder who is the more perceptive. In infancy we debate over who is the more curious. In preschool we look for the sex with the greater verbal ability. In middle childhood we ask who received higher grades. In adolescence we speculate on which sex has the higher math aptitude, and in adulthood we argue about who makes the better driver.

In Chapter 4 our review of the evidence unearthed few differences in ability between boy and girl infants and toddlers, beyond

Figure 7–1. Dennis the Menace, cartoon,
©*by Field Enterprises, Inc.*

the fact that girls seem to talk earlier and use longer sentences than boys. In Chapter 6, we concentrated, above all, on possible sex differences in personality characteristics such as aggressiveness and dependency, so salient in the childhood years. In a discussion of possible sex differences among elementary school children, we again turn to abilities, taking them as our focus at this time, since it is now that the school puts children's abilities into the spotlight. There, they are scrutinized to determine the child's strengths and weaknesses, to direct the child in the optimization of his or her strengths and the bolstering of weaknesses, and to make decisions about the direction in which to steer the child. As we see more clearly which of the sex differences in ability are real and which are imagined, we can understand more fully the extent to which decisions and directions are guided not by the individual's strengths and weaknesses but by virtue of his or her membership in one sex or the other.

General Intelligence

Dennis the Menace found poor ole' Margaret a crashing bore—she was just too darn smart! According to our stereotypes Dennis was a pretty typical boy: he hated girls, particularly smart ones. Margaret, on the other hand, was a not-so-typical little girl who, we might reasonably predict, would appear to become less and less smart as she became more and more "wise," as it slowly penetrated her agile brain that girls, to be truly feminine, "aren't s'pposed to be" as smart as boys.

The fact is that during the preschool and elementary school years, no differences in general intelligence are found. Given that the tests have been purposely constructed to control for sex differences (i.e., to include as many items favoring one sex as the other), the lack of differences is not surprising. The only time sex differences appear is when the assessment tool includes an overabundance of male- or female-favored items. For example, tests with a preponderance of verbal items generally find girls scoring higher. On the majority of tests purporting to measure general intelligence, however, boys and girls do equally well.

Verbal Ability

Did you ever try to count the number of fish swimming in a crowded tank? Undoubtedly, there were more than one could deal with by staring through the wall of glass. That's how it is to look at studies of verbal ability: for every wiggly fish, there is a correspondingly slippery test or measure.

Some are measures of spontaneous speech productions, some are measures of abilities elicited via a test or by an experimenter. Studies of spontaneous speech focus upon an infant's progress in babbling, the toddler's first word, the number, range, and length of a child's vocalizations, verbal output or fluency, comprehension, and vocabulary. Studies of tested abilities look at the child's performance on standardized tests of language skill, such as the Illinois Test of Psycholinguistic Abilities, and the Peabody Picture Vocabulary Test.

After groping around the muddy waters of research findings, we find that verbal abilities differentiate the sexes in the earliest and latest stages of childhood. We have already seen that in the infancy period girls babble more and talk earlier than boys. Boys seem to catch up to girls in the preschool period on most verbal measures and remain equal to girls until puberty.

Reading

An undisputed difference in verbal ability among elementary-school boys and girls in the United States involves reading skills. Remedial reading classes in the early elementary school years overflow with boys having difficulty learning to read, though by age 10 most have caught up. It has been estimated that three to ten times as many boys than girls have learning and behavioral disorders, part of which is the failure to read or to read well. Developmental psychologists interested in explaining the reading disabilities of so many young boys have offered hypotheses ranging from a biophysical immaturity to a cultural determinism. Neurophysical factors are increasingly being called upon to account for the strong predominance of boys with disorders such as dyslexia and hyperactivity. But evidence from other countries, specifically England and Germany, two countries that we might expect to be similar to ours, suggest that cultural factors play an important role as well (Johnson, 1973–1974; Preston, 1962). In those countries, where the elementary school teachers are mostly male, researchers find boys excelling in reading skills and sometimes even doing better than girls. Preston (1962) thought that one reason for the superiority of the German boys over the German girls in his study was that in Germany reading is thought of as a normal, everyday sort of activity for males. In the United States, reading may not be thought of as a masculine activity. In fact, when Jerome Kagan (1964) asked American schoolchildren to rank various everyday and school-related objects on how masculine or feminine they were, he found blackboards, chalk, and other school-related materials were rated as feminine.

To find out whether attributing masculine or feminine characteristics to reading actually affects reading performance (since the study by Kagan only implies this) Judith Schickedanz (1973) first questioned third graders about whether reading was a masculine or feminine activity and then looked at their reading ability. Schick-edanz found that third-grade boys who perceived reading as a masculine activity read better than boys who thought reading was a feminine activity. These findings, in conjunction with the issue of whether or not American schools and not just reading per se are overly feminized (see discussion to follow), suggest that a problem clearly exists. Young boys are not participating fully or competently in an activity that profoundly affects their performance on other intellectual tasks, their enjoyment of reading for leisure, and their utilization of the skill in the practical concerns of everyday living—like writing away for the ventriloquist's voice-thrower kit, checking the bulletin board for notices of used bikes, or understanding the subtitles at a French movie.

Mathematical Ability

Just when it looks as if the girls are monopolizing the 3 R's, we arrive at 'Rithmetic. Girls and boys are equal in mathematical ability through their preschool and most of their elementary school years. However, around the end of elementary school, boys begin to do better in math, an advantage that continues through high school and college.

During middle childhood, a variety of experiences trigger the eventual divergence in math scores for girls and boys. Cultural stereo-types peg math as a masculine activity, just as they characterize read-ing as a feminine activity, parents encourage math ability in boys and discourage it in girls, and boys are pressured to achieve in fields that utilize math while girls are channeled into less strenuous fields. Re-search tells us that positive attitudes about problem-solving are actually related to masculine sex-role identification, reinforcing the link between masculinity and math (Milton, 1957). Children's math performance is related to parents' ideas about the value of school math courses (Alpert, Stellwagen and Becker, 1965), and parents value math courses more for their sons than their daughters.

Further, math achievement appears to be directly related to sex-typed interests and the anticipated utility of math skills: "Members of each sex are encouraged in, and become interested in and pro-ficient at, the kinds of tasks that are most relevant to the roles they fill currently or are expected to fill in the future. According to this view, boys in high school forge ahead in math because they and their parents know they may become engineers or scientists; while the girls know they are unlikely to need math in the occupations they will take up when they leave school." (Maccoby, 1966, p. 40) As for the role of sex-typed interests as possible causes of difference in mathematical achievement between the sexes, Thomas Hilton and Gosta Berglund (1974), after questioning boys and girls, found that boys more frequently read books on science and scientific magazines (after their reading skills have improved, of course!), are more interested in math than are girls, who report that they find it boring, think of math as potentially useful to them in terms of earning a living, and talk about science more with their friends and parents. Just as interest in math facilitates achievement in math, so does high achievement stimulate interest in this subject; with such a reciprocal influence between the two, it is no wonder that by the end of elementary school, boys are forging ahead in math-related skills.

Creativity

On the rosters of creative beings in the fields of art, science, and letters, women's names are few. In order to determine whether the heavy representation of males among the ranks of the creative is due to male superiority in creative thinking or to differential aspects of the life situations of men and women, investigators have attempted to devise tests to tap an individual's creative potential.

First, creativity researchers (e.g., Wallach, 1977) ask creative people to describe the sorts of intellectual skills they employ in their creative productivity. After determining the thought processes that might be relevant to creativity, they set out to measure the extent to which these processes, called "divergent thinking," enable a person to formulate unique and novel ideas by reaching out and beyond material he or she already possesses into a realm of expansive possibilities. A favorite test of this process is the "Uses" test. The investigator might give an individual something like an ordinary cardboard box and ask him or her to think of as many interesting and unusual uses for the box as possible. From the responses, the investigator determines a person's *fluency* by the number of uses given and *originality* by the uniqueness of the responses (which could vary from an ordinary "carry groceries in it," to an unusual "paint the inside black with the constellations on it, place it on your head, and learn astrology night and day; as the seasons change, simply rotate the box").

On the tests of creative ability relying on verbal skills, girls over 7 years of age sometimes show an advantage. But at younger ages, and on tests not relying on verbal skills, boys and girls do not differ on measures of creativity.

Visual–Spatial Ability

Picture the Boston skyline from Cambridge in the west. Because the streets in the old city wind this way and that, the buildings are not neatly lined up, as they are in New York or Kansas City. Some of the skyscrapers face you head on, some are at an angle, some are partially occluded. How many building surfaces do you see? Now imagine a fisherman by the sea to the south of the city. How many surfaces does *he* (or she!) see? Being able to visualize the fisherman's perspective of the buildings, to determine how they relate to one another at a new angle, and to calculate the number of visible surfaces is akin to succeeding in a visual–spatial abilities task. Though male superiority on such tasks is not yet established in the elementary school years, by adolescence and adulthood its existence is well documented, as we shall see in Chapter 9.

Analytic Ability

The term "analytic ability" has been used to refer to a myriad of different intellectual skills. What to include and what to exclude as an analytic ability is a problem. The ability to respond to a particular aspect of a stimulus situation without being influenced by the background or context is called "disembedding." To test disembedding, researchers such as Herman Witkin and his colleagues (1972) do things like invite individuals into a tilted room with a tilted chair: the subject's job is to set one of them, the room or the chair, upright. Or, in a situation called the Rod and Frame Test (RFT), they might give the subject the task of straightening a rod to an exact vertical when it is bordered by a tilted frame. Also, recall the puzzle books on which you worked as a child. Usually, they include a scramble of lines within which you were to search for things like (a) a lion, (b) a turtle, (c) a snake, and (d) a parrot. You had to discern the outline of the parrot among the mass of lines and fill in its form. The task similar to this is called the Embedded Figures Test (EFT). Individuals who are invulnerable to the tilt of the frame or the scramble of lines are labeled "field independent," whereas those who are susceptible to the influence are labeled "field dependent." On both the RFT and EFT, college-age and adult men excel. Males are more field independent, females more field dependent. These tests have been modified so that children can take them and, lo and behold, the sex differences found in adulthood are not found in early or middle childhood. Boys and girls begin to diverge at the end of elementary school for disembedding tasks, just as they did for visual–spatial ability tasks.

Many are reluctant to consider these findings as evidence for superior analytic ability among males, however. Rather than represent a general intellectual capacity for analytic reasoning, more specifically the capacity to focus on an element rather than the whole, these skills may be indicative of more specific visual–spatial ability in which adolescent and adult males have already been found to excel. Disembedding and visual–spatial ability *are* highly related; individuals who do well on one almost always do well on the other. Further, the development of sex differences takes the same course for the two, with males having an advantage, but not until the end of childhood and beginning of adolescence.

Analytic reasoning has also been studied as the ability to restructure a problem or to "break set." Interestingly, this ability is akin to creativity, as it involves flexibility. An example of this sort of problem is given by A. S. Luchins, who, in 1942, devised a series of tasks such as the following: Suppose someone asked you to fetch 6 quarts of water from the river with only a 4- and a 9-quart pail. How would you do it? (Answer: Four of the 6 quarts will be easy: All you have to do is fill the 4-quart pail. Separating out just 2 quarts is what's hard. To accomplish this takes several steps. First try to fill the 9-quart pail three times with the 4-quart pail. You'll find that you can't; but what you'll end up with is a full 9-quart can and 3 3 quarts left over in the 4-quart pail. Good. Throw out the water in the full 9-quart pail and pour the 3 quarts into it. Now try to fill up the 9-quart pail again. You'll find you can empty the 4-quart pail into it only one and a-half-times, leaving you with 2 quarts in the 4-quart pail. Empty the full 9-quart pail once again and transfer the 2 quarts into it, then refill the 4-quart pail and add its contents. There you have 6 quarts!) In honor of the originator of these problems, they are today called the Luchins jars. In Luchins's original study, males outperformed females. J. D. Cunningham (1965) reran the Luchins jar study with children 7 to 12 years of age, and as in the study with adults, the boys outperformed the girls.

Achievement

Accomplishments abound in the middle childhood years: children master subways and bus routes, school subjects and game rules, birdhouse building, and bike riding. Aware of what it means to do something well, to approach some standard of excellence, they strive toward whatever goals they have set for themselves.

How vigorously they strive depends on thousands of factors such as the activity involved (e.g., delivering for a paper route, or reading a book), the difficulty of the activity (distributing the newspapers in a high-density urban apartment complex compared to distributing from farm to distant farm, or absorbing oneself in a comic book versus tackling an adult classic), the reason for engaging in the activity (to save up for a ten-speed bike, or to finish a homework assignment), the conditions under which the activity is to be accomplished (rain, or shine), the value of the goal (a pocketful of money, or just plain fun), the expectancy of success (finding subscribers to the *New York Times* in Orange County, California, or finishing *War and Peace* in a week), children's individual perseverance ("never say, die!" versus "who cares anyway?"), or simply how one feels at the time (exhausted, or hungry). Unfortunately, one of the major factors not mentioned in the list above that determines whether or not a child achieves is gender.

How do researchers measure achievement in children? After all, in childhood no college degrees have been earned, no high ranks on the corporate ladder have been reached, no big-money purses have been captured on the race track or tennis courts. Usually, researchers rely on school grades, interest and participation in school activities, children's aspirations for future occupations, and their expectations for success.

When school grades are taken as an indication of achievement, they favor girls, who do better throughout the elementary school years. Girls also show a greater interest in school-related activities, perhaps because they perceive the school as a feminine domain and school success as a feminine endeavor. Achievement in particular subjects such as mathematics and reading is influenced to some extent by whether the subject is perceived as masculine or feminine, with pupils doing better in whichever they see as more appropriate for their sex. As we have seen, when reading is perceived as feminine, boys perform poorly in it, but when it is perceived as masculine, they excel.

Perceptions affect not just achievement, but expectations of achieving; not just success, but the expectancy for success. Already, the sex-role stereotype of a lesser competence among females begins to take its toll, for young girls have lower expectancies for success than boys. Sex differences in expectancies, which are discussed in detail in Chapter 9, emerge as early as 7 years of age. If one were to ask a boy how well he would do on a task, chances are that he would rate himself higher than a girl would beforehand—even though boys and girls actually perform similarly on it. Girls' estimates of their skills and of their chance of success are consistently lower than boys' in similar situations (Crandall, 1969).

The fact that a child's perception of the sex-appropriateness of a task and of stereotypes generally held about members of his or her sex affect both achievement behavior and expectancies for success is consistent with the model given in Chapter 2, Figure 2-1. A study by Aletha Stein, Sheila Pohly, and Edward Mueller (1971) provides an empirical demonstration. Elementary school boys and girls were all given the same set of three tasks. For one task, the experimenters gave the children words with sets of blanks under them. The children, using a number code provided by the experimenter, had to translate the letters of the word into the proper string of numbers. For example, if the code informed the child that A = 1, B = 2, C = 3, and D = 4, then the word *C A B* would translate *3 1 2*. In another task, the experimenters gave the children pictures of objects drawn with double lines and their task was to draw around the object, keeping their pencil between the lines. At the same time, the experimenters manipulated the children's perceptions of the tasks as masculine, feminine, or neutral in order to see if their perceptions would in fact affect their achievement behaviors. Even though the *very same tasks* were identified as related to boys' school subjects (e.g., shop or industrial arts), girls' school subjects (e.g., home economics), or subjects in which boys and girls do equally well (e.g., band music), the researchers found that the children's motivation as well as performance were affected by their beliefs that the tasks were sex-appropriate or sex-inappropriate for them. With respect to their expectancy of success, for example, when the boys thought they were working on a masculine task, they reported a much higher expectation that they would do well than if they thought the task was feminine. With respect to the value they placed on good performance, they were more likely to have declared that doing well was important for them when they thought the task was masculine than when they thought it was feminine. When the girls thought they were doing a masculine task, however, they had lower expectancies of success, and felt it was less important anyway, than when they thought they were working on a feminine or neutral task. Measuring actual achievement behavior by the amount of time the children devoted to completing each of the tasks, they found that boys spent the most amount of time on the masculine task, an intermediate amount of time on the neutral task, and the least amount of time on the feminine task. But girls spent the same amount of time on each. In this study, sex typing of activities influenced both boys' and girls' expectancies of success; but it affected only the boys' actual achievement. Presumably boys, more pressured by parents, peers, and society in general to behave in sex-appropriate ways, are more attracted to tasks sex-typed as masculine, value their performance in them more highly, and are willing to spend more time at them than girls are to feminine tasks. And, because of the greater status and power of males generally, both boys and girls—by the amount of time they give to the masculine tasks—show that the masculine label is a source of attraction for them.

SCHOOL AS A MEDIATOR OF SEX-ROLE DEVELOPMENT

Early September marks the first day of school for 10 million children in the United States. Kissing the folks good-bye, they leave the house, greet their lunch-boxed friends, and begin their not yet routinized journey. Taking quick steps in syncopation, they arrive well in advance and loiter on the fringe of the playground, waiting. R-r-ring! They scramble, giggling nervously as they storm the doorway. "Good morning, boys and girls," greets the teacher cheerfully, and the process of sex differentiation is underway.

The process of sex-role socialization in the schools is not always as blatant as the use of sex-laden appellations (as "Okay, girls, let's show the boys how well we can file to the auditorium") or two lines (boys on the right, girls on the left) or any number of countless, seemingly trivial events, each with the power to convey a lifetime of cultural expectancies. It could be, and often is, subtle.

The Official Curriculum

Not very long ago, any school's list of course offerings made it plain that pupils were being systematically shuttled to or excluded from particular areas of learning. The official curriculum barred boys from cooking classes and girls from shop; it placed boys on the playing fields for football and track events and girls on the gym mats for slimnastics routines and modern dance. Then, along came Title IX, which forced schools to put their course offerings in the washer, to agitate them so every course would open to every student, and to spin out all its sex-discriminating ink marks. Administrators, teachers, and students read that, according to the law of our land, "no person shall, on the basis of sex, be excluded from participation in, be denied the benefits of, or be subjected to discrimination under any education program or activity receiving Federal financial assistance."

Without the official curriculum to blame, yet aware of the still compelling influence the school exerts upon children's acquisition of sex-typed behaviors and beliefs, concerned individuals have turned to a phenomenon they always knew existed but that they see clearly only now that it stands alone namely, "the hidden curriculum" (Frazier and Sadker, 1973).

The Hidden Curriculum

Overlaying the official curriculum are a daily series of interactions between pupils and their teachers, concentrated periods of attention toward textbooks and instructional materials, total immersion in the school's rules and rituals, prolonged exchanges with peers, and glimpses into the administrative hierarchy. Combined, these aspects comprise the hidden curriculum through which the child and all his or her classmates must pass.

Administration

Though you can probably count on half a hand the number of contacts you had with your school principals, chances are that you remember each of them well. Every child knows that principals are the V.I.P.'s of the school building. In 1928 the majority of those V.I.P.'s (55 percent) were women. By 1958 the percentage of female principals had dropped to 38 percent; and by 1971 it had plunged to 21 percent. As superintendents, women in 1971 fared even worse than as principals, occupying less than 1 percent of the school superintendent positions in the United States.

Neal Gross and Anne Trask (1976), who conducted an extensive investigation of the sex factor in the management of schools, cite a number of possible reasons for the underrepresentation of women in the position of school principal: outright discrimination, male preference policy, an effort to combat "momism" (the state of affairs in which the schools are overrun with women and boys are deprived of role models), the failure of colleges to prepare female educators for administrative positions, and the low career aspirations of female teachers. Whatever the reason, the fact remains that the unbalanced number of male and female school principals affects the child. First, while it does provide male models for the boys and girls alike, it provides them disproportionately: the male role models are stationed in the high echelons, while the female role models occupy mostly the lower-level positions. Pupils may use this information to determine their own career aspirations, develop notions about the functions of men and women in the adult working world, and acquire respect and admiration for those individuals holding the positions of authority and power.

Teachers

Unlike school administrators, teachers are ever-present figures for the child. Indeed, the average elementary school child spends more waking hours with his or her teacher than with Mom and Dad.

Needless to say, teachers' attitudes toward pupils play an important role in the hidden curriculum, particularly insofar as they affect behavior. To find out the extent to which teachers' attitudes toward boys and girls corresponded with sex-role stereotypes, Teresa Levitin and J. Chananie (1972) asked teachers to rate several children according to how much they approved of, liked, and might respond to these children. They then gave the teachers descriptions of six hypothetical children: "Joan (Bob) is a good student. She (he) often tries harder than the other children in her (his) class. Tom (Alice) is an assertive child. He (she) is sometimes disobedient to the teacher and often aggressive with the other children in his (her) class. Carol (Jim) is a dependent child. She (he) is obedient to the teacher and often acquiescent with other children in her (his) class." (p. 1,311) Rating the achieving Joan or Bob, the aggressive Tom or Alice, and the passive Carol or Jim, the teachers, not surprisingly, exhibited the expected professional commitment to achievement in the classroom: they showed their highest approval for the achieving child. Though they gave their lowest approval to the aggressive child, they showed a differential tolerance of aggressive behavior in the hypothetical Tom and Alice. An aggressive boy like Tom would be the subject of their forgiveness; an aggressive girl would bear their ill will. Teachers also expressed a differential tolerance of dependent behavior, taking more kindly to dependency in a girl than in a boy.

In a series of studies (Fagot and Patterson, 1969; Fagot, 1977), Beverly Fagot and her colleagues examined teachers' responses to children's sex-role behavior in particular. They found that regardless of the sex of the child performing the behavior, teachers respond positively (e.g., by commenting favorably, asking or responding to questions, joining in and helping) to a greater proportion of feminine behaviors than masculine behaviors. (By "feminine," they mean behaviors usually preferred by girls; by "masculine," behaviors usually preferred by boys.) The explanation most often called upon to account for the teacher's more favorable attitudes toward feminine behavior has to do with a phenomenon sometimes called "momism" in the schools. The emphasis on "propriety, obedience, decorum, cleanliness, silence, physical and, too often, mental passivity" (Sexton, 1965) in the schools has, according to some, led to a feminization of the schools. We shall return to this issue momentarily.

With a teacher's preference for "feminine" behaviors on the part of his or her pupils, girls in a classroom are more likely to conform to the role of ideal pupil than boys. Elaborating on the interaction between a child's sex role and his or her role as pupil, Patrick

Figure 7–1.

Lee (1977) has explained that, at the same time girls conform to the *pupil* role, they reinforce their conformity to their *feminine sex role*. The circularity of the process strengthens the sex-typed tendency for girls to behave receptively rather than actively. And their increasingly entrenched receptivity and increasingly diminished activity suit the school situation perfectly, providing the girls with an easy school adjustment. Boys, by contrast, find themselves caught in the middle of society's expectations for an active and assertive manner characteristic of the "ideal male" on the one hand, and the school's expectation of a receptive and passive manner characteristic of the "ideal pupil" on the other. The school experience for boys, then, is stressful and alienating and the boy's response is a poorer school adjustment.

A word of caution about Lee's analysis of the situation: The apparent ease with which a girl makes the transition into the school environment may actually disguise an anxiety as profound as that affecting the boys. For example, it could be that boys and girls react differently to the stress associated with school demands. While a boy who is called upon in class to respond to a question for which he doesn't know the answer might become disruptive and aggressive, a girl in a similarly frightening and uncertain situation might become withdrawn and passive. So, rather than think blithely that the problem extends only to boys, educators must be alert to the possibility that the very qualities that make the girl such an "easy" pupil may be dysfunctional to later demands *and* an indication of current coping problems.

In the course of maintaining classroom decorum, teachers treat boys and girls differently. For example, they direct more disapproval and blame toward boys than toward girls. When William Meyer and George Thompson (1956) studied differences in sixth-grade teachers' approval and disapproval of boys and girls, they found that the classroom observers and the pupils themselves (who had nominated classmates approved of and disapproved of by their teacher) agreed that more disapproval went to boys. In addition, when teachers criticize boys, they use a harsher tone of voice than when commenting upon similar behaviors among girls. But all is not gloom and doom for the boys: they also receive more praise, more academic response opportunities, more instruction, and more work-related contacts, that is, more contact with teachers generally, than girls.

If we look at teacher interactions with individual children rather than with boys as a group versus girls as a group, the picture becomes much clearer and we can see better what is really going on in the classroom. It quickly becomes obvious that boys, because of their greater potential for problem behavior, are salient to the teachers; and when they actually evoke that potential and exhibit disruptive or aggressive behavior, the teacher responds by scolding. Or the teacher employs a more task-oriented strategy for manipulating the situation, such as calling upon the troublesome lad to answer a question, in order to distract him from his ongoing out-of-line behavior, to discourage him from imminent out-of-line behavior, or simply to assist him in his concentration on the task at hand (Martin, 1972). All this teacher attention to the problem boys (of which there are more than problem girls) has the effect of bringing up the frequency-of-interaction scores with boys in general. So, rather than contend that teachers scold all boys more than they scold girls, it might be better to say they scold *some* boys more than they scold all the girls put together.

However, as we have mentioned, it's not just the naughty end of the continuum that catches the teacher's eye. The goodness end does too. Studies finding the high frequency of teachers' being critical toward boys have also found that they praise boys more (Meyer and Thompson, 1956). When boys behave in a manner appropriate to the school environment (in a manner some would describe as "feminine"), they reap the rewards for their good conduct to an even greater extent than they bear the burden of bad conduct (as we saw in the Fagot and Patterson study cited earlier). Even in preschool, boys receive more positive and negative attention from their teacher than girls do (Berk, 1971).

The Feminization of the Schools

Are the schools exerting a feminizing influence over our school-children? Judging by the spate of articles worrying about the "Feminization of American Elementary Schools" (Brophy and Good, 1973) and wondering whether "Schools Are Emasculating Our Boys" (Sexton, 1965), one would think so. The focus of concern (such as the predominance of reading disabilities, problems with acting out, underachievement, and other school-induced anxieties among boys) is genuine. But the conceptualization of these concerns, namely as an emasculation or feminization process, is a reflection of sex-role stereotypes. Parents might recoil at the training in docility, obedience, and conformity that schools impose upon their sons, contending that they account for the boys' supposedly anxiety-related problems. But if docility, obedience, and conformity are undesirable traits for boys, surely they are undesirable for girls as well (for whom, as we have seen, the effects of anxiety might be less obvious). If feminization is bad for boys, it is probably bad for all children. Rather than look to the teacher–child interaction as the sole source and therefore the only potential remedy to problems associated with sex typing, then, perhaps parents and educators should look to the school as a cultural institution fostering dependence and passivity, qualities often antithetical to successful adulthood.

Readers and Textbooks

The hidden curriculum of sex-role stereotyping also abides in the readers and textbooks at the font of all grammar school knowledge.

Starting with Dick and Jane, pupils swim through countless stories in their struggle to acquire reading skills. Because children's readers serve the teaching and learning experience of reading above all else, their contents often escape our attention. We care less about substance than function, so long as they lead the child through a smooth and logical progression from primitive to at least a respectable reading level.

But reading is not simply a mechanical act of translating a string of letters into words and a string of words into sentences. Reading can be a pleasure, a pain, an insight, or understanding, and it can instill one with ambition, pride, shame, empathy, joy, or sadness. Through books, one can learn not just a series of facts, but a way of life. One can glimpse into the lives of others to learn how they deal with their world, how they behave in particular circumstances, what sorts of consequences befall them as they act as they do. Furthermore, books serve the even more general function of inculcating society's values, of teaching the child about the culture as a whole, of providing the child with role models toward whose likeness the child might strive, and of inducing the child in subtle ways to accept the role prohibitions and prescriptions set forth in the text.

Because of the possible enormity of the subsidiary effects of reading, many investigators have decided to look beyond the simple story line and to scrutinize closely the multiple and complex messages being conveyed to children in even the simplest of readers.

One of the most probing studies involved examining 134 elementary school readers which were submitted to a group called Women on Words and Images (1972) by various suburban school districts in New Jersey. Simple counting would have provided startling and convincing enough evidence that something was amiss. Out of the total of 2,760 stories included in these readers, boy-centered stories outnumbered girl-centered stories nearly three to one; adult male-centered stories outnumbered adult female stories three to one; and male biographies outnumbered female biographies six to one.

Going beyond mere numbers and looking at qualitative differences such as the sex of the adult role models, the group noted that young readers were exposed to an abundance of male roles; the male characters occupied 147 different jobs, including architect, band conductor, computer operator, gas station attendant, hunter, innkeeper, janitor, lifeguard, museum manager, news reporter, principal, radio reporter, store owner, actor, and veterinarian. It would be the simplest thing in the world for us, as adults, to close our eyes and conjure up a visual image of a woman in each and every one of those positions (try it!), probably because we have actually known women who hold these jobs. But in the books studied, not one woman worked in these fields. Instead, they were presented as occupying a minimal number of positions, chief among them motherhood. Parenthood, for women, is portrayed as an *exclusive* occupation, one which allows for no other occupation at the same time—in spite of the fact that in the United States 51 percent of mothers with children under 18 years of age worked outside the home in 1977 (U.S. Department of Labor, 1977). With over 15 million mothers in the work force, one would expect more than merely 26 occupations to be acknowledged (these included parenthood, and also cleaning woman, dressmaker, fat lady, governess, housekeeper, recreation director, school nurse, secretary, and even witch!). The only jobs both males and females can do, according to the stories in this study, are to write, baby-sit, bake, cook, paint, teach, and heal.

Besides the fact that girls, who represent 51 percent of the schoolchildren, see other girls as central characters in only 11 percent of the stories, those they do see are decidedly deficient. If one were to line up all of the storybook characters and cull out those displaying passivity, docility, and dependency, chances are six to one (119 to 19) the character would be a girl. The report by the Women on Words and Images (1972) describes girls as "spectators of life": "They are given things, told things, provide a ready-made audience and instant admiration for whatever's going on. In illustration after illustration, as well as in the stories themselves, girls look on with hands behind their backs." Generous and self-effacing, girls proceed about their business (which is usually cooking and cleaning). One step out of the kitchen and they behave clumsily, foolishly, fearfully, or aimlessly, though always prettily.

By contrast, boy characters are portrayed as ingenious, clever, creative, resourceful, persevering, industrious, strong, brave, heroic, helpful, masterful, acquisitive, adventurous, fortunate, competitive, powerful, explorative, mobile, imaginative, autonomous, assertive, aspiring, independent, and skillful. (It is interesting to note that the characterizations of boys and girls given in the readers is just like those given by the young children in their fantasy play; see Chapter 6). If the contrast in portraits were not damaging enough, stories sometimes involved one sex actually demeaning the other sex. Of the 67 denigrations, 65 were directed against girls.

Even in so straightforward a subject as mathematics, a hidden message snakes its way through the figures, problems, and illustrations. In the first hundred pages of a first-grade mathematics textbook, for example, a researcher (Mlinar, 1977) found pictures of Indian girls, dolls, and Eskimo girls doing nothing at all, of queens ruling kingdoms with their kings, of witches (again!) casting spells, and of girls buying balloons and skipping rope. Among the males pictured were sailors sailing, band members marching and playing music, kings ruling kingdoms with their queens, bakers baking, pirates plundering ships, circus performers performing, knights jousting, men observing the stars and selling balloons, clowns clowning, boys swimming and raising pumpkins, and Indians being chiefs and war-dancing. While historically males have held the monopoly on knighthood and piratedom, there is no reason why women could not have been portrayed as modern day sailors, as musicians, bakers, circus performers, clowns, astronomers, balloon sellers, pumpkin raisers, or swimmers, not just to even out the representation of males and females who occupy the world on a 50–50 (rather than 1 to 15) basis, but to expand the role options being presented to the girl pupils (note that there was not a *single* role to which a young girl could realistically aspire), and to indicate to boys and girls alike that women are not categorically passive, do-nothing individuals, but are capable of acting and of earning a living, as nearly 90 percent of them actually do at some time in their lives!

Jumping ahead to seventh grade, the math texts were no different: if one were to judge by the illustrations, women and girls spend a significant portion of their lives sewing and cooking while men indulge in a myriad of enterprising, praiseworthy, money-making, and significant activities. And for all the years in between—second, third, fourth, fifth, sixth—schoolchildren confront the same distortion.

The science textbooks are no better in offering schoolchildren a view of what the future can hold for aspiring individuals. Authors usually let the children know that science is a male activity right from the start. In the introduction, the child reads that a scientist is a human being like himself and that *he* has the same sort of everyday problems. But the scientist distinguishes *him*self by discovering solutions to the problems around *him*. The plea for nonsexist language often meets with derision because it seems trivial: but the fact is that the use of the word "she" would serve as a constant reminder to the elementary school girl of the possibilities before her (not to mention conferring respect upon women in general on the part of boys and girls alike). *She,* too, can, in reading the text, think of herself as a scientist, a problem-solver, a fact-finder, and a contributor to her world.

Instead, a girl gets eight years of textbooks depicting women sewing, watching television, serving cakes, and ironing, and men spraying trees, driving combines, reading papers, putting antifreeze into their cars, adjusting equipment, working as satellite ground controllers and camera operators, researching radioactive substances, observing scientific demonstrations, and generating electricity (examples taken from science textbooks). And the more she looks, the more she sees.

Many publishers now acknowledge the problem. In a monograph about the image of women in textbooks prepared by Scott, Foresman and Company for the New Jersey Teaching Association, an effort was made to confront sexism, defined as "all those attitudes and actions which delegate women to a secondary and inferior status in society." The monograph demonstrates the subtlety of textbook sexism by presenting a few examples which, upon the first reading seem relatively innocuous—until one sees the alternative. Then, the factual distortion, the innuendos, the misleading quality, or the simple unfairness are glaring. Presented with both possibilities, ask yourself which statement seems more true, which more accurately portrays the way things *really* are or were.

Examples of Sexist Language:	*Possible Alternatives:*
early man; Neanderthal man; . . .	early humans, early men and women; Neanderthals; Neanderthal men and women; . . .
business men; congressmen; mailmen	business people; Members of Congress; mail carriers
the common man; the man on the street; the man who pays property tax; the typical American . . . he; the motorist . . . he	ordinary people; the person who pays property tax; one who pays a property tax; typical Americans; motorists . . . they
the ancient Egyptians allowed women considerable control over property	women in ancient Egypt had considerable control over property
a farmer and his wife; a horse owner and his family	a farm couple; horse owners and their children
Marie Curie did what few people—men or women—could do	Marie Curie did what few people could do
Mary Wells Lawrence is a highly successful woman advertising executive	Mary Wells Lawrence is a highly successful advertising executive
The candidates were Bryan K. Wilson, president of American Electronics, Inc., and Florence Greenwood, a pert blond grandmother of five	The candidates were Bryan K. Wilson, president of American Electronics, Inc., and Florence Greenwood, credit manager for Bloomingdale's department store
	The candidates were Bryan K. Wilson, a handsome, golden-haired father of three, and Florence Greenwood, a pert blond grandmother of five

From "Guidelines for Improving the Image of Women in Textbooks," by Scott, Foresman and Company

Many people have not seen the use of the generic "he" as an issue. It's too cumberssome to include "she" all the time, we argue. Besides, we claim, children fully understand that when we say "he" we mean everybody and when we say "men," we mean men and women both. L. Harrison and R. N. Passero (1975), in an attempt to confirm our convictions that children automatically include females in their reading of the traditional generic terms, presented third-grade pupils with hypothetical written situations below which were a series of different-sex line drawings. The children were to circle the appropriate drawing or drawings. The investigator presented each situation in two forms: one using a generic term like "men" or "salesman" and another using a neutral term like "people" and "salesperson." When the traditional generic term was used, from 49 to 85 percent of the pupils circled only the drawings depicting male figures, but when neutral terms were used, only from 3 to 31 percent of the pupils circled all the male drawings. And, when Harrison (1975) conducted a similar study with junior high school students, there emerged the same tendency on the part of the children to exclude women from consideration in their interpretation of the situation. Giving them seven different situations, Harrison asked the students to draw a picture of it and to provide the figures with first names. To one group, he gave the instructions: "Draw three examples of early man and the tools you think he used in daily life," a traditionally generic way of stating the situation analogous to the style of history textbooks. To another group, he directed: "Draw three examples of early people and the tools you think they used in daily life," an inclusionary manner of speaking. And, to a third group, he requested: "Draw three examples of early men and women and the tools you think they used in daily life," a manner of stating the situation which specifically includes members of both sexes. The findings clearly indicate that females are not included in children's understanding of generic terms. Instead of interpreting the "generic he" generically, in referring to a class of people that includes men and women alike, children react to the language literally. If a sentence *says* "he," it *means* "he." Interpreting the "he" of history, science, and literature literally would certainly distort the child's view of the world and virtually fill it with images of men in every conceivable position to the utter exclusion of women.

Teachers who would like to stay alert to sex-role stereotyping in readers and textbooks might replicate the studies discussed here by noting the number of stories in which the main character is a male or female; the number of illustrations depicting males and females; the number of boys versus girls in active play, using initiative and solving problems, being passive, earning recognition, or receiving help; the sorts of activities and jobs engaged in by men and women jointly. In math books, particular attention might be given to the number of boys and girls in active outdoor roles, in passive indoor roles, as producers or as consumers, the number of girls and boys in work problems dealing with money and machines and the number dealing with recipes and marketing. In science texts, teachers can watch for the number of boys and girls *doing* versus *watching* experiments and the number of men and women conducting experiments or doing research (it's commonly noted that boys "do" science while girls just "learn" it).

MEDIA AS MEDIATORS
OF SEX-ROLE DEVELOPMENT

Television

With the average elementary school child in front of the tube after school, in the evenings, on Saturday mornings, and Sundays too, he or she is likely to log more hours there than behind a schoolroom desk. Few children would be able to boast nearly so much time in one-to-one interaction with a parent. For the length of time children are watching television, the image they receive of men and women (if not the world in general) is out of the hands of parents and teachers and in the hand of the scriptwriters and advertising agencies.

Analyses of popular, commercially produced children's television programs show television does more than its part to perpetuate sex-role stereotypes. First, number serves to differentiate the sexes, with male roles exceeding female roles two to one. Second, behavior differentiates the sexes, with males being portrayed as aggressive and as constructive (i.e., building, planning, and the like) and females being shown most often as deferent. Third, the consequences that befall men and women, boys and girls, differ, with rewards raining down on the males and inconsequentiality upon the females with the exception of punishments for high levels of activity (Sternglanz and Serbin, 1974).

The stereotypes lurk even among such noncommercial vanguards as "Sesame Street." Concerned about the image they convey to children, particularly in inner-city areas, Sesame's scriptwriters have made a determined effort to present an abundance of male role models. Not only do the males fill the air time, but they do so warmly, devotedly, cooperatively, masterfully, laughingly, constructively, humorously, and easily; in other words, they show a wide range of psychological dimensions unconstrained by the male sex-role stereotype and luxuriously individualistic. Their activities, too, defy the stereotype. Sure, they play sports, build birdhouses, and solve problems, but they also teach, comfort, cook, and sew. The ladies of "Sesame Street," however, fare poorly. Besides being nearly invisible, they are usually not the most admirable creatures: nagging, vain, and contrary.

Having read numerous reports (Vogel, Broverman, and Gardner, 1970, Eaton and Chase, 1972; Bergman, 1974) on the status of sexism on "Sesame Street," one of the authors decided that before summarizing the findings, she would flip on the TV set for a personal update. She watched for twenty minutes. First, she saw a skit enacted by two male puppets. One portrayed a letter carrier and the second a learned professor specializing in studies of the ET family. The professor had recently ordered the letters S, W, and M, which the letter carrier was in the process of delivering. As each letter arrived, the professor taught the carrier the marvelous secrets of the ET family (namely, that by placing the letters in front of it, one could make wonderful words, like SET, WET, and MET). Next, the author saw the letter C illustrated by a cartoon cowboy skillfully lassoing a mirror image of himself. Then she saw the number "2" being demonstrated by a male fiddler singing a folk-dancing tune about twos as pairs of animals promenaded by. As a woman sang of a girl's accomplishments as she grows, the author saw a film of babies, toddlers, and finally preschoolers. One of the shots, of a pregnant woman and a small girl in a laundromat, was accompanied by a female voice singing merrily, "I can help my mommy fold the clothes and sweep the kitchen floor." After the film, she saw a young man teaching children how scissors, axes, saws, and knives all go together because they can cut. Then, two male puppets played construction workers relaxing in a sarsaparilla bar after work. Next, she saw a male painter dangerously high up on a skyscraper scaffold, painting the words "WET PAINT." She saw two men and a woman learning the meaning of the sign WET PAINT—the hard way (i.e., by sitting on a park bench and leaning on a lamp post and a fence). Finally, just before turning it off, she saw a puppet skit involving a moustached, aggressive male agent and his amiable client, a set of teeth, discussing how to give his act more sparkle and shine. The solution: to find a beauty. "Okay, Gladys, send in the first beauty," calls the agent to his unseen receptionist. First, a very seductive washcloth enters and promises to "do an act you'll never forget." But the agent explains that she is probably better at other parts of the body besides teeth. Next, an equally alluring hairbrush struts in, but she "gets the brush-off." Finally, a friendly little toothbrush plods in and promises to brighten him up. It's love at first sight: the set of teeth vows that, if she will brush him, he will shine. Confirmation enough that even "Sesame Street" has miles to go before boy and girl viewers will enjoy nonstereotyped images of men and women.

Male to female ratios, varying ranges of occupational roles, and differential psychological attributes and behaviors depending on a character's sex are usually obvious and easily remedied, but not always. Sex stereotyping can be an insidious business. For example, in instructive episodes, like teaching young viewers to develop a sensitivity to incongruity, the scriptwriter might present the query "What's wrong here?" and show the child a short skit of a woman weighted down with luggage while her husband walks beside her empty-handed. The child's task is to judge as problematic the fact that the woman is carrying the luggage rather than the man. In fact, it is not sex, but size and strength that are the relevant considerations (unless etiquette rather than cognitive functioning is the chief concern). What the child should be noting is that having someone who is lighter and weaker (like Laurel of the Laurel and Hardy pair) carry the suitcase while someone who is bigger and stronger walks idly alongside represents the real disharmony. The writer's mistake, easily made because the *averages* for male and female height suggest that the male would be the heavier and stronger, was to disregard the *individuals* by tying height and weight inexorably to gender, which Nature herself has not done.

Television serves as an important source of information for children of all ages. Evidence is accumulating, however, that it functions differently for children of different ages. Watching "The Flintstones" or "I Dream of Jeannie," the average preschooler would simply absorb the information conveyed by the televised models nondifferentially. By the elementary school years, however, boys will attend to the models discriminatively. They will be more likely to notice, to spend more time watching, and to remember the actions of models the same sex as themselves (Grusec and Brinker, 1962; Slaby and Frey, 1975).

Why? As we saw in Chapter 5, children pass through several different stages in their acquisition of sex-role identity. Ronald Slaby and Karin Frey explain, "As they come to understand that everyone including themselves is either a male or a female and that this condition is stable and consistent throughout life, it becomes increasingly relevant for them to learn and to adopt the social roles concerning male-appropriate and female-appropriate behaviors" (p. 854). In the process of what Maccoby and Jacklin have called "self-socialization," the children begin to seek out and pay special attention to individuals with whom they share gender.

Content analyses, regardless of the reason, agree: boys and girls observe a view of men and women more stereotyped than life itself. One might expect, then, that the more time a child spends watching television, the more sex-typed he or she will be. To find out, Terry Frueh and Paul McGhee (1975) had parents complete a television-viewing form derived from the *TV Guide* indicating which programs their child had watched in the previous week, as well as the number of hours the child usually watched television each week, and the typicalness of the previous week's television viewing for the child. Then they gave each child a scale to determine how sex-typed they were. Indeed, they found that long hours of television viewing were associated with strong traditional sex-role development for both boys and girls. As for all correlational findings, we cannot tell whether long hours of television viewing led to stronger sex-typing among the young viewers, or whether strongly sex-typed children watch more television than less sex-typed children. We only know that the lengthy television viewing seems to go hand in hand with a strong sex-typing.

Advertisements

Like the toast in a club sandwich, advertisements invariably border and intrude upon the program content. While you might be eating (watching) a club sandwich (television) for the turkey (program), it's the bread (advertisements) that makes the whole thing possible! Many wonder how the view of the world presented by television advertisers might be affecting children's own developing world view, influencing their material values, and contributing to their conceptualization of the sexes (Hendrick and Seal, 1977).

When one examines what children see before, during, and after their favorite weekend television programs, as F. Earl Barcus (1975) did, one finds males heavily overrepresented in the advertisements. Monitoring 25½ hours of children's programs on five commerical Boston stations, Barcus found that 56 percent of the characters in the ads were male and 24 percent were female. (The remaining 20 percent were animals of unspecified sex.) And of the off-camera "voice-overs," 90 percent of the voices used to endorse or sell a product were male.

The use of male casts and male voice-overs in advertisements represents an international effort on the part of the advertisers to raise sales. They, too, have done their reading: they know that little girls have less of a preference for the feminine sex role than boys have for the masculine sex role and are more willing to cross over (e.g., to act "tomboyish," to play with "boys" toys, etc. [Hartup and Zook, 1960; Rabban, 1950]). Whether this stems from an awareness of the lesser power and lower status of females in our society or from a greater tolerance among parents for sex-inappropriate behavior and toy choices by girls, the fact remains that a product endorsed by a boy is likely to have a wider audience than one endorsed by a girl. As advertising executive Mel Helitzer explains:

> The sex of children used in commercials is a critical consideration. More often than not, a boy refuses to be sold on anything being demonstrated by a girl. A good rule of thumb is that, when in doubt, leave out the girls. Most general products can be sold to both sexes by the use of boy models, and, even with girl viewers, boys tend to provide greater interest than girl models. (1970, p. 13)

Acknowledging not only the greater latitude of potential girl purchasers, but the greater restrictiveness of potential boy purchasers, the advertisers bend to it. Their portrayals show that boys are where the action is; they accompany the commercial geared to boys with rock music, primary colors, and upbeat language. Their portrayals of girls, in which the music is soft, the colors are pastel, and the language is flat, further reinforce and cater to the sex-role stereotypes (Leonard, 1976). Young viewers find the boys outdoors in active involvement with the toy, probably developing an interest and expertise in a technical or athletic skill. They find girls at home, in their bedrooms 88 percent of the time (versus 6 percent for boys), probably engaged in a repetitive behavior like putting a skating outfit on a doll and taking it off, dressing the doll in a ball gown and taking it off, getting the doll into her nightgown and taking it off (Chellay and Francis, 1974).

Advertisements directed toward parents might affect the child indirectly. As we saw in Chapter 6, toy packaging and advertisements influence the parents' toy-purchasing behavior. Similarly, the United Dime Savings advertisement that depicts a distinguished gentleman in a pinstripe suit leaning over to shake the hand of a small boy client might prompt a parent to open a savings account for his or her son and initiate him early to the responsibility of handling one's finances. A gelatin advertisement that offers a special dessert for every sort of child lists the "mother's helper" (depicted by a smiling, braided young girl drying dishes), a "star" (depicted by a little girl in a ballerina costume, with a haloed head and a magic wand in her hand), a "daredevil" (depicted by a young boy holding his skateboard), an "A student" (depicted by a homely, bespectacled girl holding up her report card), and a Little League "superstar" (depicted by a baseball-outfitted boy eating his dessert). Madison Avenue captures the stereotypes closest to our hearts—little girls whose finest moments occur in the kitchen helping mama, on the dance floor where she can dress up prettily, and in the school where she can earn approval from others with her high grades; little boys whose glowing hours occur rolling down a hill at 80 mph on a skateboard, or on the playing field slugging a homer—and uses them to sell Jello. The problem is not that the portrayals are false: one is more likely to see a girl in a dance outfit than a boy, and a boy in baseball gear than a girl. The problem is that in looking at the ads, one would think it could never be otherwise.

Best Sellers

Every spring the *New York Times Book Review* comes out with its seasonal review of the latest in children's books. In one review (Davis, 1978) one finds Arne Kristiansen 400 miles from the North

Pole, alone in a town from which all the inhabitants have fled in anticipation of a Nazi takeover, planning how single-handedly to warn his father who is off on a scientific expedition; 13-year-old friends, Seth and David, tackling the legend of the bones on Black Spruce Mountain; Paul Williams displaying "strength, good humor, (and) at least as much courage as the next fellow" when the Golden Flyer train he is riding out West becomes snowbound high in the Sierras; 14-year-old Mark Kline overcoming "kidnapping, a dark sea journey in the hold of a fishing boat, and a collision with a party of desperados to win his struggle to find (his older brother) Carl"; and Eugene d'Ennoncourt Havighurst, II, who survives "The Night of the Hurricane." As the reviewer explains, "Survival is the very stuff of the adventure tale. Man against nature, man against overwhelming odds. . . . " Just as a reader might come to take him literally, the reviewer of current biographies available to children tells of Harriet Beecher Stowe, who, against society, in spite of equally overwhelming odds, sparked a social upheaval which ended in the abolishment of slavery; of Mother Jones's trek through the coal mining country, organizing workers, fighting against child labor, and instigating reforms, and of Margaret Fuller's role as an intellectual leader in the nineteenth century. The reviewer writes, "Is all that consciousness raising by defenders of women's rights beginning to take subliminal effect?" (Fask, 1977, p. 48). Perhaps, but it's slow going. For example, in the silhouettes accompanying each of the reviews, the *New York Times* illustrator depicts twice as many boys as girls (three boys reading, one swinging from a tree, one painting a picture, one drawing, one clapping a (smaller) girl's back, one reading to a (smaller) girl, one flipping pancakes, one looking through a telescope, one swinging from a rope, and one watching; as compared to the girls, one of whom is swinging on a swing, one clapping the (taller) boy's back, one looking at the (larger) boy reading; one crouched down observing the boy swinging from the rope). And in the publishers' ads alongside the review, there are again twice as many boys as girls and twice as many men as women. And, two out of the four women plus a mama bear are wearing aprons.

In a study entitled "Jack Went Up the Hill . . . But Where Was Jill?" Shirley St. Peter (1977) questioned whether sex-role stereotyping in children's books had actually diminished since the advent of Women's Lib, which she reckoned began with the publication of Betty Friedan's *The Feminine Mystique*. To find out, St. Peter compared children's books before 1966 and after 1966. Using what has by now become a standard checklist, she looked at the sex of the central characters, the sex of the figures portrayed on the front covers, the sex of the individuals featured in the titles, the number of activities of males and females in the illustrations, the presence of expressive and instrumental role activities, and so on.

Pre- or post-liberation, the commercial children's books were like the readers and textbooks discussed previously: females were underrepresented in central roles, titles, and illustrations, and males were underrepresented in expressive roles; males were overrepresented in instrumental roles and women in housewife activities—more so after 1966 than before!

Others have confirmed the trend toward greater rather than less sexism in children's books. An examination of award-winning picture books over a fifty-year period reveals a decrease in sex bias during the 1940's, which is sustained throughout the 1950's, only to revive in the 1960's and 1970's. In prewar periods, the number of male and female stars, characters, and illustrations were nearly equal; in postwar periods, a disproportionate number were male. And, the disproportion seems to be increasing still.

To turn to the classics will not help: Fairty Tales such as Cinderella, Snow White and the Seven Dwarfs, Little Red Riding Hood, which have enchanted and delighted countless children for so many years, also portray women and girls in a most unfavorable light. Who will ever forget the Wicked Witch of the West? Or Cinderella's stepmother? Although we can find men in wicked roles, 80 percent of the negative characters in Grimm's fairy tales are female.

Even the heroines are portrayed unfavorably—weak, helpless, ever suffering, childlike. Three of the predominant themes are (1) being trusting and innocent, as in Snow White's accepting the apple and Little Red Riding Hood venturing into the woods alone; (2) shining in domestic activities, as in Snow White's cleaning and cooking for the dwarfs and Cinderella's acting as a house servant for her stepmother; and (3) having to be rescued by the white knight as in Snow White's Prince Charming and Cinderella's shoe prince (Belotti, 1976).

PEERS AS MEDIATORS
OF SEX-ROLE DEVELOPMENT

Right from the start, the peer group is a different creature for boys and girls—it has different size and shape, inhabits a different terrain, and performs a different act for each of the sexes. The male peer group, as we have already noted, runs in packs; the female group plays in pairs or clusters of three. The male group takes to the street sooner and teams up with whomever it happens to encounter along the way; the female group is more commonly found in or near the home and restricts its company to invited guests. No one knows why early peer group formation happens this way. Perhaps the earlier autonomy granted to boys by parents permits them to leave the house and make their acquaintances elsewhere, while the greater restrictions placed on girls necessitates arranging for their playmates to visit. Maybe the protective attitude toward young girls leads to their playmates being "selected" rather than "discovered." Maybe boys have a biological predisposition to seek male company, as a sociobiologist might suggest (Tiger, 1969). Or, it could be that the greater verbal ability of girls lends itself to the conversational mode possible only in one-to-one or small-group interaction, while the greater aggressiveness of boys prompts them to congregate with enough others to form a competitive grouping for team sports and games. In any case and for whatever the reason, the peer group in middle childhood is different for boys and for girls.

One feature most middle childhood peer groups share is homogeneity; they are either all-boy or all-girl. Whether boys and girls seek out others of the same sex in order to learn the appropriate sex-typed behavior, or whether their notion of their own sex role includes the idea that one is required to hang around others of the same sex as oneself is unknown. But what is certain is that, particularly for boys, the peer group represents a powerful mediator of sex-role acquisition. Recall that the preschool children's fantasy play revealed extensive portrayals of the mother role but only scanty enactments of the father's role. The lack of exposure to the father in both his family and occupational roles implied by the children's characterizations would, according to any one of the theories discussed earlier, prove especially troublesome for boys who look to the father, as the same-sex parent, for cues about how a fellow is to behave. The frequent absence of the male role model at home and at school means that the average boy is likely to turn to his peer group for guidance in the area of sex-role development. By hanging around others like oneself, a child can fill in the gaps in his or her knowledge about what individuals of the appropriate sex do, how they ought to act, what sorts of interests they could pursue, and the like. With the same-sex peer group, the child can practice his or her sex role.

"Unfortunately," Ruth Hartley points out (speaking of boys), "both the information and the practice he gets are distorted. Since his peers have no better sources of information than he has, all they can do is pool the impressions and anxieties they derived from their early training. Thus, the picture they draw is oversimplified and overemphasized. It is a picture drawn in black and white, with little or no modulation and it is incomplete, including a few of the many elements that go to make up the role of the mature male." (1959, p. 459) This would explain some of the exaggerated sex typing of activities and interests. As we saw in our discussion on the effects of sex-appropriate and inappropriate interests on achievement behavior, when boys thought they were working on a task that boys of their age liked and did well on, they gave the task more of their time and valued their performance on the tasks more highly than they would have without the information that the task was for boys. Uncertain about less obvious aspects of the male role, the boys cling tenaciously to those aspects of which they are certain. Of course, girls too care about doing the "sex-appropriate thing," but not to the same extent.

Another consequence of the indirect and elusive means of acquiring sex role provided by one's equally knowledgeable and therefore equally ignorant peer group is sometimes a tendency to deprecate girls. In a clumsy effort to differentiate themselves from the group called girls, some boys often resort to placing all things female (with the possible exception of mother, who is in a class by herself) on a shelf marked "Yuk!"

Most girls, with an abundance of role models close by, particularly mother and teacher, have less difficulty in seeking out cues about what girls and women do and rely less on their peer group for sex-role related information. For general purposes, same-sex peers are just as important to girls as they are to boys, however. In the course of a year's observation of peer groups, Patterson and Fagot (1969) noted boys reinforcing other boys and girls reinforcing other girls a total of 359 and 463 times, respectively. But they saw only 71 cases of boys reinforcing girls and only 63 cases of girls reinforcing boys. The persuasiveness of the same-sex group, implied by these figures, would surely override any "feminization effect" of the teachers' reinforcing behavior toward boys discussed earlier. In fact, Patterson and Fagot tell of the peer group dynamics centering on one boy they observed whose behavioral choices were predominantly feminine. Not only did his peers offer strong doses of negative reinforcement, but they played with him less than any other child. Forceful intervention combined with systematic exclusion represent just two potent tactics of the socializing agents called peers.

SEX-ROLE PERCEPTION IN MIDDLE CHILDHOOD

By the time children reach school age, they are skilled in the fine art of sex typing: they can designate male and female toys, occupations, interests, and activities (Vener and Snyder, 1966). Footballs are for boys; dolls, for girls. Doctors are men; nurses, women. Sports are masculine; fashion, feminine. Running around is male; sitting still is female. Having figured the system out by 4 or 5 years of age, they can, according to Freud, rest up until they can put both their sex roles and their sexuality into action. But for now, some would say, they subside into a latency period, during which all their energies are diverted to the more neutral pursuits of gaining mastery and acquiring skills. A glimpse at the child's changing perception of sex role, however, indicates that the period is not as latent as one might suppose. Refining their notions of masculinity and femininity and considering their own place in the scheme of things are part and parcel of their strivings toward mastery and a general competence in dealing with their world. Now is the time the child looks around and about. What he or she sees, at home, in school, on television, in the neighborhood, has just been discussed. Some of the effects of this child's-eye view of the world and the absorption of its message may not appear until adolescence or adulthood. But some become obvious early, coloring the child's perceptions of adults both in home and out, and of his or her own self both in the future and now.

In the previous chapter, we let the children's actual portrayal of sex roles in fantasy play inform us about their perspectives. By elementary school, we need only ask the children, for they have achieved a level of verbal ability and comprehension sufficient to convey accurately their impressions about the male and female role in our society. When Ruth Hartley (1959) asked 8- and 11-year-old boys what men need to know and to be able to do, the boys responded that men "need to be strong; they have to be ready to make decisions; they must be able to protect women and children in emergencies; they have to have more manual strength than women; they should know how to carry heavy things; they are the ones to do the hard labor, the rough work; they must be able to fix things; they must get money to support their families; they need 'a good business head. . .'; they also need to know how to take good care of children, how to get along with their wives and how to teach their children right from wrong" (pp. 190–191). In the family, men "are the boss; they have authority in relation to the disposal of monies and they get first choice in the use of the most comfortable chair in the house and the daily paper. They seem to get mad a lot, but are able to make children feel good; they laugh and make more jokes than women do. Compared with mothers, fathers are more fun to be with; they are exciting to have around; they have the best ideas" (p. 191).

Adult women, according to elementary school boys, "are indecisive; they are afraid of many things; they make a fuss over things; they get tired a lot; they very often need someone to help them; they stay home most of the time; they are not as strong as men; they don't like adventure; they are squeamish about seeing blood; they don't know what to do in an emergency; they cannot do dangerous things; they are more easily damaged than men; and they die more easily than men. Moreover, they are 'lofty' about 'dirty' jobs; they feel themselves above manual work; they are scared of getting wet or getting an electrical shock; they cannot do things men do because they have a way of doing things the wrong way; they are not very intelligent; they can only scream in an emergency where a man would take charge. Women are the ones who have to keep things neat and tidy and clean up household messes; they feel sad more often than men. Although they make children feel good, they also make boys carry heavy loads, haul heavy shopping carts uphill; keep them from going out when they want to go out or demand that they stay out when they want to come in. They take the pep out of things and are fussy about children's grades. They very easily become jealous and envy their husbands" (pp. 191–192).

Grace Baruch (1974) conducted a similar study with girls and found the same sex-role differentiation, with males viewed as competent, logical, and active, females as gentle, neat, and affectionate. The portraits of males and females, fathers and mothers, that Hartley and Baruch have been able to draw through their interviews with elementary school children resemble the portraits drawn earlier through the play observations. But by middle childhood the portraits are more complex and less concrete.

Children's stereotypes of male and female adults extend outside of the home and family into the realm of work as well. They perceive occupational roles held by adults as sex-linked. To be a boss, a taxi driver, a factory worker, a mayor, or a lawyer is to be a man; to be a nurse or housekeeper is to be a female.

The problem with a sex-stereotyped view of the work world is that it carries over into the children's own lives by affecting their career aspirations and their hopes and plans for the future. The all-American boy wants to be a craftsman, engineer, doctor, or sportsman; nothing less will do. Being a pilot would be great; but being a flight attendant would be tantamount to failure. Girls want to be teachers, artists, stewardesses, nurses, and veterinarians.

Sex differences in the expression of vocational aspirations start early. Asking children from 6 to 8 years of age what they would like to be when they grew up, William Looft (1971) found the boys chose a broad range of occupations such as football player, policeman, doctor, dentist, pilot, and astronaut, while the girls confined themselves to a narrow range of traditionally female jobs like nurse, teacher, mother, stewardess, and salesclerk. In an extension of that study, Lynn Hewitt (1975) found that with age, boys', but not girls', job perspectives become increasingly broad as they learn of the infinity of choices available to them. Girls, with age, do not experience this growing awareness of occupational alternatives.

Not only do boys and girls have different occupational aspirations, but they perceive their eventual familial role somewhat differently. Iglitizen (1972), who conducted interviews with elementary school children, found that girls were very much more likely than boys to note that marriage would be a predominant focus of their lives, although only 6 percent of the girls listed wife and mother as their only roles. Boys were more likely to place family life in the background or to ignore it completely. In describing a typical day of the future, a boy would be more likely to get right down to business: "I would talk to my clients on what their problems were. If I thought his thoughts were right I would explain the right procedures to take depending on his problems, and I would fight for his thoughts." Now, that kind of thinking will get a bloke a fast promotion! Describing her day, a girl might concentrate instead on the traditionally female responsibilities, sometimes to the detriment or even neglect of her professed occupation: "I would start the morning after getting out of bed by eating breakfast. Then I would clean the house. If I was done before lunch I would probably visit a friend. Then eat lunch. After lunch I would probably go shopping. Then I would come home and rest for awhile. When my husband came home (if I was married) he would tell me how his day went and I would tell him how mine went. If he was in a real good mood he would take me out to dinner. When we were done with dinner we would go to a movie. Then we would go home and go to bed." The traditional stereotype has overshadowed if not overpowered all but the domestic affairs, providing the child with no awareness of the training and work required to achieve success as an artist, the occupation she had indicated that she would like to pursue.

Perceptions of sex differences among children of their own age are as stereotyped as their views of adult men and women and of their own future selves. Their image of elementary school boys and girls mirrors the image we see in the picture books they had leafed through as preschoolers, the readers and textbooks they study in school, the novels they read at their leisure, and the television they watch after school. They expect boys to be outdoors more than girls, not to be cry babies or sissies or softies, to get into trouble, to have adventures, to be athletic, and to possess many skills and abilities. They expect girls to stay close to home, to play quietly, to be easily frightened and to cry about it, to stay clean and neat, to fuss over dolls, to talk about clothes, and to know how to cook and sew.

By the elementary school years, a child has achieved a sufficient level of intellectual functioning to understand that, if he is a boy, he will be a boy forever, and if she is a girl, nothing will alter that fact. The child will have acquired the notion of "gender constancy" (Emmerich et al., 1977).

Children's perceptions of sex role can have an effect on their more general perception of themselves as individuals, and on their self-esteem. Believing boys to be more skillful can lead boys to rate themselves as more competent than girls would rate themselves, and such reasoning could lead them to assume leadership positions on the basis of that belief. When Nicholas Pollis and Donald Doyle (1972) asked first graders to throw a bean bag to hit a concealed target, boys estimated that they (the boys) had performed better than the girls had performed. Even the three girls who had achieved perfect scores thought that they had probably done poorly; and the other children agreed. Since popularity in the peer group is so often based on perceived or real power, it is not surprising that 80 percent of the girls in this study scored below the median on a sociometric test of popularity, while only 31 percent of the boys did.

PUBESCENCE
The Coming of Age and Sex Roles

chapter eight

Puberty, marking the end of childhood and the beginning of adolescence, is a period of rapid and sometimes bewildering changes. As the adolescent watches these changes occur, he or she may be alternately fascinated and terrified, pleased and disappointed, self-confident and self-conscious.

Puberty is both a public and a private event, one that the adolescent feels to be deeply personal but that is sometimes painfully evident to and broadly acknowledged by parents and friends. In her diary, Anne Frank conveys the most secretive nature of puberty and the adolescent's frequently ambiguous feelings toward it:

> Each time I have a period . . . I have the feeling that in spite of all the pain, unpleasantness, nastiness, I have a sweet secret and that is why, although it is nothing but a nuisance to me in a way, I always long for the time that I shall feel that secret within me again. (1972, p. 117)

The public nature of puberty is nowhere more evident than in the locker room, where the progress of one's sexual maturity is subject to comparison and comment. Peers (sometimes subtly and sometimes not so subtly) tease, make sexual jokes, and once in a while, behave cruelly. The movie *Carrie* begins with a locker room scene: Carrie, an awkward, unpopular, and sheltered teenager, begins to menstruate for the first time while showering after gym class. Not having been told about menstruation by her mother and not privy to girl talk, she is terrified by the experience. Her peers, enacting every adolescent's worst fears, do not sympathize with her or explain to her what is happening, but laugh at her and tease her unmercifully.

Puberty is not only a biological experience, it is a social one as well. Puberty marks the coming of age, the introduction to adulthood. The girl is a woman and the boy a man, at least in terms of appearance and sexual maturity. By achieving sexual maturity, adolescents are able to participate in adult activities. To commemorate the beginning of adulthood, many societies have elaborate rituals and ceremonies, often referred to as "the rites of passage," as the child is introduced into the religious or secular community. Because the rites that celebrate the entrance into adulthood vary so widely across cultures, we will look at their meanings in different societies.

But first, we have a problem. How do we, or anyone else for that matter, know exactly when puberty takes place? We all know some 12-year-olds who have fully matured and others who have not matured at all! For girls, the task is easy. Most cultures, including our own, use the first menstruation (called *menarche*) to mark the beginning of puberty. Almost all of the rites of passage for girls focus on menarche.

Menarche may pass with celebration, disdain, or no comment, depending on the culture (Delaney, Lupton, and Toth, 1976; Hays, 1964). The Apache Indians look upon a girl's first menstruation favorably, considering it an awesome, supernatural blessing. Eskimos isolate the girl from contact with people for 40 days. Margaret Mead's description of the cermony of the Arapesh illustrates the elaborateness and importance of the occasion in some cultural groups:

> A girl's first menstruation and the accompanying ceremonial take place in . . . her husband's home. But her brothers must play a part in it and they are sent for; failing brothers, cousins will come. Her brothers build her a menstrual hut, which is stronger and better-constructed than are the menstrual huts of older women. . . . The girl is cautioned to sit with her legs crossed. Her woven arm and leg bands, her earrings, her old lime gourd and lime spatula are taken from her. Her woven belt is taken off. If these are fairly new they are given away; if they are old they are cut off and destroyed. There is no feeling that they themselves are contaminated, but only the desire to cut the girl's connection with her past.
>
> The girl is attended by older women who are her own relatives or relatives of her husband. They rub her all over with stinging nettles. They tell her to roll one of the large nettle-leaves into a tube and thrust it into her vulva: this will ensure her breasts growing large and strong. The girl eats no food, nor does she drink water. On the third day, she comes out of the hut and stands against a tree while her mother's brother makes the decorative cuts upon her shoulders and buttocks. This is done so gently, with neither earth nor lime rubbed in—the usual New Guinea method for making scarification marks permanent—that it is only possible to find the scars during the next three or four years. During that time, however, if strangers wish to know whether a girl is nubile, they look for the marks. Each day the women rub the girl with nettles. It is well if she fasts for five or six days, but the women watch her anxiously, and if she becomes too weak they put an end to it. Fasting will make her strong, but too much of it might make her die, and the emergence ceremony is hastened. (1935, pp. 92–93)

Boys are another matter. There is no such discrete and public marker for puberty. In our culture, some scientists see the boy's first ejaculation as comparable to the girl's first period. Many cultures that celebrate rites of passage separate all the boys in a certain age group (usually 12 to 14 years) from the rest of the community. There, the boys are "taught" to be men by the village elders, as was poignantly illustrated in Alex Haley's book and movie, *Roots* (1976). Kunte Kinte, an African boy, was whisked off to the woods with his peers one day, to learn hunting, fighting, tribal customs and values, and to be circumcised. Upon returning to the village, as he ran toward his mother, she reminded him that he was a man now, upon which he greeted her like an adult rather than a child. Moving into his own hut and having his own food and hunt utensils, he was ready to embark upon a productive life within the community.

The rituals followed tell us a great deal about how different societies view puberty. As we have seen, some societies greet puberty with joy, others with fear, and still others with avoidance. The pubertal child learns very quickly his or her society's attitudes and expectations concerning puberty and ultimately adulthood. The rite of passage is a ritualized way of saying: "Now you are an adult. It is time that you act like an adult (rather than a child) and take on an adult's activities and responsibilities." Since adult roles and responsibilities are sex-linked in almost all cultures, the pubertal child is learning about *sex roles,* not just adult roles. In fact, the message is not "Now you are adult," but "Now you are a man or a woman, with male or female roles and responsibilities."

What about our own society's rites of passages? Although we cannot compete with the Arapesh or the African tribe described, some American families do celebrate the event. As one girl described her first period:

> When I discovered it . . . (my mother) told me to come with her, and we went into the living room to tell my father. She just looked at me and then at him and said, "Well, your little girl is a young lady now!" My dad gave me a hug and congratulated me and I felt grown up and proud that I was a lady at last. (Shipman, 1971, p. 331)

Unfortunately, the event is not always acknowledged with pride. Another girl recalls her experience:

I had no information whatsoever, no hint that anything was going to happen to me. . . . I thought I was on the point of death from internal hemorrhage. . . . What did my highly educated mother do? She read me a furious lecture about what a bad, evil, immoral thing I was to start menstruating at the age of eleven! So young and so vile! Even after thirty years, I can feel the shock of hearing her condemn me for "doing" something I had no idea occurred. (Weideger, 1975, p. 169)

Although Americans have no formalized rites of passage, some of the customs brought to America by European immigrants are still practiced, although they are becoming increasingly uncommon.

In spite of our society's lack of a rite, adolescents in our society do receive information about societal beliefs concerning puberty. In terms of menarche for girls and probably ejaculation for boys, much of the information is contradictory and negative. On the one hand, menarche and ejaculation are thought to be traumatic and upsetting events, while on the other they are symbols of sexual maturity, of becoming a woman or a man. Even though they signify sexual maturity and adulthood, girls are told to hide the fact that they are menstruating by "acting normal" and "not letting anyone know," and boys are given similar messages about ejaculation.

Societal beliefs and customs, as illustrated in the preceding examples, set the stage for puberty. Biological changes that occur at puberty are interpreted and given meaning by the society. Given that puberty marks the beginning of sexual maturity, it is not surprising that many of the societal beliefs center on the development of sex roles. In this chapter we will examine the biological and psychological changes associated with puberty as well as the societal views of these changes and their implications for sex-role development.

PUBERTY AND BIOLOGY

The biological aspects of puberty include growth rate changes, sexual maturation changes, and hormone changes. Growth rate and sexual maturation changes have been extensively documented by James M. Tanner and his associates in Great Britain (Tanner, 1962, 1970, 1971), and hormonal changes have been extensively documented primarily by John Money and his associates in the United States (Money and Ehrhardt, 1972). Their work, which we will briefly describe, provides a fairly complete picture of biological changes during puberty.

Growth Rate Changes

Only at one time in the organism's life is growth more rapid than at puberty: during the fetal period and the first two years of life. Growth rates slow down during childhood only to accelerate during puberty. This acceleration is psychologically more significant than earlier growth since the adolescent, unlike the fetus or infant, scrutinizes the body changes carefully, intensively, and self-consciously.

During the peak year of the adolescent growth spurt, which usually arrives two years earlier for girls than boys, children shoot up between 6 and 12 centimeters (or 2 to 5 inches). Though the age of growth spurt varies across cultures, the two-year difference between boys and girls holds. In the United States and Great Britain, the girls' spurt usually comes at 12, the boys' at 14. This difference is illustrated by what is known as velocity curves, or the amount a child grows each year. In Figure 8-1, velocity curves for supine length, or height, is shown for boys and girls in Great Britain. The adolescent growth spurt is seen in the rise in numbers of centimeters of growth per year in the 12- to 14-year age period; the girls' earlier spurt is clearly illustrated (Tanner, Whitehouse and Takaishi, 1966).

The growth spurt affects all body parts, not just height, and different parts develop at different rates and times. The head, hands, and feet reach adult proportion earliest. So, when adolescents complain of large hands, or of tripping over their own feet, they're right; but they can be reassured that the rest of their bodies will catch up, and that their hands and feet will be proportionately smaller at the end of puberty. Next, leg length increases, followed by body breadth and shoulder width. As Tanner states, "a boy stops growing out of his trousers (at least in length) a year before he stops growing out of his jackets" (1971).

The muscles also grow in size and strength during puberty, especially for boys. While girls, because of their earlier growth spurt, may have larger muscles for a short time, boys will ultimately have larger muscles, as well as larger hearts and lungs, lower resting heart rates, and higher blood pressure.

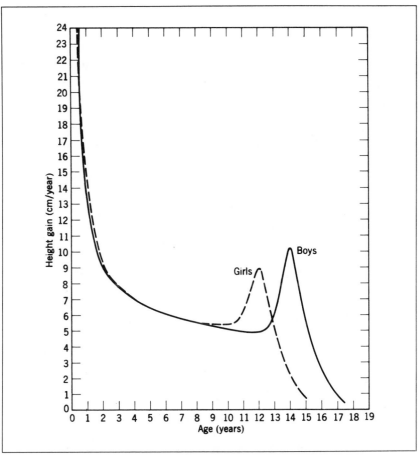

Figure 8-1. Typical-individual velocity curves for supine length or height in boys and girls. These curves represent the velocity of the typical boy and girl at any given instant. From Tanner, Whitehouse, and Takaishi (1966).

Sexual Maturation

Like growth rate changes, the sequence of events in sexual maturation is fairly well known and extremely well documented. Although the averages are well established, individual variation is the rule. Therefore, if a particular adolescent has not developed in the exact sequence to be described, it does not mean that he or she is developing abnormally. Normal sexual maturation can take many different paths, but all lead to the same outcome: the development of a functioning reproductive system.

The boy's sequence is as follows. First, sometime between 9½ and 13½ years of age, the testes enlarge. About a year later the penis begins to grow. And a year after that, the boy typically experiences his first ejaculation. Hair begins to increase on all parts of the body at the same time as the testes and penis are becoming mature. Pubic hair appears first, followed by body and facial hair a few years later. Facial hair starts at the corners of the upper lip and ends of the sides of the face and border of the chin. Hair development continues throughout the entire pubertal period. The breaking of the voice, a phenomenon that causes many an adolescent boy to blush, is the last obvious sign of puberty. It is caused by the enlargement of the larynx, causing the voice to deepen. Thus, voice changes do not herald the beginning of puberty, as some people believe, but mark its end.

For girls, the first sign of sexual maturity is breast budding, which involves the breasts becoming elevated and the nipples enlarged and which occurs around 10 to 14 years of age. The second sign is usually the appearance of pubic hair. Then, the internal (uterus and vagina) and the external (clitoris and labia) genitalia mature. Only after these three signs of maturation occur does menstruation begin. Following menstruation, body hair appears, hips broaden, and fat deposits increase (Tanner, 1971; Money and Ehrhardt, 1972).

As the preceding descriptions suggest, it is difficult to pinpoint the precise onset of sexual maturation, as physical changes occur gradually and overlap. However, the most obvious changes—menstruation in girls and ejaculation in boys—actually occur late in the sequence.

The relationship between growth rate and sexual maturation changes are different for girls and boys. The growth spurt occurs before the girls' genitals begin to develop but after the boys' genitals do. Therefore, a girl who is worried about becoming too tall can be reassured that if she has begun to menstruate, her height spurt is over. Conversely, a boy who is worried that he will not grow any taller because his genitalia are already developing still has his growth spurt to look forward to.

It is vital to remember that these biological changes can occur very rapidly or very slowly. For girls, the time between breast budding and menarche can take anywhere from 1½ to 6 years. The beginning to the end of puberty for boys lasts anywhere from 2 to

5 years. In addition, puberty may begin in elementary school or in senior high school. We can take three normal, healthy 14-year-olds, and one of them might look like a preadolescent (an 11-year-old), one a midadolescent (a 14-year-old), and one a late adolescent (a 17-year-old) in terms of height, genitalia, and secondary sexual characteristics (Tanner, 1971). Yet all three will be normal. They might have different social experiences and conflicts, however, depending on their physical maturity, as we shall see later on.

Hormonal Changes

In addition to sexual maturation and growth rate changes, puberty brings hormonal changes, which, in part, account for the other biological changes that occur. Three types of sex hormones circulate in the body: androgen (called the masculinizing hormone), estrogen (called the feminizing hormone), and progesterone (called the pregnancy hormone). Scientists used to believe that only females produced the "female" hormones (estrogen and progesterone), and males the "male" hormone (androgen). However, it has been found that we all produce some of each. Where are these hormones produced? The adrenal glands of both men and women produce small amounts of the male and female hormones. The reproductive organs produce the bulk of the sex hormones—the male testes producing androgen, the female ovaries producing estrogen, and the corpus luteum (the sac in which each month an immature egg grows and matures before being released from the ovary) producing progesterone. Finally, the placenta of a developing fetus in a pregnant woman also produces large amounts of estrogen and progesterone. Hormone production declines when the reproductive organs become dysfunctional. This is especially true in women whose menstrual cycles have ceased at menopause (Money and Ehrhardt, 1972).

Hormones and Secondary Sex Characteristics

As we saw in Chapter 3, the sex hormones determine whether a fetus will develop male or female sex organs. They also determine whether an individual will acquire the appropriate secondary sex characteristics at puberty. During the fetal period, boys have a greater amount of androgen circulating in their developing bodies than do girls; the absence of androgen results in the development of a uterus and a clitoris in girls, and its presence results in a prostate and a penis in boys. After birth, hormone levels are quite low, although both boys and girls have small amounts of androgen, estrogen, and progesterone circulating in their bodies throughout childhood. Around the age of 11 hormone levels begin to rise. Scientists do not know what actually triggers the production of sex hormones at this time, although they do know that certain sections of the brain are responsible for the production.

The appearance of the secondary sex characteristics, as well as the growth spurt, are determined in part by the sex hormones. Androgen promotes muscle development, beard growth, chest hair, and larynx enlargement. Estrogen is responsible for breast development, hip widening, fat deposits, salt and water metabolism, and an increased sense of smell. Progesterone prepares the body for pregnancy through enlargement of the breasts and alteration of the uterus.

The impact of the sex hormones on sexual maturation may be demonstrated by cases of atypical sexual development described by John Money and Anke Ehrhardt (1972). In rare cases, some of which were described in Chapter 3, a few male babies are assigned a female gender at birth because of their lack of a penis, and a few female babies are assigned as boys at birth because of their having an enlarged clitoris that looks like a penis. If these children are not given hormone treatments at puberty, they will develop incorrect sexual characteristics. The biological males who are reared as girls are given estrogen treatments, which enlarge the breasts and hips, reduce acne, and prevent facial hair. Thus, estrogen treatment retards masculine development, allowing these children to develop just like their sisters. In the opposite situation, female babies reared as boys are given androgen at puberty, which retards the widening of hips and fat deposits, breast development, and menstruation, and encourages hair growth and voice deepening. Again, the secondary sexual characteristics become appropriate for the child's assigned sex.

As we saw earlier, each of us has a small amount of the opposite-sex hormone circulating in our bodies, since the adrenal gland produces all of the sex hormones, albeit in small amounts. The high amounts of the same-sex hormones override the effects of the small amount of opposite-sex hormones. For example, the small amount of androgen present in females does not masculinize the female body, unless the higher amounts of estrogen are, for some reason, not present. Thus, after menopause, when the estrogen level drops in women, the small amount of androgen in a woman's body may be expressed in a slight lowering of the voice and appearance of some facial hair.

Hormonal Cyclicity

In women, all three sex hormones are produced cyclically, while in men, the sex hormones seem to be produced more continuously. The cyclic nature of estrogen and progesterone regulates women's menstrual cycles, specifically ovulation and menstruation. To describe the monthly changes in women's hormone levels, let us look at a woman who has a 28-day cycle, or a period every 28 days. We know that cycle length varies from woman to woman and even from cycle to cycle in individual women. A cycle may be as short as 20 days or as long as 40. Some women experience irregular cycles which vary from month to month. However, the hormonal changes described for a 28-day cycle are similar for cycles of varying length.

Figure 8-2, taken from Neils Lauersen and Steven Whitney's book, *It's Your Body* (1977), illustrates the monthly ovarian hormones, brain hormone, body temperature, and ovarian changes (we will not be discussing the brain and ovarian changes here: Lauersen and Whitney present a more complete picture of cycle changes). As can be seen in Figure 8-2, Day 1 is defined as the first day of the menstrual flow, Day 28 the day just preceding menstruation. On Day 1, the lining of the uterus mixed with a small amount of blood is shed; this is the menstrual flow. Estrogen and progesterone production is low. The hypothalamus section of the brain signals the ovaries to begin producing more estrogen. At this time, one of the thousands of immature eggs in the ovaries begins to grow and develop. From Day 1 to Day 14, estrogen production increases, the egg grows, and the uterine lining develops. On Day 15 the egg, now fully mature, is relased from the ovary and travels through the fallopian tube to the uterus. If the egg is not fertilized during the next few days, it disintegrates. With ovulation there is often a dip in estrogen production.

After the egg is released, the corpus luteum (the sac described earlier) develops from the follicle of the now released egg. It produces progesterone until it disintegrates just prior to menstruation. Estrogen production also rises in conjunction with the rise in progesterone. After Day 24, both hormones drop, signaling the end of the cycle and the beginning of menstruation. The time from ovula-

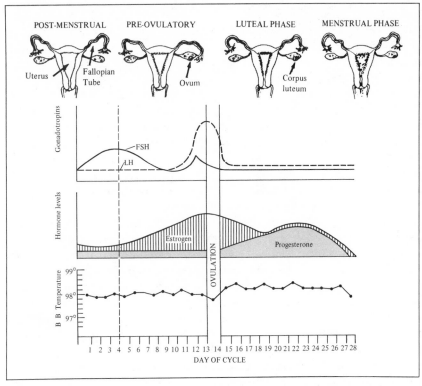

Figure 8-2. This graph illustrates the close relationship between the brain hormones (gonadotrophins), the ovarian hormones (estrogen and progesterone), and their influence on ovulation, the menstrual period, and the Basal Body Temperature (BBT). At the top of the illustration, one ovum is seen developed in the preovulatory phase. Note also that the end of the fallopian tube is reaching down toward the ovum to ensure that the tube will catch the ovum during ovulation. (Reprinted with permission from It's Your Body: A Woman's Guide to Gynecology, *Dr. Niels Lauersen and Steven Whitney. Copyright © 1977 by Dr. Niels Lauersen and Steven Whitney. Used by permission of Grosset & Dunlap, Inc.)*

tion to menstruation (Day 15 to 28), called the *luteal* phase, is much less variable than the time from menstruation to ovulation (Day 1 to Day 14). The luteal phase lasts 12 to 14 days, regardless of whether a woman s cycle is 25, 35, or 45 days in length. Also, women seem to have cyclic variations in androgen production, with peaks at ovulation and premenstrually. Recent research suggests that males may also have monthly variations in androgen production. And both sexes have *daily* cycles of high and low hormone production which are affected by external factors. For example, stress has been found to affect hormone levels in humans (Levine, 1971).

Even more complex is the interaction between hormone levels and various situations; because of such interaction, it is difficult to make cause-and-effect statements about hormones and behavior. An example of this complexity is found in the work of Robert Rose and his colleagues (Rose, Gordon, Bernstein, 1972; Rose, Holaday, and Bernstein, 1971). Working with male rhesus monkeys, these scientists found that higher levels of androgen were associated with dominance in the male rhesus monkeys' peer group. Rose and his colleagues then asked: Which came first, the high dominance or the high androgen levels? They found that the question could not be answered simply, as the monkeys' hormone levels differed in terms of situational factors. For example, androgen was high when monkeys were placed with sexually receptive female rhesus monkeys. Androgen was low when the same monkeys were placed in an already established group of males or were defeated in a group of males. Thus, hormone levels are variable, being affected by situation, time of the day, time of the month, and feeling states.

Hormones and Behavior

In Chapter 3 we talked about the impact of biology on behavior, and in Chapter 6 we looked at the influence of hormones on aggression. Two reproductive aspects of behavior have also been linked to hormone production—sexual drive and menstrual-related behavior.

The most consistent finding in the literature on sexuality has to do with the influence of androgen upon sexual behavior. Small amounts of androgen seem to be necessary for sexual drive in both males and females of many species. In work with rhesus monkeys, several investigators found that adult females were not as sexually aroused if their androgen level was experimentally suppressed. If small amounts of androgen were then injected, the females' sexual arousal returned to normal. However, injection of larger amounts of androgen did not result in an even greater arousal, suggesting that the small amount of androgen normally circulating in the female rhesus monkey is enough for sexual activity (Everitt and Herbert, 1969, 1970). In humans, clinical evidence from the work of John Money and others points to the same conclusion. Menopause, and its corresponding decrease in estrogen, does not lower adult women's sexual drive, presumably because the adrenal glands are still producing small amounts of androgen. Likewise, if adolescents or adults have very low levels of androgen due to some problem, they tend to have lower sex drives (Money and Ehrhardt, 1972).

Prenatal hormones also seem to affect sexual behavior through altering sensitivity of adult animals to male and female hormones. Presumably the presence or absense of androgen prenatally affects portions of the brain, which, in adulthood, becomes particularly sensitive to certain hormones. This phenomenon has been demonstrated only with rats, so caution must be taken in extrapolating to humans. Nevertheless, the findings are as follows: If female rats are given androgen at birth, as adults they are likely to exhibit much male sexual behavior, such as mounting, especially when receiving more androgen at this time. If they are given androgen as adults but not as infants, the increase in mounting behavior is much less. Conversely, if male rats are made insensitive to androgen at birth through castration, an injection of estrogen during adulthood elicits typical female sexual responses. Without the early androgen insensitivity, estrogen injections at adulthood do not result in female sexual responses. Thus, early hormonal experiences affect later sexual behavior, as the effect of male and female hormones on an organism's adult sexual behavior is at least partially determined by the presence or absence of androgen in the beginning of life (Harris, 1964; Levine, 1966; Levine and Mullins, 1966).

The second hormone-behavior relationship to receive a great deal of attention is menstrual-related symptomatology. Most or all women have been thought to experience fluctuations in somatic, emotional, and behavioral characteristics corresponding to phases of their menstrual cycle. Some of the symptoms thought to be associated with menstruation are increases in pain, water retention, negative moods, fits of crying, difficulties in concentration, and decreased school and sport performance. Similar symptoms are thought to occur one to three days before the start of menstruation, the most well-known being "the premenstrual blues." These changes are believed to be hormonally based, tied to the decrease in progesterone and estrogen production that precedes menstruation (Parlee, 1973).

However, the link between hormone fluctuations and menstrual symptoms has not been proven. In addition, behavior fluctuations are not even universal. School and sport performance do not suffer premenstrually or menstrually. World records have been set and Olympics won by young women who were menstruating or were premenstrual. Furthermore, almost none of the many, many studies of performance and menstruation find any effects of cycle phase. The existence of mood swings and the premenstrual blues also finds little support in carefully controlled studies. As Diane Ruble and Jeanne Brooks-Gunn (1979) have summarized, when women are asked to plot their moods daily for several months, the majority do not have mood swings associated with the menstrual cycle. Studies reporting mood swings have been those in which women were asked to *remember* if they experienced such swings, not actually to chart them daily. Apparently women selectively remember negative moods, being more likely to remember them when they have an event to which to "tie" them, like the onset of menstruation. Other bouts of negative moods during the month are likely to be forgotten.

Another menstrual symptom is weight gain. Again, in certain controlled studies, very few women actually gain weight before their period, although many women believe they do. Only a very few symptoms, specifically abdominal or back pain, and painful or tender breasts, consistently have been shown to occur with menstruation and to occur in many (but certainly not all) women. Even these symptoms are in part culturally determined. Not all cultures report the same menstrual symptoms (even though women in all cultures have the same hormone cycle). For example, in the Philippines, menstrual-related symptoms include body tingling, black and blue spots, and pain, while in Korea they include change in heartbeat, indigestion, absentmindedness, and insomnia (WHO Task Force, 1975). In a study by Diane Ruble (1977), college women who were expecting their periods in about seven or eight days were brought into the Princeton University Infirmary. A woman in a white laboratory coat hooked them up to some very complex machinery, telling the students that the tests being performed could predict when the students' periods were to begin. One-third were told that they would begin in two weeks, one-third in seven or eight days, and one-third in one or two days (remember that all were due in about a week). All of the women believed the experimenter, as most women experience slight monthly irregularities. The women who were told they were premenstrual reported more abdominal pain and tender breasts than women who were told they were not premenstrual. Of course, all of the women were in the same cycle phase, and none were premenstrual. Taken together, all of these findings suggest that most premenstrual symptoms do not actually exist, and that only abdominal pain and tender breasts can be explained biologically.

Interestingly, women are *believed* to be debilitated by menstruation by the hormones that "rage" through a woman's body. In 1970 a physician who at that time was a member of the Democratic Party Committee on National Priorities, voiced a too common view about women and menstruation. "If you had an investment in a bank . . . you wouldn't want the president of your bank making a loan under these raging hormonal influences at that particular period" (*New York Times,* 1970). When women are actually asked about the effects of menstruation, few report being debilitated. For example, in a study on menstruation conducted by Jeanne Brooks-Gunn, Diane Ruble, and Ann Clarke (1977), only one-third of a group of Princeton University women said that menstruation was even somewhat debilitating and almost none said that it was severely debilitating. The few women who report severe effects tend to be those who experience extreme cramping, which is often accompanied by nausea, fainting, and chills. This condition, called spasmodic dysmenorrhea, typically occurs first in adolescence, presumably after ovulation begins, and decreases in severity with age, pregnancy, or birth control medication (Lauresen and Whitney, 1977).

In summary, then, androgen may be related to sexual drive in that a small amount of this hormone is necessary even in women, although higher levels of androgen do not increase one's sexual drive. The hormonal changes underlying the menstrual cycle have a much smaller effect on women's behavior than previously believed. Most symptoms show no cyclic variation, and almost all that do seem to be influenced by cultural beliefs. Given our model in Chapter 2, Figure 2-1, the importance of cultural beliefs on something like menstrual symptoms does not seem surprising.

Timing of Biological Change

The onset of puberty is controlled by the brain and is initiated by the increase in sex hormones. One of the most startling facts about the event has to do with its earlier onset now than in generations of the past. In Europe and the United States the age of menarche has declined four months per decade since 1850. In 1833 an adolescent girl did not menstruate until she was, on the average, 17 years of age; today, European and American girls first menstruate at 12 or 13 years of age! Why has this precipitous drop occurred? Nutrition has a lot to do with the drop, although general health and heredity are also important. To see the importance of nutrition, we need only look at Africa, where girls in some of the poorer areas do not menstruate until 15, 16, or 17 years of age, while more well-to-do African girls begin menstruating at the same time as European girls do (Brooks-Gunn and Ruble, in press; Tanner, 1971).

How does nutrition affect menarche? It seems that the growth spurt and menarche are partially controlled by weight, both absolute weight and relative weight. Rose Frisch (1973, 1974) has shown that girls will not menstruate until they reach a certain relative weight for their height, which is measured in terms of percentage of body fat. Thus, girls, whether they are early, average, or late maturing, will menstruate only after a critical weight is achieved. Weight is also important for the maintenance of menstruation. Girls who have a condition in which they stop eating (called *anorexia nervosa*) cease menstruating as soon as their weight drops 10 to 15 percent below the critical weight for menstruation. Some women athletes, whose proportion of body fat is low, also stop menstruating. Both groups begin menstruating again as soon as body weight and body fat rise.

Thus, the earlier puberty that we have seen over the last century is due to the fact that children are growing and gaining weight more quickly than ever before. However, in the United States we are probably close to reaching the lowest age possible for puberty to occur in normal groups of children, because of the weight constraints discussed by Frisch. Interestingly, in rare cases puberty has been found to occur in very young children. Called *precocious puberty,* this condition is due to an abnormality in the brain. In some cases, a young girl of 5 may develop breasts and begin to menstruate. Indeed, a 5½-year-old girl is said to have delivered a healthy baby by Caesarean section. Money and his associates have followed a group of these children and found that, despite their earlier sexual maturity, these children did not begin to date or have intercourse until their adolescent years. Being sexually mature during childhood was obviously difficult for these children, as they did not fit in with their age-mates nor with sexually mature adolescents. During childhood, these children sought a compromise, making friends among children slightly older than themselves but not among sexually mature adolescents. At the "normal" time of puberty, around 11 or 12, they began to spend time with older adolescents (Money and Ehrhardt, 1972).

PSYCHOLOGICAL EFFECTS
OF PUBERTY

As we indicated previously, puberty involves psychological as well as biological change. Two types of change are typically studied: psychological changes associated with menarche and the psychological effects of early and late maturation.

Menarche

To study the psychological effect of menarche, researchers compare the personality traits of girls who have begun to menstruate and girls who have not. Some people believe that menarche is a positive event, one that pushes the adolescent toward maturity, while others believe that menarche is a negative event, one that pulls the adolescent back into childhood patterns.

The "push toward maturity" belief is exemplified by studies that find prepubertal girls to be more confused and disorganized, more prone to attacks of giggling, and less interested in heterosexual activities than girls who have begun to menstruate (Brooks-Gunn and Ruble, in press). Many girls recall the onset of menarche as a growing-up process that moves them away from childhood activities. For example, one 15-year-old said:

> It was like growing up overnight. I felt that I was not a little kid anymore. I couldn't ride my bicycle anymore, really I'm not kidding you. (Kagan, 1972, p. 97)

Similarly the heroine (Ginny) of Lisa Alther's novel *Kinflicks* (1976) is told by her mother at the onset of her first menstruation: "No more football. . . . You're a young woman now." Ginny's thoughts following that revelation were as follows:

> No more football? She might as well have told Arthur Murray never to dance again. . . . I went upstairs, and as I exchanged my shoulder pad for a sanitary pad and elastic belt, I knew that menstruation might just as well have been a gastrointestinal hemorrhage in terms of its repercussions on my life. (p. 33)

Alternatively, the onset of menstruation has been characterized as an event fraught with negative affect, insecurity, and regression. As one girl reported, "I expected to turn into a beautiful fairy princess . . . felt ugly when I did not." (Weideger, 1975, p. 169) Another girl said, "I was afraid to tell my mothers or friends; I was so ashamed." Fortunately, such negative experiences, or at least such intense ones, are becoming less common today, what with better advance preparation and more open attitudes.

In all probability, the event is a mixed blessing, having both positive and negative effects. In survey data collected by Jeanne Brooks-Gunn and Diane Ruble (1977) on adolescent attitudes about menstruation (from which some of the anecdotes and quotations here have been taken), almost all girls agreed that "menstruation was part of becoming a woman," but only one-third thought "menstruation was something to be happy about." In addition, as the quotation from *Kinflicks* so clearly illustrates, menstruation signals the beginning of sex-role restrictions and expectations as well as maturation.

Timing of Maturation

As we have seen, timing of maturity varies widely during adolescence. Some adolescents will be sexually mature and have reached their adult height by age 12; others will not reach this stage until age 17. Such difference in maturation rates are thought to affect psychological development. Early maturation may increase the adolescent's standing in his or her peer group while late maturation may prove detrimental. Even if this is not true, adolescents may *believe* their standing is affected, as they are continually comparing themselves to their peers and to the societal ideals for maturation.

Interestingly, when the psychological effects of maturation have been studied, different patterns have emerged for boys and girls. For boys, whose ideal is the muscular, athletic build, one might expect the early maturers to be more popular and more confident than late maturers. Mary Jones and Paul Mussen (Jones, 1957, 1965; Mussen and Jones, 1957; Mussen, 1962) studied a group of early and late maturers from puberty through adulthood and found the early maturers to be perceived by others as more good looking and grownup, the late maturers as more bossy and restless. When questioned themselves, the late maturers reported feeling more inadequate and less self-confident than the early maturers. Thus, the early-maturing boys were not only stronger and taller, but were more confident, more accepted, and perhaps more secure about their masculinity.

What happened to these two groups of boys when they grew up? A follow-up of these boys when they were in their 30's found the early maturers were more responsible and dominant, more likely to be in executive positions, and less rebellious and impulsive than the late maturers. Thus, it seems that they were better adjusted. Or were they? In addition to the characteristics listed above, the early maturers were less flexible, tolerant, and sensitive to others' feelings, had less of a sense of humor, and were more moralistic than the late maturers. Using both sets of characteristics, we see that the early maturers had more of the traditional masculine characteristics, while the later maturers had some masculine and some feminine characteristics. The boys who matured later can be described as more androgynous (possessing both masculine and feminine characteristics), which, as we saw in Chapter 2, is related to more flexible and adaptable behavior. Perhaps the early maturers, by possessing a masculine body very early, are treated in more sex-stereotyped ways, are channeled into masculine and all-male activities, and more readily accept the traditional masculine role than boys who mature a bit later.

Although early puberty clearly brings prestige to the boy (even though this prestige may be a two-edged sword, it does exist during the adolescent years), the relationship between maturity and prestige is less clear-cut for the adolescent girl. First, early-maturing girls tend to have more muscular body builds than late-maturing girls, who tend to have more slender builds. The ideal body type for girls is petite, which would tend to favor the late, not the early maturer. Second, popularity seems to be related to being "in phase," rather than being early or late. In one study by Mary Faust (1960), sixth- to ninth-grade girls were divided into four groups—prepubertal, pubertal (menstruating for less than one year), post-pubertal (menstruating for one to three years), and late adolescence. Girls who were "in phase" for their grade were the most popular. This meant that the prepubertal girls were most popular in sixth grade, the post-pubertal in junior high school. Third, adolescent girls tend to congregate in small, intimate groups, where differences in maturation may not be as noticeable or important. Boys spend more time in large groups that focus on physical activities, and the late maturer sticks out like a sore thumb. Thus, early maturation is not necessarily valued for the adolescent girl. As one girl who matured very early said, "I felt clumsy, my feet were too big, my body too tall." For the girl, being "in phase" with her age-mates is most desired, so both the early maturer and the late maturer are at a disadvantage.

SOCIETAL VIEWS OF PUBERTY

The effect that societal views have on the child's developing attitudes and expectations is very clear in puberty, especially with regard to sex-appropriate behaviors and roles. Four societal views affecting the adolescents' perceptions of their bodies concern ideal body type, physical attractiveness, menstrual-related beliefs, and beliefs about ejaculation.

Ideal Body Type

The fact that our society holds very clear ideals for body type can be seen on television shows, in advertisements, and in fashion. It would be difficult to live in this society and not know what the ideal body is for a man and for a woman. The ideal man has a muscular, athletic build and is on the tall side (but not too tall); the ideal woman is slender and shorter than a man. Given the diversity of body shapes and sizes, few of us measure up to these ideals. However, the ideals *do* affect us, even as adults. We diet to become slimmer and we exercise to become more muscular—or, more often, we worry about dieting and talk about exercising. The adolescent is even more affected by the body ideal; not knowing how his or her body will turn out, every change, real or imagined, is closely scrutinized.

We know that adolescents learn about the ideal body type very early. In some studies, adolescents are given silhouettes of three body types (slender, muscular, and heavy) and asked to rate each in terms of the ideal for boys and girls. The muscular silhouette is usually rated as ideal for boys, the slender one for girls. In addition, adolescents rate males who are muscular as being more popular and having a more positive personality than males who are more slender or heavier (Dwyer and Mayer, 1969; Lerner, 1969).

Boys and girls alike are concerned about whether or not their own bodies reflect these ideals. Girls, wishing to be petite, are much more concerned about being overweight than underweight. In fact, girls often believe they are overweight when they are not; they confuse being average in relative weight for height, with absolute weight. Such confusion can lead to inappropriate and potentially dangerous dieting. The most extreme example of such dieting is found in girls who literally starve themselves. This condition, which we have already mentioned, is called *anorexia nervosa;* it often starts as a "normal" diet in a girl who is of average weight-for-height, but progresses to an almost morbid fascination with losing weight (Bruch, 1978). Weight plummets to the point where menstruation ceases and health is endangered; in some cases, hospitalization is necessary to prevent starvation. The body image of these girls is so distorted that they believe they are still overweight even when they have become grossly underweight. Although anorexia nervosa has many causes and is clearly a sign of psychological difficulty, the rise in the number of anorexics has corresponded with the increasing emphasis on thinness in our society. Even though anorexia nervosa does not occur in most girls, being thin is so important that one out of every three adolescent girls is on a diet at any point in time.

Interestingly, the importance of being thin does not diminish after adolescence. Believing oneself to have been a heavy adolescent has lingering effects, as the following example illustrates. A friend, who at 30 is of average weight, reminisces about her adolescent years, portraying herself as a chubby adolescent. When we look at pictures of her during adolescence, the truth is quite different from her perception. She was not overweight, but average and even somewhat gangly. Today, she persists in dieting, even though her weight is, as it was fifteen years ago, average for her height and age.

Boys, on the other hand, wish to be tall and muscular; they worry about being underweight, having thin arms, having underdeveloped chests, and being too short. Athletic ability, which is related to the muscular build, is another major concern of boys. A male acquaintance of ours tells of spending hours lifting weights and eating huge amounts of food in high school to "build bulk." When he recently bumped into an old friend from his weight-lifting days the friend remarked on how much smaller he was; this diminution in size was seen as negative by his friend.

Physical Attractiveness

Physical attractiveness is another major concern of both adolescent boys and girls. An overwhelming number of American adolescents worry about their appearance—their clothing, hair, complexion, facial features. In one large study of adolescents by Alexander Frazier and Lorenzo Lisonbee (1971), one-half of the boys and four out of five girls had concerns about physical appearance. Complexion, especially acne, was the biggest worry of boys and girls.

Alix Schulman poignantly describes the teenager's battle with acne in her *Memoirs of an Ex-Prom Queen* (1976).

> The first imperfection of my skin—the first beginning of my slow, extended decline—had appeared the summer I turned sixteen on the night of a large family dinner party at our house. I admit I behaved badly.
>
> That night my father's newest employee, a clerk fresh out of Harvard Law whom I was very eager to meet, had been invited to dinner. (p. 84) . . .
>
> [While carving the roast, my father] leaned over and dropped the first hacked slice of meat onto my plate. Then, on his way back up, he began to scrutinize my nearby face. With more disapproval than curiosity he suddenly said, "What's that?"
>
> "What's what?"
>
> "That on your cheek—there." He pointed at me with the carving knife.
>
> I winced away. I knew perfectly well what he was talking about. What he had picked out publicly to confront me with was something that, after causing me no end of anguish that afternoon I had decided was simply a pimple—a round, brown, ephemeral blemish which I had clumsily tried to cover up with dabs of my mother's make-up snitched from the jars lined up on her crowded dressing table. But, a novice in such methods, I had succeeded only in altering its color. It was no disguise for my father's eagle eye, though it might easily have hidden the imperfection from Alan Steiger, the young lawyer. (p. 86)

Rather than helping adolescents accept acne as part of being an adolescent, teenage magazine advertisements and radio commercials help perpetuate the concern over acne, advocating that the teenager declare all-out war against acne by plummeting the pimple or eradicating the eruption.

Other concerns of the teenager include irregular teeth, glasses, dry skin, and large noses, with girls tending to voice these concerns more regularly. The large numbers of adolescents seeking orthodontic treatment and contact lenses reflect these concerns. The biggest concern of all is the generalized feeling, "I am ugly." As the hero of Paul Zindel's juvenile novel, *My Darling, My Hamburger* (1971), relates:

> He wouldn't ask anyone else, he knew. It was too close to the prom. He put another piece of meat into his mouth. *Oh, God, what was wrong with him?* He thought everything had been going along fine. He would've asked her to go steady. Maybe that's why she broke the date, he thought. She knew they were getting to that point. Perhaps someone else had asked her. Perhaps she had just been using him all these months, just waiting for someone else to come along. Anybody. Anybody was better than Dennis Holowitz. *I'm so ugly,* he thought, grinding the meat between his teeth. *Ugly, I'm sick. I'm ashamed. My clothes are ugly. My face is ugly. My body is ugly. What am I doing alive? I always come back to this point. It's always there. This ugliness. I can't fight it. I'm running out of strength.*
> (pp. 82-83)

This concern about looks is due to more than the existence of an ideal for physical attractiveness. Popularity, that goal to which adolescents agonizingly strive, is based on many factors, physical appearance being one of the most important. Physical attractiveness has been shown to be related to popularity in studies of children (starting at age 6!), adolescents, and college students. In one study of junior high school students, the most important characteristics for popularity for girls were, first, "being good looking" and second, "being tidy" (Grunland and Anderson, 1957). Even though other factors do become important in determining popularity, acceptance, and dating preferences in older adolescents, attractiveness still plays a major role. Even in adulthood, attractiveness affects people's lives: for example, being considered attractive is an asset when looking for a job (although professional women are sometimes discouraged from being too attractive). In an extreme example, women patients in mental hospitals are more likely to get individual therapy if they are young and attractive (Chesler, 1972). Thus, adolescents' concern over physical appearance, although seemingly excessive, stems from their concern over popularity and from our culture's obsession with attractiveness.

Menstrual-Related Beliefs

Societal beliefs about menstruation undoubtedly affect the adolescent girls' expectations and experiences. In a survey of fifth- to sixth-grade and seventh- to eighth-grade girls, Jeanne Brooks-Gunn and Diane Ruble (in press) have studied experiences and expectations about menstruation, finding that prepubertal girls in elementary school already knew about cycle-related symptoms. By junior high school, prepubertal girls, having more knowledge about menstruation, expected to experience all of the cycle-related changes our society subscribes to. The junior high school girls who were menstruating reported experiencing all of these symptoms (but none of the symptoms that other cultures believe exist). The premenstrual elementary school girls had less negative attitudes about menstruation than the premenstrual junior high school girls. Perhaps the young girls receive preparatory information from school emphasizing the positive aspects (that menstruation is a sign of womanhood), have less knowledge of sex-role restrictions placed on the menstruating girl, wish to be "in phase" with their age-mates and therefore look forward to the event, and discuss menstruation less with mother and friends than do girls in junior high school.

How are such beliefs acquired by young girls? When we asked about sources of menstrual-related information, we found that almost all girls learned about menstruation from their mothers, with fathers contributing no knowledge at all. Older sisters, when available, were also good sources for two-thirds of our sample. Female friends were also an important source of information, while male peers were not. Finally, health education classes provided information to over three-quarters of these girls, media sources for only one-third of the girls.

Ejaculation

We know much less about boys' experiences and beliefs concerning sexual maturity than we do about girls' experiences. This is not surprising, given that the most obvious male sign of sexual maturation is the ability to ejaculate. Ejaculation is more blatantly sexual than menstruation, and this fact accounts for the lack of research and discussion on this subject. However, the taboo-like nature of the subject tells us a great deal about society's view. As Gordon Shipman (1971), one of the few scientists who have studied the subject, explains:

> Imagine an American boy coming to the breakfast table exclaiming, "Mom, guess what? I had my first wet dream last night. Now I'm a man." It is not without significance that such an imaginary episode is greeted in American culture with laughter. (pp. 333-334)

The taboo on celebrating manhood denies the boy any feelings of pride or achievement. In Shipman's sample, only 6 percent of the boys questioned felt positive feelings about their first ejaculatory experience. Remember that in Brooks-Gunn and Ruble's sample of girls, all of them, even those who had negative attitudes about menstruation, felt menstruation had signaled the attainment of womanhood and were pleased about this.

The restriction on discussing ejaculation but not menstruation is illustrated by the fact that boys have learned the same beliefs and expectations regarding menstruation that girls have learned. In a study by Anne Clarke and Diane Ruble (1978) of seventh to eighth graders, boys and girls had the same attitudes about menstruation, learned about it from similar sources, and knew about the cycle-related symptoms that supposedly exist. The boys were also relieved that they did not have to menstruate.

PREPARATION FOR SEXUAL MATURATION

How well are boys and girls prepared for the advent of sexual maturation? As might be expected, preparation differs for boys and girls. With the more tolerant attitude about menstruation than ejaculation, we would expect girls to be better prepared than boys.

Preparation for menstruation has changed radically in the past half century. When Theodora Abel and Natalie Jaffe (1950) examined preparation practices in several European cultures in the first half of this century, girls were found to have little advance warning. For example, no preparation was given in various segments of German, Polish, and Irish society. In contrast, Italian girls were likely to have heard their female relatives discuss menstruation, which was a topic of great importance and therefore discussed freely. After the onset of menstruation, mothers in all cultures explained menstruation to their daughters. However, the completeness of the explanations varied greatly. As an extreme, Polish peasants did not tell their girls how to wear sanitary cloths nor how to keep them in place; the girls were expected to know how to do this without being taught.

When these cultural groups immigrated to America, adolescents were more likely to be given information prior to the event, since it was thought to be old-fashioned not to do so. Also, families wanted their girls to learn their own culture's customs and beliefs, not another group's beliefs. Advance preparation in America changed dramatically after the second World War. Of adult women interviewed in the late 1950's who had begun to menstruate in the 1940's, one-third of them had no advance warning about menstruation. Of our adolescents interviewed in the 1970's, only a small minority had no advance warning.

The fact that many girls were not prepared for menstruation opened the door for theories about the ill effects of being unprepared. Besides fear and shame, Natalie Shainess (1961) found in clinical interviews with adult women in the late 1950's that the premenstrual blues were much more likely to occur in women who had not been prepared by their mothers. Interestingly, only 15 percent of this sample remembered their mothers being happy, excited, or pleased when their daughters began to menstruate. Unlike the case with the Shainess sample, menstrual distress, as reported by our adolescents, was not related to advance preparation or maternal feelings (as most girls were prepared and had mothers who were somewhat happy about the experience). However, report of menstrual distress was related to maternal report of menstrual distress. If girls believed their mothers experienced menstrual symptoms, they too anticipated or reported being negatively affected by menstruation (Brooks-Gunn and Ruble, 1978). Menstrual distress was also higher in girls whose families seemed to be less open about menstruation. Girls whose fathers did not know when they began menstruating reported more menstrual distress than girls whose fathers knew. Thus, even in the 1970's, preparation, in terms of maternal symptoms and an open family atmosphere, do relate to girls' menstrual experiences.

The type of preparation society provides to girls is illustrated by the booklets distributed by the personal products industry and used in health class. Lynn Whisnant, Elizabeth Brett, and Leonard Zegans (1975) analyzed the contents of these booklets, uncovering a confusing blend of messages. Menstruation was characterized not only as a normal, natural part of life, but as an embarrassing event, one that needs to be concealed; and as a hygienic crisis, one that needs to be combatted by frequent bathing and napkin changing. According to one booklet, menstruation is "a natural, normal part of life. Treat it naturally, normally, and you won't be embarrassed or upset each time it comes." (*Accent on You,* p. 13) Another booklet states, "It's absolutely impossible for anyone to know you are menstruating unless of course you act stupid about the whole thing." (*Growing Up and Liking It,* 1976, p. 15) The message about acting normal has been accepted; almost all of the girls in the Brooks-Gunn and Ruble sample said that they tried to act normal during their period and worried about others finding out.

The booklets also give fairly explicit and rigid instructions for combatting any physical changes that may occur and, by doing so, they seem to deny that some girls (although fortunately only a minority) experience moderate to severe cramping. Again, one of the booklets admonished girls that much of the discomfort associated with menstruation is in the mind; fretting about your period will only cause pain.

One of the authors, having experienced spasmodic dysmenorrhea (severe cramping) since early adolescence, had many negative experiences associated with menstruation, including being taken to an emergency room by a distraught father who did not know what else to do, and to this day, the prospect of being "caught" somewhere where there may not be a bed, and a heating pad, available for the four to five hours the pain lasts, causes apprehension. Having a positive mental attitude or plunging into activities, often given as remedies for this condition, will *not* appreciably reduce spasmodic dysmenorrhea. However, helping allay the girl's fears about the pain and about being abnormal and teaching her how to cope with pain (as is done in childbirth classes) has been shown to alleviate such pain.

Cultural beliefs about menstruation are also portrayed in media advertisements. The advertisements for medication suggest that pain is experienced by all women. Some product manufacturers go so far as to suggest that menstrual-related problems are experienced throughout the month.

As might be expected from our earlier discussion of ejaculation, boys are not as well prepared for sexual maturation as are girls. Parents do not give advance warning about ejaculation, and boys do not tell their parents about their first experience nor do they ask their parents for information after the fact. Most information is gained from their male peer group, in the form of jokes. In fact, in the one study on this topic by Gordon Shipman mentioned previously, only 6 percent of the boys were told about ejaculation and what to expect prior to the event. Contrast this with the fact that only about 6 percent of all girls are not told about menstruation before it occurs!

Thus, it is not surprising that one in five boys reported being frightened by their first experience. Shipman found this was true whether they had experienced their first ejaculation as a wet dream or through masturbating. Some boys believed they had wet their bed and were ashamed and confused about their "immature" behavior, while other boys believed masturbating was immoral and wrong. Even the sharing of locker room jokes about the subject does not lessen feelings of isolation and shame. It is as if the adolescent boy does not know that all of his male friends (at least four out of five of them) are also masturbating.

Ironically, boys may be better informed about their sisters' sexual maturation than their own. We saw that junior high school boys know all about menstruation. In fact, they seem to know almost as much as junior high school girls!

Clearly, adequate preparation for sexual maturation is necessary for both boys and girls. Preparation reduces fear and anxiety and increases acceptance of body changes. The adolescent girl of the 1970's is much better prepared for menstruation than her mother and grandmothers were. Unfortunately, the adolescent boy of the 1970's is not as well prepared as his sister, and still hides behind secrecy, jokes, and shame.

PUBERTY AND SEX ROLES

Throughout this chapter, we have introduced you to puberty—the biological changes, the psychological effects, and the societal beliefs. All of these changes, as we have seen, affect sex-role identity. Puberty heralds the advent of adulthood, the taking on of male and female roles. All of the observation, modeling, and cognitive construction of sex roles during childhood become more real; adolescents do not only practice sex roles, but they begin to live them! Our examination of pubertal changes leads us to the following conclusions.

Puberty, by focusing the adolescent on his or her body and the changes that are occurring, sharpens distinctions between male and female. Not only are they more aware than ever before of physical differences, but adolescents compare their bodies with those of their peers. How fast is my body developing? Will I be short or tall, graceful or awkward, slender or heavy, well-muscled or not? Will I have large or small breasts, slim or wide hips, broad or narrow shoulders? Will I fit the society's ideal of a masculine or feminine body or not? The concerns have some basis in reality, as adolescents' standing in their peer group is affected by adherence to specific body types. Also, timing of maturation and body type in adolescence may even have a carry-over effect to adulthood. As we saw earlier, personality characteristics and adherence to standards of masculinity and femininity laid down in adolescence can continue through adulthood. To complicate matters, body type probably influences how others respond to one throughout life, thereby strengthening early self-perceptions. The slender, the muscular, and the curvacious adolescent and woman, however similar they may be, are treated differently.

Puberty may also bring restrictions and prohibitions that were not present during adolescence. Ginny, and countless others like her, have hung up their shoulder pads and football cleats with the advent of puberty. On the other hand, boys, if not already on the playing field, are given shoulder pads and football cleats regardless of their own proclivities and their own maturation. Although many activities are appropriate for young adolescents, coordination and size may make team sports painful experiences for some, with some sports (especially football) being potentially harmful for youngsters or late maturers. The movie *Bad News Bears* illustrates the dilemma of boys and girls. The team's "hot" pitcher happens to be a girl who, with the advent of puberty, wishes to stop pitching, to wear makeup and bras, and to date older boys. Several of the team's "losers" are boys who are very small or very fat and who, not incidentally, have fathers who dream of past fame on the playing field or, never having achieved it themselves, desire glory for their sons.

Girls find themselves in another predicament during puberty. Not only are they expected to give up sports, but they find their sexual maturity is a concern rather than a joy to their parents. Sexuality invites trouble, be it adolescent boys' harmless attentions, the neighboring men's lingering glances, or the older adolescent male's invitations for dating, drinking, or whatever. And, in the back of many a parent's mind (especially in urbanized areas) is the potential for rape. Girls are told to protect themselves, never to walk at night alone, always to call if out after dark, never to go out with strangers; these parental cautions, unfortunately, are warranted in many American communities, but they are also transmitting information about how female bodies are perceived in this society.

Puberty also heralds a change in goals. In childhood, girls and boys alike strive to do well in school, to be popular with friends. However, the biological changes of puberty, coupled with societal beliefs, send them off in different directions: boys to the athletic field and girls to the dressing room.

All of these body-related occurrences lead to a heavy dose of sex typing, a dose that may be more of a jolt for the adolescent girl than for her brother. In *Kinflicks,* Ginny likened the advent of puberty to a "gastrointestinal hemorrhage in terms of its repercussions on my life." The girl is expected to cease active sports, or at least to trade them in for more ladylike ones, to diminish her tomboy activities, to spend hours in front of mirrors, to conceal her sexuality for fear of rape, and to learn the ways of womanhood. The boy, having had more sex-role restrictions placed on him during childhood, may feel less pressure. Nevertheless, he is expected to become an athlete and to become assertive and aggressive in certain situations regardless of his proclivities.

ADOLESCENCE
Toward an Adult Sex Role

chapter nine

Adolescence is, above all, a time of change—not only changes of the body, but changes in the way the world treats the adolescent and the way he or she interacts with it. Now, the soon-to-be-adult must face the impending independence from the family, absorption into the peer culture, and the quest for career, lover, and mate. Erik Erikson (1968) characterizes the concern of adolescence as a "search for identity," with the major foci of the search being autonomy, social affiliation, intimacy, and the establishment of realistic goals for oneself.

The cultural beliefs and societal pressures illustrated in Chapter 2 and the parental, educational, peer, and media socialization forces discussed throughout this book combine to influence the merging adolescent's identity formation and tie the process of "becoming" inexorably to sex roles. For example, the questions we as parents, teachers, or community members ask of boy and girl adolescents, and, implicitly, the demands we make of them, are different. What we ask of boys is, "What do you want to do?" and what we ask of girls, "What will you be?" As Nancy Chodorow (1971) has pointed out: boys and men "do," while girls and women "are." In societal terms, the young man must *earn* his identity, and constantly reestablish it through career success, monetary rewards, and a steady demonstration of leadership and competence. The young woman, on the other hand, *acquires* her identity by becoming a wife, a mother, and a provider of emotional support and nurturance. The young man's identity derives from active pursuit, the young woman's from passive acquiescence. Even our perceptions of biological differences support the distinction between "doing" and "being," as is illustrated in the following passage from Karen Horney (1932), the early twentieth-century psychoanalyst.

> The man is actually obliged to go on proving his manhood to the woman. There is no analogous necessity for her: even if she is frigid, she can engage in sexual intercourse and conceive and bear a child. She performs her part by merely being, without any *doing*. . . . The man on the other hand has to *do* something in order to fulfill himself. (p. 359)

Socialization practices reinforce the distinction between "doing" and "being." As Simone de Beauvoir (1968) so eloquently states:

The young boy, be he ambitious, thoughtless, or timid, looks toward an open future; he will be a seaman or an engineer, he will stay on the farm or go away to the city, he will see the world, he will get rich; he feels free, confronting a future in which the unexpected awaits him. The young girl will be a wife, grandmother; she will keep house just as her mother did, she will give her children the same care she herself received when young—she is twelve years old and already her story is written in the heavens. She will discover it day after day without ever making it. (p. 278)

In a word, men choose while women are chosen. Nowhere is this more evident than in adolescence, the time of career, educational, peer, and mate choices. In this chapter we will examine these choices vis-à-vis careers and achievement orientation, educational influences and peer group and dating experiences.

SEX DIFFERENCES IN ADOLESCENCE

Career Aspirations

Each step forward in work as a Successful American, regardless of sex, means a step back as a woman. (Mead, 1968, p. 303)

A central feature of the American identity is one's work identity. When Danny Cummings moves next door, his new neighbors are more likely to remark, "Oh, he's with Squibb" or "Another lawyer" than "I hear he goes fishing every Saturday" or "He really enjoys playing with his kids." When students meet at a mixer they ask one another, "Where do you go to school?" and "What are you going to do when you finish?"

The adolescent's career aspirations determine his or her answers to these questions. But they are subject to a myriad of forces—societal, familial, educational, and others—that we have seen affect so many aspects of the developing individual. When Margaret Mead wrote the statement with which we began this section, she was talking about the fact that success in the work place and in intellectual endeavors simply does not accommodate to our society's notions of womanhood. Women are said to face a double bind: if they pursue their career aspirations, they risk jeopardizing what we call "femininity," and if they abide by society's notion of femininity, they chance losing out on a career. Rather than challenge this argument, however, countless young women base their vocational and life style choices upon it.

Concerns about occupations become paramount in adolescence. Under the influence of chronic myths (men "do," women "are"; career success is incompatible with femininity), young people prepare for a lifetime of work by considering their career options and acting upon their choices. Their new maturity separates them from the fantasy choices of the past. Batman and the Presidency fade from view as realistic career possibilities. Choices become more conventional in the sense that they are tied to parental aspirations and educational levels, to community, school, and social class expectations, and to the availability of role models, all interacting with one's own ability level (Borrow, 1968).

Just what occupations are selected as potential career choices? Lenore Harmon (1971) asked 1,200 college freshmen women about their career choices as children and later as adolescents. Over one-half of the young women had considered and were still considering being a housewife. The other two most common career choices were in education and social service. Occupational choices varied with age: during early elementary school, they remembered housewife or actress as the favored choice; during the latter part of elementary school, they envisioned themselves as artists, nurses, and missionaries; by junior high school, they wanted to be elementary school teachers, dance instructors, and beauticians; at the beginning of high school, models, stewardesses, and teachers; and by the end of high school, social workers and teachers. The older they became, the more sophisticated and more reality-oriented were their career choices. However, regardless of age, the choices were sex-stereotyped; very few girls wanted to be doctors, lawyers, executives, or scientists. When boys of their age are asked about career choices, such occupations are always high on the list. In addition, boys do not mention that they want to be fathers or husbands, while girls explicitly state that they wish to be mothers and wives.

In an earlier chapter we discussed how children's perceptions of sex roles determined the sorts of careers they envisioned for themselves and for others and how as a result of these perceptions girls set much lower career goals for themselves and considered a much narrower range of options. Further, our society seems to foster lower aspirations in girls than other societies do in their girls. More than in Chile, Western Germany, and Turkey, 16- to 19-year-old girls in the United States aspire to careers lower on the totem pole than the same-aged boys of their culture (Seward and Williamson, 1969).

Up until adolescence, the differential perceptions and hopes of children are just worrisome (Chapter 2 explained the power of perception upon action). Now, in adolescence, the children reach an important juncture—thoughts, speculations, and perceptions must be transformed into plans and actions. Now the mechanisms underlying what we as adults see as disparities in the work force become obvious. First, boys act sooner than girls on formulating and on implementing their career plans. Second, boys perceive their vocational identity as primary, girls see it as secondary. In a massive study by Elizabeth Douvan and Joseph Adelson (1966), girls kept their vocational plans tentative and flexible during adolescence, presumably because these plans were highly contingent on and secondary to their marriage plans. The girls were, generally, more people oriented than career oriented, concerning themselves with affiliation rather than vocation. Third, when girls do choose a vocation, it is service oriented or a helping profession, in keeping with the female sex role.

A few girls in the past have chosen so-called masculine occupations. Are these girls different from those who choose more traditionally feminine occupations or no career at all? Among the factors that distinguish traditional versus career-oriented girls are the employment status of the mother, the relationship of the girl with her father, the social class of the family, and the interests, maturity, and vocational plans of the girl herself. The career-oriented adolescent girl is likely to have a mother who is employed, to have a strong relationship with her father, often participating in activities with him, and to come from middle or high social status. In addition, the girl is likely to perceive career orientation as consistent rather than inconsistent with the female role, to be achievement oriented, and to exhibit vocational plans and interests that are similar to those of boys of her own age (Tyler, 1964; Rezler, 1967; Putnam and Hansen, 1972). Male support from peers as well as father is also important. A similar profile has been found for the woman who actually has entered a masculine profession. In a study of highly successful women executives, Margaret Hennig (1973) interviewed one-quarter of all the women presidents or vice-presidents of nationally recognized business firms in 1968 (there were only 100 such women in the

United States at that time). All of the successful women were first-born, either the only child or the eldest of a two- or three-daughter family. All were middle class, were from the East Coast, had fathers in middle-management positions and mothers in the home. One-half of the women's mothers had more education than the fathers. Their childhood relationships with their parents had been affectionate and close, as had their parents' own relationship with each other. They felt they had a special relationship with the father and shared interests and hobbies with him. Both parents supported the girls' exploring "masculine" interests, as well as recognizing and accepting their femaleness. Pursuing a career was not seen by their parents to be incompatible with the female role.

Career choices, then, are sex-related. From an early age, girls have learned, via cultural beliefs and socialization, that their options are limited. This realistic assessment of their world was illustrated in the example we saw in Chapter 2:

> That girls learn very early the societal expectation for them was perhaps captured most poignantly by the expression of that single girl who initially said she wished to be a doctor when she grew up; when asked what occupation she *really* expected to hold in adulthood, she resignedly replied, "I'll probably have to be something else, maybe a store lady." (Looft, 1971, p. 366)

Achievement-Related Abilities

Perhaps sex differences in career aspirations have a basis in actual ability differences. We have reviewed the status of sex differences in ability during middle childhood and found few. Now we shall present an update for the adolescent years.

Verbal Abilities

With puberty, girls surge ahead of boys on spelling, comprehension, verbal creativity, and verbal understanding of logical relationships. In one of the few longitudinal studies of verbal abilities to follow children through adolescence, not only were girls superior to boys, but their advantage increased markedly between the ninth and twelfth grades (Droege, 1967).

Mathematical Ability

While the girls show an advantage in verbal skills, boys show one in math. Most studies of high school students report boys ahead of girls in math skills. Part of this difference may be due to boys' greater number of math courses. To control the possible factor of more extensive math training among boys, some investigators (e.g., Flanagan *et al.*, 1961) have looked at the math scores of boys and girls who have taken an equal number of math courses. Still, they found that the boy adolescents scored higher than the girls. Math skill seems to go hand in hand with science, in which boys show a greater interest and a better performance than girls (except on portions of the tests relying on verbal abilities, in which girls do better [Walberg, 1969]).

Spatial Ability

Spatial ability, which is usually defined as the ability to visually manipulate objects in space, is tested in a number of ways: by separating a figure from its background, by fitting together pieces of a figure, or by translating two-dimensional representations into three-dimensional ones. Sex differences in this ability, like those in verbal and math abilities, appear in early adolescence and increase throughout the adolescent period. In trying to explain sex differences in spatial ability, both a biological and an environmental explanation have been advanced.

Geneticists have suggested that this sex difference is due to the existence of a recessive gene that controls spatial ability. Each cell in our body contains 46 identical chromosomes. These 46 are paired so that each cell contains 23 pairs, one of each pair coming from our mother and one from our father. On each chromosome are thousands upon thousands of gene pairs that contain the genetic code for all aspects of our development. The question is, which one of the gene pair will be used for the genetic code? Nature has provided the answer by assigning some genes as dominant, some as recessive. A recessive gene will be expressed only if there is no dominant gene available.

In the early 1960's, Richard Stafford (1961) hypothesized that the spatial ability gene was carried on the X chromosome and that this gene was recessive. The male, having an X and a Y chromosome, would be more likely to express the recessive spatial ability gene, since a recessive gene on the X chromosome would have no competition from a dominant gene, as the Y chromosome contains no spatial ability gene (the Y chromosome contains little genetic information; besides gender, the only other gene code that has been identified on the Y chromosome is one for hairy ears). The female, on the other hand, has two X chromosomes. In order for her to express spatial ability, both X chromosomes would have to possess recessive spatial ability genes. Thus, in order to express spatial ability, the male only needs one spatial ability gene, the female two. In order to explore this possibility, genetic psychologists looked at the similarity between parents and children on spatial ability tests. Since a boy received his X chromosome from his mother, not his father, and since the spatial ability gene was thought to reside on the X chromosome, mothers and sons would be more similar than fathers and sons on spatial ability tests. Father–daughter correlations should be higher than mother–daughter ones because the daughter has to receive the father's *only* X chromosome and may receive either of the mother's X chromosomes. In family studies of spatial ability, several different research teams have found the predicted parent-child relationships, suggesting that spatial ability is influenced by a sex-linked recessive gene, which males are more likely to express.

Besides the genetic influence, hormones are also thought to affect spatial ability. Researchers have found that females with only one X chromosome (XO pattern, called Turner's Syndrome) usually do not do well on visual–spatial tasks. We would expect them to do as well as males, since, like males, they have only one X chromosome (with no corresponding dominant gene for poorer spatial ability on the second, but in this case absent, X chromosome). Darrel Bock and Donald Kolakowski (1973) have hypothesized that this seeming paradox is explained by the fact that Turner's Syndrome girls have miniscule amounts of or no androgen in their bodies (normal girls have small amounts of androgen). Without some androgen present, they believe, the spatial ability gene is unable to express itself. However, large amounts of androgen are not related to high spatial ability; rather, the *presence* of androgen is related to the *presence* of spatial ability. The influence of hormones on spatial ability as well as on verbal and math ability is currently under investigation, although no conclusive statement about hormonal effects has yet been offered (Waber, 1977; Peterson, 1976).

That spatial ability is linked to a genetic sex difference does not mean *all* males do better than *all* females on spatial ability tasks. Bock and Kolakowski estimate that 50 percent of all men and 25 percent of all women have a spatial ability gene present. These investigators hypothesize that spatial ability may be influenced by two or even more factors. Thus, even the genetic psychologists caution that sex differences in spatial ability are only partially explained by genetic factors.

Social psychologists have discovered that socialization and educational practices also play a part in spatial ability acquisition. Socialization is implicated by the fact that spatial ability differences do not appear until puberty, after appreciable socialization has occurred. Cross-cultural work has identified some of the socialization practices that seem to facilitate spatial ability, specifically, the freedom to explore and the lack of parental dominance.

John Berry (1966) investigated this idea by finding two societies, one permissive and one restrictive. Eskimos, who allow great independence and freedom for both their boys and girls, score high on spatial tests as adults, whether they be male or female. The Temne of West Africa, who place limits on their children, especially girls, have, as adults, lower spatial ability, with females doing less well. Further, cross-cultural studies have shown that within a culture, people who are in transition from a traditional life style to a more modern industrial one have higher spatial ability than those who are still living a more traditional style, with education being thought to be the crucial factor. Within cultures, attempts to link parental practices with child spatial ability have not been successful, however (Maccoby and Jacklin, 1974).

Some investigators have also suggested that spatial ability is related to training. Women, so the reasoning goes, who have less opportunity to participate in activities that rely on spatial ability, are less likely to develop this ability.

These findings suggest that both biology and socialization affect the development of spatial skills. Genetic, and possibly hormonal, differences predispose more men than women to do well in spatial skills, while socialization differences channel more men than women to engage in and practice activities that facilitate spatial skills.

General Ability

Let us now turn to more general tests of ability, including intelligence and achievement tests. As we have mentioned, most IQ tests were originally developed so that no sex differences would appear. However, we would expect small sex differences within tests, especially on verbal and math items. The Scholastic Achievement Tests (SAT's), taken by the majority of high school seniors wishing to enter college, include both verbal and math aptitude tests. When comparisons of high school seniors' test scores on these tests were made from the middle 1960's to the middle 1970's, sex differences were found. They were most prevalent in the 1960's, with boys earning higher scores on the math, girls on the verbal tests. By 1972–1973, however, the girls' verbal advantage disappeared, although the boys' math advantage did not. The decline of the girls' verbal advantage has been attributed to the larger number of girls taking the SAT's (making the pool of girls less selective) and the fewer number of boys taking the SAT's (making the pool of boys more selective) (College Entrance Examination Board, 1977).

The Overall Picture

Adolescent boys and girls do differ with respect to visual-spatial, math, and to a lesser extent verbal ability. These differences are consistent, but the distributions of boys' and girls' scores overlap to a high degree. This means that while on the average boys do better in math, for example, not all boys do better than all girls: some girls score very high in math ability, and some boys score very low. This phenomenon was illustrated in Chapter 6.

Interestingly, in terms of schoolwork, girls actually perform better, earning higher grades than boys (Maccoby and Jacklin, 1974). Their higher grade averages do not translate into higher vocational goals or a higher rate of college or graduate school attendance, though. Given these findings, we must ask again: why do women achieve so much less in our society than men, and why are there so few women professionals? The answer usually given is that males are more motivated to achieve than females. Let us turn to the achievement literature to see if this is true.

Achievement

For better or worse, our society has been noted for its high achievement orientation. Those who view it as a positive feature of the American way of life define it as an internal motive to gain and maintain a standard of excellence. Those who see it as negative stress competition and greed.

Achievement Motivation

David McClelland and his associates (McClelland, 1961; McClelland *et al.*, 1953) have theorized extensively on achievement and have conducted prodigious research on the subject. They hypothesize that three factors contribute to one's motivation to achieve: *motive*, a stable predisposition for excellence that is learned early in life; *expectation*, the probability of succeeding on a particular task; and *incentive*, the attractiveness of the goal. All three are necessary in order for an individual to express achievement motivation and, as we can surmise from the discussion of achievement in Chapter 7, all three are affected by sex-role learning. Expectations, for example, differ: girls expect to perform poorly more often than boys. Incentives, too, differ: a goal which is attractive to boys may not be attractive to girls, and vice versa. Even motives have been thought to differentiate the sexes, as we shall see.

Studies of achievement motivation have focused both on societies and on individuals. Examining achievement motivation at a societal level, McClelland (1961) hypothesized that achievement motivation was related to entrepreneurial activity. High amounts of achievement motivation in a society, he reasoned, would lead to rapid and persistent economic growth and development. To provide support for his hypothesis, McClelland analyzed the amount of achievement motivation portrayed in literature, children's stories, and fairy tales, and correlated it with the growth and decline of various societies. He found that development was related to a society's high achievement motivation, as reflected in the stories, and decline to a society's low achievement motivation.

On an individual level, researchers tried to determine the antecedents and correlates of achievement motivation. McClelland, along with John Atkinson and others, found that the high-achieving man was motivated by internal rather than external standards. The achievement-oriented entrepreneur, for example, was driven not by a vision of barrels full of money nor awards from the Junior Chamber of Commerce, but by the idea of achievement for the sake of achieving. Other attributes of the achievement-oriented man included his ability to set realistic goals, his preference for moderately rather than extremely difficult tasks, and his improved performance on tasks in which some risk is involved and in which the outcome can be influenced by ability rather than luck. Achievement-oriented men could be characterized as self-reliant, competent, independent, and autonomous, all part of the stereotype of masculinity (Atkinson, 1958).

As you might have noticed, studies on achievement motivation describe achievement-motivated *men*. What about women? In an 800 page volume on achievement motivation (Atkinson *et al.,* 1958) women were relegated to only a footnote. Why? First, males, monopolizing the professions such as medicine and law, seemed to be the only ones achieving. Second, women, having low levels of achievement (or so the scientists believed), would be poor subjects of research on achievement motivation. To substantiate this claim, researchers pointed to the results of the original work on achievement in which they "aroused" the achievement motivation of their subjects before measuring it. First, they gave subjects an anagrams task, informing them that their performance would reflect qualities of leadership, intelligence, and the ability to organize, if they had any. Presumably, then, the subjects would feel they had a lot riding on an impressive performance. Then they were asked to examine a picture and write a story about it. Achievement motivation is usually measured by a projective technique of this sort (called a TAT, Thematic Apperception Test). The picture showed a young man sitting alone in a classroom leaning on his desk with his head resting on his hand. The subject, if he or she had a high achievement motivation, would speculate that the young man was daydreaming about becoming a reknowned scientist as he worked out an intricate mathematical problem in his head. Someone with a low achievement motivation might write about how the young man had to stay after school for some trivial disciplinary offense and thought only of how many more minutes he would have to sit there. The content of the subjects' stories was analyzed for the amount of achievement imagery in them and each subject was given a score. The investigators found that men who had been aroused demonstrated higher levels of achievement motivation than those who had not. Women, however, showed no more achievement motivation with the arousal than without it. Unaroused women exhibited *more* achievement imagery than unaroused men. But, because they lost their advantage after the arousal caused the men's achievement motivation to rise, women were said to have a lower achievement motive than men (Veroff, Wilcox, and Atkinson, 1953; French and Lesser, 1964).

The hypothesis then emerged that women have an affiliation motive rather than an achievement motive, since, the researchers reasoned, they strove toward social acceptance and were primarily people oriented. To confirm this idea, the investigators decided to arouse the women socially, so women were given a social arousal condition rather than an achievement arousal one, and, lo and behold, the scores went up. For a long time, this finding was taken as proof that the achievement motivation of men and women is qualitatively different—and perhaps it is. Traditionally, women have had limited outlets for achieving. Chief among them have been the home and family. The findings may simply be reflecting women's realistic assessments of a situation in which high expectations and incentives lay primarily in the social sphere. Worth noting, too, is the fact that all of the subjects, regardless of sex, used less achievement imagery when the picture was of a woman. Again, the subjects may have been revealing realistic attitudes stemming from their awareness of societal sex roles (Maccoby and Jacklin, 1974; Monahan, Kuhn, and Shaver, 1974).

Reviewing the findings, Eleanor Maccoby and Carolyn Jacklin pointed to a potentially important practical situation dealing with the role of "push" in a boy's development:

> When n Ach [achievement motivation] is measured projectively with male pictures, females in high school and college show a high level of achievement imagery whether given an "arousal" treatment or not; men show a high level only when aroused by reference to assessment of their intelligence and leadership ability. There may be a clue here to boys' lower grades in school—it appears that it takes stronger efforts to motivate them. (1974, p. 138)

Unfortunately, we do not know whether or not sex differences in achievement motivation are due to societal portrayals of sex roles, differences in men's and women's motivational levels, or differences in the amount of push boys and girls, men and women, receive. We do know, however, that achievement orientation as measured by actual behavior rather than projective techniques does differ for men and women, with these differences beginning to appear in adolescence.

Since adult men who are high in achievement motivation show a preference for moderately risky situations and a great deal of task persistence, riskiness and persistence are two variables that have been studied in childhood. While persisting on a task does not seem to be related to sex (Maccoby and Jacklin, 1974), riskiness does. Paul Slovik (1966) found that adolescent boys will play a game that involves risk longer than adolescent girls, to the point of winning less money. Younger children do not exhibit this sex difference.

Differences in achievement among adolescent girls and boys show up in their goals as well. When James Coleman (1961) asked high school seniors how they wanted to be remembered by their peers after they left high school, more boys than girls expressed a desire to be remembered as brilliant students (regardless of whether they were really brilliant or just average). In their freshman year, no differences had existed in the percentage of boys and girls who felt this way; they emerged only later, apparently as the girls picked up the message that there are better things to be remembered for (e.g., attractiveness, friendliness) than brilliance.

There is some evidence that girls who do achieve have incorporated the idea of achievement into their notion of the female role, while those who do not achieve, have not. Gerald Lesser, Rhoda Kravitz, and Rita Packard (1963), in a study of achievement motivation in a high school for gifted girls in New York City, found that high achievers showed a high achievement imagery after arousal when shown pictures of females, while underachievers who were equally bright showed increased achievement imagery when males were pictured on the TAT test.

Adolescent boys and young men are more likely to possess attributes of achievement orientation and to succeed in the work place than girls and young women. Yet, sex differences in the psychological concept of achievement motivation employed by researchers have not been firmly established, and those differences that do exist seem to reflect realistic assessments of societal sex roles rather than internal, personal motivational systems.

Fear of Failure

If motivational forces cannot explain sex differences in achievement orientation, maybe another phenomenon—namely, fear of failure—can. John Atkinson (Atkinson and Feather, 1966; Atkinson and Litwin, 1960) was one of the first to discuss fear of failure, which he believed to be related to achievement motivation. In an effort to attain a standard of excellence, one can succeed, or one can fail. The chance of succeeding, and of enjoying the resulting feeling of pride at one's accomplishment, is welcome. But the possibility of failing, and of suffering the feelings of shame which accompany failure, is distressing. Therefore, fear of failure should have an inhibiting effect on achievement motivation. If girls and women are low on achievement motivation, researchers hypothesized, they should be high in fear of failure. Their investigations show that high test anxiety and general anxiety, which are thought to be indicative of fear of failure, *are* related to low performance on intelligence and academic tests, regardless of sex. Seymour Sarason and Kenndy Hill (Hill and Sarason, 1966; Sarason, Hill, and Zimbardo, 1964) have done the most extensive work on test anxiety and general anxiety in children. In a five-year longitudinal study, they found similar levels of anxiety among the boys and girls in first grade, but higher levels of anxiety among the girls than boys in third grade and thereafter. Two factors that may be influencing the girls' higher anxiety scores are: first, their greater willingness to admit anxious feelings, since a boy of that age would recognize that the acknowledgment of fear or anxiety runs counter to the sex-role stereotype of a brave young fellow; and second, the similarity of the anxiety test items to the realistic concerns of young girls (e.g., "Do you get scared when you have to walk home alone at night?").

Fear of Success

Matina Horner (1970, 1972, 1974) went a step further in accounting for the lower achievement of women. She suggests that not only might the possibility of failure trigger feelings of fear of anxiety, but so might the possibility of success. After all, success, too, has its costs. Recall the quotation from Margaret Mead, for example: one step up the ladder of success might cost two steps down the ladder of femininity. And even if it doesn't, the thought that it *might* could be discouraging enough to prevent some women from proceeding with the first step. When society considers intellectual striving as inappropriate for women, women who exhibit such behavior unfortunately will be seen as deviant.

If such societal beliefs exist, how do individual women cope with the fact that femininity and individual achievement are seen as "desirable but mutually exclusive goals"? Horner hypothesized that women may cope by fearing success rather than failure. To test this notion, she gave 90 college women the following verbal lead: "After first-term finals, Anne finds herself at the top of her medical school class," and 88 men the same lead with John substituted for Anne.

Her subjects then wrote stories about Anne or John. Three different types of fear of success imagery were found: fear of social rejection, concern about one's normality or femininity, and denial. The first and most common category, fear of social rejection, included stories about the loss of friends or male support as a result of Anne's success. As two of Horner's original subjects wrote:

> Anne is a wonderful girl who has always succeeded. She never had to work. Anne didn't really care. She went to med school because she couldn't marry. . . . She really cares nothing and wants to get married. No one will marry her. She has lots of friends but no dates. She's just another girl. She tries to pretend intelligence is not part of her. She doesn't hide it—just ignores it. She will get a great job in a marvelous hospital. I don't know if she will every marry. (1970, p. 60)

> Anne doesn't want to be number one in her class. She feels she shouldn't rank so high because of social reasons. She drops down to ninth in the class and then marries the boy who graduates number one. (p. 60)

In the second category, concern about one's normality, the subjects perceived the protagonist as having internal fears, doubts, and guilt about herself.

> Ann is completely ecstatic but at the same time feels guilty. She wishes that she could stop studying so hard, but parental and personal pressures drive her. She will finally have a nervous breakdown and quit med school and marry a successful young doctor. (p. 61)

In the third type, the subjects actually denied or distorted the protagonist's success or attributed it to luck or cheating.

> Anne is a *code* name for a nonexistent person created by a group of med students. They take turns taking exams and writing papers for Anne. . . . (p. 62)

> Anne is talking to her counselor. The counselor says she will make a fine nurse. She will continue her med school courses. She will study very hard and find she can and will become a good nurse. (p. 62).

All three types of fear of success were much more common in the women's stories about Anne than the men's stories about John: two-thirds of the women's but less than one-tenth of the men's stories contained fear of success imagery.

From this and other studies by Horner, we can paint the following picture of Anne. She is lonely, without social graces or prospects, guilty, fearful, or a liar and a cheat. Further, she is physically unattractive, masculine, competitive, driven, and conceited—not a very admirable character by anyone's standards.

Horner, like McClelland and Atkinson, was also interested in the effect of an achievement arousal condition upon fear of success. Not surprisingly, Horner found that women who were fearful of success performed a task better in a noncompetitive situation (i.e., when they were alone). The performance of women who were low in fear of success, however, improved when they were in a competitive group setting (like the high-achievement-oriented men in the studies discussed earlier). In addition, women who were high in fear of success felt it was not as important to do well on the task as those low in fear of success.

Fear of success hit a responsive chord in researchers and clinicians alike who were concerned with women's low achievement. In less than a decade from the appearance of Horner's dissertation, over 200 articles on fear of success had appeared. Some of these studies confirmed her original findings, while others did not. Let's look at some of the major findings from the voluminous work.

One question of interest was whether or not fear of success appeared in younger girls and adolescents. In one study, Grace Baruch (1974) asked fifth and tenth graders to write a study to the following lead "Anne (John) has won first prize in the Science Fair for her (his) exhibition on car engines." The girls wrote a story about Anne, the boys about John. Baruch chose a cue that would be similar to that of Horner but appropriate for elementary and high school students. Also she wanted to portray a girl in a sex-inappropriate activity. Baruch identified two predominant types of fear of success stories among the children: the Fear Present Story, which contained fear of success imagery throughout, and the Coping Story, which contained fear of success imagery until the end of the story, at which time the protagonist dramatically overcame the negative consequences of being a successful female.

Equal numbers of boys and girls wrote fear of success stories (Fear Present) at each grade level, with the number increasing for both sexes from fifth to tenth grade. The *content* of the stories differed, however. The fifth-grade boys' stories were filled with revenge and mistreatment, the tenth-grade boys' stories (over two-thirds) with cheating. A fifth-grade boy wrote:

> John brought his exhibit on car engines home and went out to play. One of Tom's friends, Jerry, took it when he wasn't looking. (p. 205)

And a tenth-grade boy:

> Dad did a damned good job last night, buying out the judges. There stood a neat piece of cardboard with a diagram on it, and a hunk of dirty metal, and John with a dumb look on his face, while all around him were the science whizzes with their contraptions clanking away, and their test tubes boiling, busily explaining things to the people. (Baruch, unpublished manuscript)

The girls in both grades wrote stories involving jealousy, rejection, and accidents.

> She is standing in front of her exhibit smiling and feeling proud yet she also feels sort of funny because she is a girl and girls don't usually think about car engines. Her girl friends all look at her because they think she is weird and all the boys are laughing at her because they don't think she's feminine. Now she feels hurt and alone and wishes she had gotten the prize for almost anything else. She even feels that she doesn't even want the prize now at all. (p. 206)

Only girls told coping stories, in which the heroine overcomes the difficulties of achieving. The stories centered around feminine issues and were more prevalent in the older grade, suggesting that issues about achieving in a man's world are not very salient prior to adolescence. The following are "typical" coping stories, the first by one of Baruch's fifth graders, the second by a tenth grader.

> All the boys were teasing her for being interested in car engines. I'll show them, she thought. I can make just as good an engine as any boy. And one boy said, "I'll bet you can't." So they were going to see. They both brought in their car engines and guess what—Anne won. Now everybody looks at her with respect. (p. 202)

> She is just bubbling over with pride. It's as if she accomplished the impossible. All the boys teased her and the girls called her a tomboy. This

probably helped her get the prize because it kept her going and made her work even harder. She wasn't really interested in car engines but she did it just to be different and to help her fellow women prove themselves as capable individuals. Wait till her parents find out about this. They scoffed at her at the beginning in a loving sort of way but it still hurt sometimes. Boy, was Anne ever proud. (Baruch, unpublished manuscript)

Thus, girls and boys differed in terms of the types of stories they told. The girls' fear of success stories were filled with social rejection and concerns about femininity, the boys with revenge and cheating. In addition, many girls portrayed Anne as overcoming the obstacle of "femininity" and enjoying her success at the science fair.

Another issue in the fear of success literature has to do with its occurrence in persons who have already chosen careers. In one study, a small number of Atlantic Richfield executives were asked to write a story about a graduate business student being offered a "top management job." Forty percent of the men and 30 percent of the women expressed fear of success imagery in their stories (Wood and Greenfeld, 1976). When Harvard Law School graduates were asked, via mailed questionnaires, to describe "George Andrews (or Barbara Robbins), partner in a large New York law firm" and "Barbara Robbins (or George Andrews), former president of the Harvard *Law Review* and current Deputy Solicitor General," 10 percent of the male graduates and 45 percent of the female graduates exhibited fear of success (Glancy, 1970). Interestingly, more of the younger women (those graduating in the 1960's) exhibited fear of success than the older women lawyers (those graduating in the 1950's).

Yet another issue involves the fact that in all of the studies mentioned so far, men responded to male cues, women to female cues. How would people respond to opposite-sex cues? In two studies of adolescents, both boys and girls gave *more* fear of success imagery to the female than the male cue, with the boys actually describing more negative consequences for medical student Anne than the girls did. One author, M. Doerr, reports:

In one class, the boys, given the story of John, foresaw a generally happy and prosperous life for him; the girls, given the story of Anne, told of her getting married or becoming a nurse. In another class, the assignment was switched: the boys were told to complete the story about Anne, and the girls to complete the story about John. Most of the girls saw a happy future for John; more intersting was Anne's fate at the hands of the boys. Two students, working independently of each other, wrote that Anne, happily leaving the classroom where the first term grades and class standings were posted and walking out into the street, was promptly run over by a truck and killed. (1973, p. 4)

These findings suggest that not only is an individual's achievement motivation being tapped, but so are societal beliefs and norms. The girl who succeeds in a "masculine" task or occupation is perceived as deviant and unfeminine, hence the negative stories by both girls and boys.

That the fear of success imagery may reflect societal beliefs is also suggested by studies that have placed Anne in a less masculine environment. Hypothesizing that Anne is characterized so negatively because she is in medical school, a setting that has traditionally seen few women, Marlaine Lockheed (1975) told students that Anne, while at the top of her class in medical school, was in a class where one-half of the students were women. Fear of success was much less prevalent when one-half of the people with whom Anne was competing were women than when she was the only, or one of the only women. Similarly, in a study by Jeanne Brooks-Gunn, students reported much less fear of success when Anne was at the top of her nursing school class rather than her medical school class.

One problem with the fear of success literature is the difficulty in replicating the large sex differences originally reported by Horner. As you might have noticed, equal number of boys and girls wrote fear stories in the Baruch study, although sex differences were found in the types of stories written. Lois Hoffman (1974) reran the original 1965 Horner study in 1971 at the same university, in the same course, at the same time of year, in the same room, with the same cues. Her results: 62 percent of the college women exhibited fear of success (the same percentage as in the original Horner study), but 76 percent of the men also exhibited fear of success. Many other studies of college students have not found such differences between men and women, or have found only small differences. The lack of sex differences is due, at least in part, to differences in story content. Baruch and others find that girls and women write of rejection and loss of femininity, while boys' stories are characterized by denial, violence, hostility, and devaluation of success. Other explanations also have been offered. David McClelland has suggested that achievement motivation may be on the decline in late twentieth-century America. In addition, the meaning of success may be undergoing change, as traditional forms of success (performing well in school, becoming a doctor) are not the goals of all young people. David Tresemer (1977) has presented evidence that fear of success actually declined from 1969 to 1975 in both male and female college populations. Whether this is due to changes in perceptions of success, changes in achievement motivation, or changes in other societal forces is unclear. Although fear of success research has been criticized, often justifiably, the concept of achievement avoidance is a useful one, one that is particularly relevant to women who are seeking careers in traditionally male fields. The belief that certain careers and forms of success are unfeminine contributes to women's reluctance to enter such fields.

Expectancies for Achievement

Another factor that might influence women's achievement levels is their expectancies for achievement. As we saw in Chapter 6, an individual's perception of a task or activity as sex-appropriate or sex-inappropriate affects his or her expectancy of success.

By adolescence, differences in the expectancy of success among young men and women become even more pronounced. Outside the laboratory, Virginia Crandall (1969) asked college students to estimate their grades for several semesters. In spite of the fact that the female students obtain grades as good as or better than the male students, their grade estimates were pessimistic and they predicted a worse performance than their past grades would indicate was warranted. Male students were more likely to predict that they would do as well as or better than they had in the past.

Part of the explanation for the young women's low expectations and apparent lack of confidence might be a belief that their own skills and hard work play a secondary role to external factors like luck, the caprice of others, and so on. Meandering through a state fairgrounds could confirm this, as Kay Deaux, Leonard White, and Elizabeth Farris (1975) found. Watching the various games men and women played and tabulating the frequencies, they found that men tended to gravitate to games of skill, like a ring toss or a shooting gallery, while women preferred games of chance like bingo. Back in the laboratory, similar results were found: three-quarters of the men preferred skill games, three-quarters of the women luck games.

The role of luck and skill in men's and women's attributions of success and failure differs considerably. For women, luck (specifically, good luck) accounts for their success. For men, luck (specifically, bad luck) accounts for their failure. When women fail, they blame themselves; when men succeed they give themselves a pat on the back. Thus, women frequently fail to credit themselves for success while they blame themselves for their failures. Reasoning that failure is due to their lack of effort or ability and that success stems from luck, women are less likely to regard achievement as a positive experience and less likely to expect feelings of genuine pride to accompany it (Frieze, 1975).

Determinants of Achievement Orientation

Our preceding discussion shows that differences in achievement orientation exist in boys and girls, men and women. Exactly how is achievement encouraged in males and discouraged in females? And how can we facilitate achievement orientation in those children, especially girls, who, with age, turn away from fulfilling themselves in this area? We shall present several forces—parental socialization practices, the availability of role models, male support, and media influences, and, in separate sections, we will consider the roles of the school and of the peer group.

Parental Socialization Practices. Parental socialization practices have been thought to influence achievement orientation. In a longitudinal study by Jerome Kagan and Howard Moss (1962), achievement and independence in middle childhood and adolescence predicted similar behaviors in adulthood. The foundations of adult achievement orientation are laid in the home, especially through the ministration of the mother. Maternal influence on achievement has been linked to independence training, the encouragement of independence, moderate amounts of nurturance and punitiveness, and low restrictiveness. In a classic study by Marian Winterbottom (1958), mothers with achievement-oriented sons had emphasized independence and encouraged achievement. What seems to be important is the facilitation of emotional, not physical, independence; the mother needs to move her child away from her emotionally while still providing affection. Rushing the child to do tasks earlier (i.e., crossing the street alone) does not seem to be related to achievement orientation. Encouraging achievement, Aletha Stein and Margaret

Bailey (1973) point out, includes rewarding the child's achievement activities, participating in and initiating these activities, and accelerating the child's growth. All of these factors were mentioned by Margaret Hennig's (1973) successful executives in describing their early years.

> Both parents offered the daughter large amounts of evidenced personal satisfaction and pleasure for her accomplishments. However, even when the subjects were as young as four and five years, both parents sought to help their daughters internalize those satisfactions and pleasures. The young female was encouraged to set her own goals, establish her own standards for measuring the success of her achievement, and, hence, experiencing her personally determined rewards and satisfactions. (p. 79)

Another maternal influence involves nurturance. High amounts of maternal nurturance, especially babying and overprotectiveness, are related to dependency and passivity in little girls, both correlates of femininity. To develop independence and assertiveness, both characteristics of achievement orientation (and masculinity), mothers need to be less nurturant (although still affectionate). Moderate amounts of punitiveness and hostility may facilitate this process, as they help to move the girls away from their mothers, especially since this moving away is more difficult for girls than boys. A restrictive household, like an overprotective one, is detrimental to the facilitation of achievement orientation; instead encouraging passivity and dependency in young children (Stein and Bailey, 1973). Maternal self-perceptions of their own competence also influence their daughter's own feelings of competence; low self-esteem perpetuates itself in succeeding generations (Baruch, 1972).

Identification with parents is also believed to affect achievement orientation. For girls, the father is thought to be especially important. As we saw earlier, Hennig's successful career women, while having close relationships with both parents, participated in male activities with the father and had a closer relationship with their fathers than less successful women remembered having. In younger girls, a similar finding has been reported. In another study by Grace Baruch (1975), girls were asked about their career aspirations ("What do you think you'd like to be when you're an adult?") and their parent identification ("Imagine that you are grown up and are leading your everyday life just like one of your parents—which do you prefer it to be?"). About 18 percent of the fifth- and 24 percent of the tenth-grade girls had high career aspirations—physician and scientist being the most popular choices. These girls, unlike their counterparts with lower aspirations, chose their father as their primary identification figure. Those few that chose their mother had mothers who were employed.

These studies do not tell us whether the identification with the father *causes* the career-orientation or whether career-oriented girls identify with their father because he has a career and the mother does not. That maternal employment also is related to achievement orientation suggests that girls may actively search for appropriate role models.

In line with the identification with the father is achievement-oriented girls' perception of themselves as possessing masculine traits. Early studies characterized the achieving women as more masculine, although the evidence suggests that these women are really more androgynous, possessing both masculine and feminine traits. As Hennig reminds us, her successful women executives were not raised as boys, but were allowed to explore all options in order to develop into integrated individuals.

Role Modeling. Role models seem to become important in the adolescent and early adult years, when vocational identity is actively sought. Sex-appropriate models for many careers and for the integration of family and work do not exist. The lack of nontraditional role models for women has been mentioned frequently as a factor in females' low achievement orientation. Mothers, if they provide a traditional maternal model, are more likely to have daughters who have feminine interests and participate in feminine activities, and who are low in achievement-orientation and have few career aspirations (Douvan and Adelson, 1966). As Baruch (1972) and others have pointed out, working mothers, especially those who derive satisfaction from combining career and family, have daughters who have higher career aspirations, are achievement oriented, and are less traditional.

Girls who do not have a nontraditional female role model in the home and who are career oriented have often turned to role models outside the home. Elizabeth Douvan and Joseph Adelson (1966) report that their achievement-oriented adolescent girls named nonfamily persons as influential in their lives while more traditional girls named family members. Successful older women do act as role models for young career women or young girls aspiring to a career. Role models are frequently mentioned in biographies of successful women. In a similar vein, Elizabeth Douvan (1976) cites a study in which undergraduates and career women report vividly remembering heroines in books they read in childhood. Thus, women seem actively to seek out sex-appropriate role models when they are not available at home.

One of the most intriguing pieces of information regarding the importance of role models to young women involves the startling number of professional women who attended women's colleges. Through the 1970's, women's colleges produced a high proportion of the scientists, artists, lawyers, and physicians in this country, with some estimates being as high as one-half of all professional women having attended a woman's college. When M. Elizabeth Tidball (1973) examined the backgrounds of 1,500 women listed in *Who's Who in American Women*, she found that twice as many graduated from women's colleges as from coeducational colleges.

Why is this so? Elizabeth Douvan suggests that the women's colleges provide more role models than coeducational institutions, since they typically have hired more women faculty members. Indeed, Tidball found that number of women faculty members was positively related to career success in the study mentioned previously. Like Douvan, Tidball believes the availability of role models is essential: the premise being that adult women achievers are required to beget future women achievers.

Like many professional women, both authors of this book attended women's college and, like the authors cited above, believe the experience to have directed us toward careers. Before attending college, experience with career women was almost nil. During college, a diversity of women professionals were available, women committed to a field of study, women who were single, were married, had children, had diverse outside interests. Such intellectual women provided a panorama of the many ways in which one could successfully combine career and other aspects of life. Douvan eloquently states:

> It was not, I think, the style or views of any particular faculty member that had such an important effect on students. It was the number of models available, their diversity, and their obvious pleasure in their active

roles—their lively exchange with each other and with women students—that impressed many of us with the gratifications available through the route of involvement-commitment and the life of the mind. (1976, p. 10)

With the movement away from single-sex institutions during the 1970's, there has come a decline in the proportion of women faculty in those women's colleges that opened their doors to men but no corresponding increase in the proportion of women faculty in the men's colleges that had opened their doors to women. In fact, the proportion of women faculty in all colleges decreased from the 1920's through the 1960's. Given the importance of women faculty for student career orientation, we would expect young college women to encounter difficulties in their search for same-sex role models and can only hope that the consequence is not a further reduction of an orientation toward and a striving for achievement.

Male Support.   Earlier in the chapter we noted that one of the characteristics of successful women and women who have high achievement orientation is the support and encouragement of males. Remember Matina Horner's college women who feared success? Many of these women had boyfriends who thought women should not have careers. One of Horner's students studied fear of success in highly motivated, intelligent girls at a prestigious college and found that women whose boyfriends disapproved of their careers tended to change their academic successes, or, even more drastically, to drop out of school. One woman commented:

He thinks it's ridiculous for me to go to graduate school or law school. He says I can be happy as a housewife and I just need to get a liberal arts education. (Horner, 1972, p. 69)

In the same sample, women with low fear of success had more supportive boyfriends. One of these women said of her boyfriend:

He wants me to be intelligent. It is a source of pride to him that I do so well. (p. 70)

Media Influences.   Judging by the media, the only segment of our society to view girls as achievement oriented are the sanitary napkin manufacturers. Kimberly-Clark's New Freedom advertisement depicts a young girl in a baseball outfit, softball in one hand, mitt in the other, right foot on base, and a glimmering bronze trophy at her side. Because the New Freedom girl is active, and "moves," she needs protection that moves with her. Tampax shows a vibrant and very wet young woman ascending from the surf, complete with snorkel and fins.

Most of the time the media present young women with a plethora of underachieving role models. When Audrey Manes and Paula Melnyk (1974) examined models of female achievement available to television viewers, they found a grim picture. The only models shown to have successful social relations with men were those who occupied the lower levels of achievement. Those at the higher levels (of which there were few) were almost always portrayed as either unmarried or unsuccessfully married. Usually, television shows attribute the marital failure to the interfering effect of a woman's employment. Less commonly, the programs actually show the married working woman to be an undesirable mate. In either case, the shows suggest that somehow the women's employment leads to the marriage's failure.

Of the few women who were depicted as both working and happily married, Manes and Melnyk report that two of them worked only part-time, two worked in their husband's business, and one announced her intention to quit as soon as possible. In five of the eight cases they cited, the working women still proved to be economically dependent upon their husbands and/or to lack a commitment to their profession.

Looking at how the nonworking married women were faring, Manes and Melnyk found more than 95 percent of them to be happily married. The investigators concluded that, while female achievers were clearly in evidence—as doctors, lawyers, executives, and so forth—the price they had to pay for financial independence was marital failure, and for this reason, young female viewers would reject them as desirable role models.

Analyses of television advertisements yield an equally unfavorable picture of women. In spite of the fact that 51 percent of the population is female, who account for approximately 75 percent of consumer purchases, only 43 percent of the central characters of advertisements were women. Of nearly 300 central characters viewed, 70 percent of the male central figures were presented as authorities on the advertised product, compared to 14 percent of the women. The other 30 percent of the male central characters acted as product users, compared to 86 percent of the females. In other words, the men "pronounced" upon the product and the women purchased it. Advertisers depicted men in roles independent of others, such as worker, professional-celebrity, or narrator-interviewer, but depicted women in roles determined by their relationship to others, as spouse, parent, girlfriend, or housewife. Men appeared in occupational setups such as offices, laboratories, stores, or athletic fields; women appeared at home. Men who used the product received as a reward the approval of their friends, and social and career advancement. Women received the approval of their family and of the opposite sex. So, the advertisements reiterate the messages children receive from textbooks, novels, television programs, movies, and so on: that women are less knowledgeable, less argumentative, less authoritative, less persuasive, less credible than men, and less likely to be rewarded with career advancement (McArthur and Resko, 1975)

Teenage magazines and paperbacks present a clear-cut image of sex-role stereotypes too. Conducting another "super-scientific" study, one of the authors walked into a local bookstore, reached for one adolescent-girl-oriented book, and read the back cover. The book: *Growing Anyway Up* by Florence Parry Heide. The cover:

> I went into their powder room and stared at myself in the mirror. So this is Florence Stirkel, how do you do, what funny eyes you have. What's that on your chin? A mole? A freckle? A simple pimple? I pulled my hair down over my face. There, now no one could see me.

Next, I grabbed an adolescent boys' book: *Rass* by Berneice Rabe. The cover read:

> Honor your father, Rass! That was fine but what about his father honoring him? Sure Rass got into trouble now and then—well, more now than then—but it was not as if he didn't work hard enough in the fields. If just once he could win his Dad's respect instead of a beating. "You've got to think" said his sister, "how you can make Dad like you. Maybe you could catch a big fish like he did when he was a boy." Rass never took advice from girls. Still, if he did catch that fish. . . .

Both convey something of the turmoil of adolescence, the discovery of who you are and where you stand. But the girl's response was simply to fade away behind a silk screen of hair. The boy's was clearly one of action, to get out there and pull in the biggest fish ever.

SCHOOL AS A SEX ROLE SOCIALIZER: THE UP AND DOWN STAIRCASE

Besides contributing all the mediating factors discussed in Chapter 7, and besides providing its students with role models, schools serve the cause of sex-role socialization in other ways: by structuring a same-sex or sex-typed peer system around academics and extracurricular activities alike, by assisting students with planning for their career training and goals, and by encouraging or discouraging students in the pursuit of their interests.

School and the Peer Group

Even the most conscientious school, like a compulsive housekeeper or a thousand dollar lawn mower, has bugs. The "bugs" act as signs that, despite its best efforts, the school's hidden curriculum is at work setting up different expectations for its boys and girls, showing pride at a different set of accomplishments for each, and channeling them into activities and interests possibly unrelated to their individual abilities. Educators are advised to look for such signs when they find they are teaching clumps of boys in one type of class and clumps of girls in another; when they join a group of guys engaged in a lively game of basketball after school, as the girls sit on the edge of the playing field watching; when they stop in on the student senate in action after school and notice that the officers seated in the front of the meeting room are all the same sex; when they observe an abundance of same-sex clusters awaiting the arrival of the school buses home; when they direct a school dramatic production for which the entire stage crew is male; when they set up a student employment center and watch all the girls sign up for the $1.00 per hour baby-sitting jobs and all the boys sign up for the $5.00 an hour yard work; and when they attend a sports event in which all the players are boys and all the cheerleaders are girls. The initial reaction to situations of this kind may be that they reflect the natural inclinations of the children involved. Girls sit on the sidelines or avoid making sets for the new play because they want to; boys turn down the opportunity to get paid for an evening of television watching or reading because they want to. But the least initiative on the part of a teacher, a coach, a school official, and eventually, even a peer will be likely to result in a switch. The coach's casual remark to the girls on the sidelines to "get off your duffs and net that ball!" *may* send them clamoring to the field (and if it doesn't work in the high school years, it should have been tried in the early and middle childhood years). The employment counselor's remark, "What do you usually do on Friday nights anyway, John?" may prompt the financially strapped John to see the virtues of a baby-sitting job. And an accumulation of comments showing respect and admiration for individuals of the opposite sex may help break up the same-sex clusters of after-school students. Who knows?

Career Planning and Vocational Education

One day, a couple of decades ago, an eighth-grade homeroom teacher broke the daily routine by marching into the classroom carrying a stack of brochures and scored career interest inventories. Though the first period bell had rung, she had not yet issued the usual command to the pupils to rise and proceed to their respective classes. So the pupils sat timorously behind their desks waiting for an explanation. "Today is the day we make our career decisions," she announced, in the first person plural (presumably to indicate her full participation in the proceedings). Her participation turned out to be passing out the pamphlets and the career inventories the pupils had taken several weeks before, speaking words of wisdom quickly forgotten, and leaving the pupils to ponder the possibilities.

Times have changed; career planning is no longer the one-or-two-shot affair it was then. The current, enlightened view holds that the establishment of career goals represents a lifelong process, beginning with the child's "First Book of Trucks" (watch who is driving them) and ending with post-retirement plans or the dispensation of one's property in a last will and testament. With this in mind, all that has come before—Chapters 4, 6, 7 and 8—takes on a new significance.

Preschool and elementary school attitudes toward male and female careers, derived through parents, teachers, textbooks, and television can now be seen as part of the child's continuing search for his or her own place in the scheme of things. The school to which parents send a child and the courses that they and the teachers encourage the child to pursue are part of his or her preparation for a position in society. Some courses will restrict options; others will expand them. Some extracurricular activities will serve career goals; others will bypass them entirely. A person's school years, particularly the high school years, when career counseling begins in earnest, are replete with decisions which will ultimately affect the student's career choices. The task of the teacher and the guidance counselor is to *be there* when the preparatory issues arise; to provide the student with a variety of actual and vicarious experiences relevant to the career-choice process; to encourage the student to explore a number of career possibilities, learn about the world of work, and imagine his or her own place in it. Ideally.

What *really* happens is that teachers stay busy teaching course content. Their course objectives permit few diversions into the area of career planning. As for the counselors, they usually find themselves more occupied with a student's present personal problems and course decisions than with the student's future occupational plans. In an extensive study of vocational education and career planning, Morgan Lewis and Lynne Kaltreider (1976) noted that the counselors in their sample did not even consider occupational counseling to be one of their main responsibilities. Whatever their perceptions of their task, when asked to indicate how their time is divided, the counselors report one-half given to conducting interviews with students and their parents, and the other half given to paper work and administrative matters. Of the time spent with students, 30 percent involved course selection, 17 percent involved assisting the student with post-secondary vocational plans, and 16 percent involved helping the student to make post-secondary educational plans. The remaining 37 percent of the time spent with students dealt primarily with their personal and academic problems.

With Title IX having assured students the freedom to choose and participate in any course offerings and career preparation programs they choose and having provided legal remedies for a school system's failure to provide equal opportunities, the counselor's role in the student's career preparation can be seen as "extra-legal." The advice a student receives or the cues he or she picks up in an interview with a counselor are not under the protection of Title IX, yet they can have an enormous impact on the student's career decision. For example, counselors might take an active or inactive role, either encouraging the student to pursue his or her interests regardless of their conformity to sex stereotypes, offering no comment in response to the student's expressed interests, or actually discouraging them. One subtle, sometimes unconscious, and often well-intentioned way counselors actively discourage students from entering nontraditional courses or fields is to "probe," just to be sure the student is really serious about his or her decision. The effect is to influence indirectly the student's view of the correct course of action. Placing male and female secondary school counselors in an interview situation with a female student who expressed either traditional or nontraditional career goals, Arthur Thomas and Norman Stewart (1971) found empirical evidence of the practice of "probing" nontraditional students. Counselors who heard the girl express the "deviant" desire to become an engineer regarded her choice as less appropriate and the student herself as in greater need of counseling than those who heard her express the "conforming" desire to major in home economics. The belief that a nontraditional student is any less sure of herself and her decision than a traditional one is certainly questionable, and the idea that an occupation can be appropriate or inappropriate for an individual by virtue of his or her sex is hard-dying, so accustomed are we to thinking of engineers as male and nurses as female. When we ask ourselves *why* engineering should be so inappropriate for a female and nursing so inappropriate for a male, we find far fewer reasons than we might have imagined!

In addition to perceiving occupations as sex-typed, counselors tend to probe nontraditionally oriented students because they feel they must provide the student with a "realistic" view of the work world and prepare him or her for the community's attitudes toward nontraditional job applicants. But Lewis and Kaltreider found that while one counselor would perceive the community as unaccepting of nontraditional job applicants, another counselor in the same school would perceive the community as fully accepting of all job applicants as long as they were qualified. Each counselor's efforts to act in conformity with his or her community was in reality nothing more than a reflection of the counselor's own view of the "appropriateness" of the student's goals.

Following students who had participated in nontraditional vocational education programs past graduation, Lewis and Kaltreider found that their pursuit of nontraditional occupational goals affected neither their job satisfaction, their wages, their rate of unemployment, nor their recollection of the treatment they received in the vocational education classes. In fact, girls who had taken the nontraditional program did find professional-technical and semiskilled jobs and were less likely to enter the clerical and service-oriented areas toward which the traditional girls had gravitated. And the nontraditional males were more likely to have found sales, clerical, and service goals than semiskilled or farm jobs. Nontraditional students—males and females alike—reported that they did not find sex discrimination a problem in obtaining the type of job they wanted.

Not just the attitudes of a student's counselor, but the counselor's selection and interpretation of career interest inventories can have profound implications for the student's planning. Some inventories, for example, have assumed that particular fields should exclude all and any males or all and any females, so they provide separate inventories according to the sex of the student. The male form might ask boys to say whether they like, dislike, or are indifferent to the occupations of military officer, geologist, or high school principal, not even mentioning these options on the female form. Similarly, the female form might provide girls with the opportunity to comment on occupations not offered to the boys, such as supervisor in a telephone office, stewardess, or fashion model (e.g., SVIB—Forms T399 and TW398). Tests which elicit preferences between flower arranging and cooking, or doing secretarial work or being an executive's wife, would hardly be able to reflect a high school girl's interest in physics or national defense. Other aspects of the inventories affecting responses are the degree to which the items tap experiences that might be relatively unique to either boys or girls in our culture (e.g., asking if you have ever been to a stag party or served as a Candy-Striper) and the extent to which gender-neutral, or inclusionary, occupational titles are used (e.g., sales representative, letter carrier, etc.). The issue of sex bias and sex fairness in career interest measurement is currently receiving wide attention and new procedures for assessing an individual's occupational interests are now being devised.

Even using a non-sex-biased career inventory, however, a counselor's own sex bias may still intrude upon the career-planning process. In interpreting the results of the inventory, the counselor can sway the student to sex-typed occupations within the interest areas identified as belonging to the student. The practice can easily influence the student who is eager for hints about what to do with his or her future. A study by Sandra and Daryl Bem (1973) illustrates how susceptible students are to sex typing of potential occupations. The Bems asked students to rate various employment opportunities according to how interested or uninterested they would be in the job. Each student received a list of twelve job descriptions in the form of advertisements. The investigators used three forms; they kept eight of the job descriptions identical on all three forms, but varied the four telephone company ads. On one form the ads were in traditional exclusionary language (e.g., frameman); on another form the ads were in inclusionary language (e.g., sales representative); and on the third form the ads were in sex-reversed exclusionary language (e.g., linewoman). The wording influenced considerably the interest that male and female students showed in the opposite-sex jobs. When the wording was exclusionary, men and women expressed an interest in the opposite-sex jobs only 30 and 5 percent of the time, respectively. In other words, the exclusionary language effectively *excluded* them, particularly the women, from showing an interest in those jobs. When the wording was inclusionary, or sex-reversed exclusionary, the subjects were much more willing to show an interest in the position.

Students harbor their own biases, with which the counselor must deal. In the Bem and Bem study just cited, even when the sex-reversed exclusionary wording was used, women shied away from jobs they recognized as traditionally male (though their interest increased from 5 to 45 percent). The facts that a student and counselor must face are that nine out of every ten high school girls will work at some time in their lives; on an average, 25 years or more. Even if she marries and has children, (1) she will probably work anyway, as nearly half of all married women with school-age children do, (2) her job will probably be full-time, since only about one-third of the 15.5 million mothers in the labor force are employed part-time, (3) she may become widowed, separated or divorced and join the nearly 8 million families headed by women, and (4) in any case, she will probably live as many as 45 years after her last child is grown. Yet in spite of these figures, which are current rather than projective, and in spite of the fact that women's participation in the labor force can be expected to increase still further (the rate of increase in 1977 was 14 percent for women versus only 6 percent for men), girls continue to think of marriage as the major consideration; when they do prepare for work and enter the work world, fully half of them end up in the same 21 job categories of the 250 listed by the U.S. Bureau of the Census. In fact, if one gathered together just the secretary/stenographers, household workers, bookkeepers, elementary school teachers, and waitresses, one would have one-fourth of the female work force (U.S. Department of Labor, 1977; Hedges, 1970).

The strong tendency for a girl to want to leave her options wide open and avoid any occupational commitment until a husband is found (by which time options that might have been open to her earlier are closed) derives from her belief that a home and career will inevitably conflict. In order to ascertain what a woman's career attitudes might be if the societal system in which she lived was modified a bit, Helen Farmer and Martin Bohn (1970) waved their magic wand and changed the world. They told a group of working women, all of whom had taken a career interest inventory, to:

> pretend with me that men have come of age and that
>
> 1. Men like intelligent women;
> 2. Men and women are promoted equally in business;
> 3. Raising a family well is very possible for a career woman.

When the women, in this frame of mind, answered the career inventory for a second time, they showed a new, invigorated career interest; their "Home" scores dropped and their "Career" scores rose.

Title IX was meant to widen the range of occupational skills available to male and female students by providing each with the opportunity to choose freely among vocational educational courses. While the law stands, narrow options continue. Many school systems have found that traditional course names such as Cooking or Vocational Agriculture act as barriers whereas new titles like Food Production Management and Earth Environment Occupations seem to break the barriers down. Guidance materials often picture males and females in traditional sex-typed jobs; tour guides at vocational educational institutions often steer the girls toward the cooking facilities and the boys toward the metal working areas; orientation meetings can benignly neglect to encourage nontraditional participation in shop courses, and students may feel reluctant to break with tradition or be the only member of their sex in a classroom.

Original schemes for encouraging course selections based on interests and abilities rather than on sex are cropping up everywhere. In Wayne, New Jersey, for example, the Passaic County Area Vocational-Technical School recruited girls into workshops in which they would learn traditionally male skills such as Electronics or Air Conditioning Repair. In Electronics, the girls learned soldering, testing resistors, reading oscillators, drawing schematic diagrams, and measuring AC voltage. At the end of the workshop, the girls were interviewed and asked whether they would consider accepting an actual job offer on the outside that involved electronics or air conditioning repair, for example. The girls "firmly and without hesitation expressed that they certainly would; in fact, one research student [as they were called] said that at this moment she is considering changing her present shop major (Beauty Culture) to her recently undertaken research shop, Electronics" (p. 11). One of the girls appealed, "for me, it's too late . . . please encourage other girls to try." Her lament is itself a reflection of her stereotyped belief that boys enter vocational education with an already extensive background; but in fact, most shop courses begin on the premise that the students know nothing at all about the subject and for that reason start with the very basics. When the workshops at Passaic were completed and the new year about to begin, the school invited the research students to help recruit newly arriving freshmen into the nontraditional courses. The girls stood before their fellow students and spoke candidly about their experiences. They invariably mentioned finding the courses easier than they expected, the equipment fun to operate, and the boys cooperative and receptive to their participation in the course.

On the Playing Fields

The battle of Waterloo was won on the playing fields of Eton.

Duke of Wellington

In athletics, too, the law now dictates that schools provide equal facilities, equipment, coaching, academic tutoring, and publicity (but not equal expenditures) for boys and girls. Still, inequities exist. When the doors opened, girls did not overwhelm the athletic facilities and clamor for Olympic standing. Why? Some long-lingering myths persist, acting to dissuade girls from full participation. She might believe she cannot or should not participate in sports during her period, though, as we have mentioned, Olympic medals have been won by women while menstruating. She might worry that her reproductive organs might fall apart under the force of effort, though vigorous activity has the beneficial effect of strengthening the muscles of the pelvic area. Even during pregnancy, physical activity can contribute to good health and to a shorter and easier labor. She, and those around her, might think females are more fragile and worry about broken bones, though the fact is that between 8 and 12 years of age a girl's skeleton is from 18 to 36 months more mature than a boy's. Breast injuries ought not to be a greater concern than injuries to a boy's reproductive organs; the same remedy (protective cups) is applicable to both. Bulging muscles used to be held out as a dire consequence of strenuous activity, but because women lack the high levels of androgen required for muscular hypertrophy, pumping iron can only help to equalize the one area in which women really do fall behind, namely, strength (Countiss, 1977).

The perpetuation of these myths, a history of sex-role socialization, and a lack of qualified coaches are the reasons girls did not rush to the playing fields.

In many cases, the sheer complexity and frequent ambiguity of Title IX kept schools from implementing new programs. In these cases, the law needed to be either clarified or enforced by the courts. When an Ohio high school prohibited a girl from trying out for the football team (not joining it, but just trying out for it), Judge Carl Rubin, the Federal District Judge of Dayton, ruled that it was unconstitutional to exclude her from a team on the basis of sex alone. Even though most girls might be physically unable to compete on the boys' team, no one can presume in advance that a girl is physically unfit. The judge said:

> It has always been tradition that "boys play football and girls are cheer-leaders." Why so? Where is it written that girls may not, if suitably quali-fied, play football? There may be a multitude of reasons why a girl might elect not to do so. Reasons of stature or weight, or reasons of tempera-ment, motivation, or interest. This is a matter of personal choice. But a prohibition without exception based upon sex is not. . . . It may well be that there is a student today in an Ohio high school who lacks only the

proper coaching and training to become the greatest quarterback in professional football history. Of course, the odds are astronomical against her, but isn't she entitled to a fair chance to try? (Sprint, Vol. 1 (1), Spring, 1978, p. 3)

As the judge said, time was when the most physical thing a teenage girl did was to bounce into her cheerleader's outfit and shout from the sidelines, but now she can get onto the playing field if she wants to, even if she has to sue to do it! Things *are* changing: in 1970, 294,000 girls were involved in interscholastic high school sports; by 1978, the figure had risen to 1.6 million, nearly 6 times as many! In 1971, only 7 percent of the high school athletes were girls, but by 1978, nearly 29 percent of them were. But things are not changing in terms of expenditures: in 1974, the girls reaped only 2 percent of the athletics budget; in 1976, almost 8 percent.

School athletics contribute to two important aspects of a child's development, each related indirectly to sex role. First, in terms of the child's physical development, athletics foster fitness, skill in movement, strength, and endurance. Just as we saw trends toward earlier action on career planning in the schools, we see evidence compiling that the earlier a child's introduction to a wide range of physical activities, the better. Physical activity as a lifelong habit promotes continued good health. Furthermore, a little muscle power among females would help diminish the sex-role stereotype of strength as a uniquely male commodity.

A second area in which athletics foster growth is in the development of social initiative. Emphasizing intrateam cooperation and interteam competition, and promoting a general awareness of how groups operate, team sports provide its participants with strategic skills and a feeling of gamesmanship and team play that will contribute to their later roles in management and business and in their general dealings with the world at large. In his book, *The Sociology of Sports,* Harry Edwards (1973) comments that "the ability to control the nerve-muscle mechanisms of the body in acts of skill fosters freedom, and increases his [sic] worth as a social being" (pp. 233–234). Learning to deal competently with the social world, the individual can apply the skills acquired on the field to those required on the job. As David Reissman puts it, "The road to the board room leads through the locker room." Until the passage of Title IX, that door was effectively closed to 51 percent of the schoolchildren.

Unlocked by law, it now stands ajar. But along the way to the board room, there still stand obstacles which girls will need plenty of dexterity and brawn to surmount.

PEERS AS MEDIATORS
OF SEX-ROLE DEVELOPMENT

Along with the deepening of the voice and the maturing of the breasts is a movement away from the family and toward the peer group. Throughout the childhood years, the family has directed the child's values, goals, and choices. With the advent of puberty, however, the child begins to look toward the peer group for direction. The switch can sometimes be abrupt, as many parents have observed. Charles Bowerman and John Kinch (1959) asked fourth-to tenth-grade children: who understood them better, who would they be like when they grew up, and with whom did they like to spend time. The children could answer family, peers, or neutral. Elementary school children overwhelmingly chose family over friends, junior high school children were equally likely to pick family or friends, and senior high schoolers preferred friends to family. Bowerman and Kinch found that the grade at which the most dramatic increase in peer orientation occurred differed, depending on sex. The big leap occurred between sixth and seventh grade for the girls (4 percent versus 33 percent preferred peers), and between seventh and eighth grade for the boys (17 percent versus 34 percent), with these differences corresponding to the sex differences in the onset of puberty.

Most adults view the increase in peer orientation with dismay, though we hasten to add that parents do still have an influence over their adolescents. In the study just described, one-third of the high schoolers were more family than friend oriented. Not only that, but parents have a great effect on achievement strivings as well as values and political orientations. As an example, we can look at the Vassar (Sanford *et al.*, 1956) and Bennington (Newcomb, 1943) studies that were conducted with women from these colleges in the 1940's and 1950's. Upon entering college, their ideologies were more similar to those of their parents, although they became less so as the students' college experiences progressed. But, when these students were polled a few years after college, their values were, in most cases, once again close to those of their parents. When adolescents are directly asked about the areas in which adults have more influence than peers, political feelings and personal problems are pointed to, while dress and grooming are seen as the peer domain. Peer groups themselves reflect societal values, even though adolescents often vehemently deny this. The emphasis just tends to be different—social acceptance, popularity, dating, conformity—with a little dash of rebellion thrown in to throw adults off guard. That is not to say that the peer group structure in adolescence is not unique, but merely that it reflects, as do all groups, societal beliefs and, of interest to us here, sex-role beliefs.

The transition from family to friends is essential for healthy development. The peer group allows the adolescent some independence from the often perceived confines of the family; it provides a forum for new ideas, for sexual exploration, and for just plain "hanging out." Autonomy is gained as the late adolescent finally breaks away from the conformity of the peer group itself. Adult intimacy, as well as sexuality, of course, evolve out of interaction and love relationships with age-mates, not parents. Thus, four goals—independence, autonomy, intimacy, and sexuality—are facilitated by peer interaction. The adolescent peer group, like the rest of society, channels boys into male sex roles and girls into female sex roles. As the adolescent moves from like-sex friendships, to clique membership, to dating, and finally to sexuality and intimacy, the message to maintain one's sex role is still the same.

Friendships

Friendships take on a different character at adolescence. The child, being more egocentric than the adolescent, talks more and listens less. The sharing of one's feelings and beliefs does not characterize friendships until adolescence, at which time intimacy flourishes.

Early adolescent boys and girls seem to have very different friendship patterns, as Elizabeth Douvan and her colleagues have found (1970; Douvan and Adelson, 1966; Gold and Douvan, 1969). Adolescent girls' friendships have been characterized as close and intimate in nature. Much time is spent talking, reflecting, and sharing intimate thoughts. Loyalty is of central concern to the 12- to 14-year-old girl, presumably because if innermost secrets are shared, the friend may have "dangerous knowledge" at her disposal. Friendships tend to be exclusive, with a few girls being exceptionally close to one another. Because of this, breakups tend to be highly emotional.

While friendships may facilitate interpersonal skills in girls, they seem to foster independence and achievement in boys. Boys tend to form larger, more activity-oriented groups. Although, and perhaps because, they are not as intimate, intense, or exclusive, boys' friendships may be more long lasting and stable. Boys participate in sports, in locker room conversation, and in verbal dueling. The latter activity, described by William Labov (1972) and Barbara Sommer (1978), involves ritualized insults, chopping or cutting, as it is called in some parts of the country. These insults tend toward the obscene, and deal with several themes, often with reference to the opponent's mother. Each protagonist is expected to be adept at producing a witty and equally obscene retort. Verbal dueling reflects the adolescent male's concern about sexuality, potency, and social acceptance. Just as female adolescents may share intimacies to clarify their sexual identity, so male adolescents may use verbal dueling and boasting.

Cliques

The cliques, the group, the club, the sorority—do they really exist? Although the labels may not, the institutions certainly do! A clique (although outdated and overworked, the label is still descriptive) may be a formal or informal group, but it is a relatively small group of adolescents who spend most of their waking hours together or at least in communication with each other. Clique members tend to dress alike, have the same mannerisms, the same style, the same jargon. Each clique has a distinct personality or stereotype—we all remember the brains, the athletes, the social reformers, the junior politicos, the elitists, the creeps, the cheerleaders, the radicals.

All cliques, of course, are not equal: the prevalence of certain adolescent values make some more desirable than others. For boys, athletics is the key to success; for girls, popularity and attractiveness. Where does academic achievement, which is after all the *raison d'être* of high school, fit into the picture? When James Coleman studied the structure of high school society in 1961, he found academic achievement to be overshadowed by social achievement. Coleman did discover that as boys move closer to college and career, academics become more important although not quite overtaking athletics. For girls, academics did not increase, and even decreased in importance, throughout high school. Brains might spell disaster for the girl aspiring to popularity and the prestigious clique. The reliance on popularity in girls seems to inhibit the development of other values.

The peer structure not only discourages intellectual achievement, but places a premium on conformity. Criticism of other clique members is also rampant; this may in part explain the adolescent pose of always being on stage for what David Elkind (1971) has called the "invisible audience." This critical audience is also self-induced, arising from the adolescent's self-consciousness. Together, the adolescent and the clique critique actions vis-à-vis rigid standards.

One investigator has provided us with a fascinating glimpse into the peer group structure of the adolescent. Dexter Dunphy (1963) observed 13- to 21-year-olds in their "natural settings" in Sydney, Australia. Dunphy spent hours with his subjects on "street corners, in milk bars and homes, at parties, and on Sydney beaches," and discovered two distinct types of social groups: cliques and crowds. A crowd, including 15 to 30 persons, was an association of 2 to 4 cliques, which themselves had 3 to 9 members. All crowd members were part of one of the cliques, although not all clique members were in a crowd. Because of this structure, Dunphy believes that clique membership increases, not decreases, the likelihood of social contact, since it is a prerequisite for crowd membership.

From his observations, Dunphy found several stages of group development, which are portrayed in Figure 9-1. First, the pre-adolescent "gang" emerges as a clique; it is of same-sex friends with no corresponding crowd forming. Second, the crowd begins to form, as the same-sex cliques begin to test out interaction with opposite-sex cliques. Next, the crowd becomes more distinct, and the high-status members of the same-sex cliques begin to date. Fourth, most members of the cliques are dating, and heterosexual cliques begin to form. Finally, the crowd disintegrates as groups of couples form.

How does an adolescent become a member of a clique? Dunphy's adolescents told him that a potential member must be somewhat pushy to break in, must have qualities defined as important by the clique, and must conform to the clique's dictates.

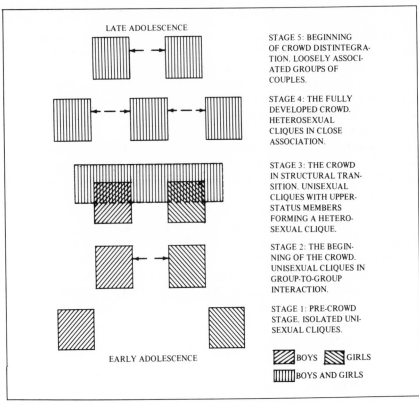

Figure 9-1. Stages of group development in adolescence. From Dunphy (1963).

All groups have a certain temperament of their own. Anyone new has to fit in; he must have similar aspects and outlooks and like similar things. (p. 239)

Adolescents were sometimes eased out of cliques because the member either had rejected the authority of the group or had failed to move along with the group in heterosexual relations. To be a clique leader, organizing social activities, being friendly to clique and crowd members, and being advanced in terms of dating were critical features.

The Dating Game

We have all played it: the excitement of a first date, the misery of not being asked out. A Saturday night spent alone or, even worse, at home was to be avoided at all costs. Dating in the 1950's and 1960's has been portrayed in movies such as *Grease* and *American Graffiti* and books such as *Kinflicks* and *Memoirs of an Ex-Prom Queen*. How much these popularized accounts of dating reflect the current state of affairs is unknown, as there are surprisingly few studies of adolescent dating patterns.

Dating is occurring earlier than ever before: girlfriends and boyfriends are common in the late elementary school years, and the norm during junior high. Sexual activity, which arises from the dating situation, has begun earlier and earlier. As we shall see, probably one-third of all girls have intercourse before their seventeenth birthday, one-half by their nineteenth birthday, and adolescent boys are even more likely to have had intercourse than adolescent girls.

Dating arises out of the group formation process that we just described. Cliques and crowds function to encourage dating and the movement from same-sex to opposite-sex friendships. Like the rules for entrance and continuation in the clique, the dating game is highly ritualized and narrowly defined; any deviance is frowned upon. You may have noticed that dating sounds like a fairly stereotypic activity, and it is! Elizabeth Douvan (1970) has provided us with the adolescent's definition of a good date.

> A good date is cheerful, easy in conversation, a good listener, neither too assertive nor too passive, and never grouchy, moody, or too sexual. (p. 38)

Besides confronting the fact that they are not the perfect date, adolescents must cope with conflicts inherent in dating. To fall behind one's clique in terms of dating is to risk expulsion from the group. Dating may provoke competition within the clique and may strain friendships. Is loyalty to a friend or having a boyfriend or girlfriend more important? Not dating at all may cause adolescents much inner anxiety about their attractiveness, their ability ever to find love or a spouse.

Different rules of the game have evolved for boy and girl adolescents, as these reflect existing sex roles. Girls are instructed in the art of getting a man, where to find him, and what to do when he's been caught. By the time she is ready to become that *Cosmopolitan* woman, her training has been extensive. Girls are not to be too active, too assertive, or too interested: just be nice and friendly and passive. They are advised to place themselves in the boy's path, while artfully acting as though there was no forethought. Once they've caught him, the same rules apply. Nancy Taylor (1975) has suggested that a good date will: "look into his eyes when he talks to you, let him suggest where to go to dinner, really listen when he talks, be on time when he picks you up, let him lead when dancing, wear subtle make-up, avoid flirting with other boys when you are out with him."

Boys, on the other hand, are to be active and assertive, although consideration is valued. Being a bit of a roué is an asset, and even being sexually aggressive is tolerated.

These sex-role descriptions may be changing, as popular books for teenagers are steering toward emphasizing sensitivity to the other's feelings rather than seductive manipulation or sexual exploitation.

Sexuality

One of the main difficulties of being a teenager is sex, at once a great discovery, a great mess, a great pleasure, a great frustration, and an all-around great muddle. (Callahan, 1976, p. 57)

Sexuality is surely one of the central concerns of adolescents. From the graffiti on bathroom walls, schoolroom conversations, personal diaries, whispered conversations, parental lectures on the "facts of life," adolescents learn about societal attitudes and practices concerning sexuality and experiment with their own sexuality.

The Sexual Revolution

"Today's Adolescents Immoral!"

"Our Teenagers Living Together in Sin."

Such media headlines have captured our attention throughout the 1950's, 1960's, and 1970's. Has a sexual revolution occurred, and if so, when did it occur? Were young people in the 1970's more sexually active than their parents or their grandparents were as youth?

Changes in sexuality have been carefully documented since the ground-breaking work of Alfred Kinsey, who, in the late 1940's and early 1950's, interviewed thousands of men and women who spoke candidly about their sexual activity (Kinsey, et al., 1948, 1953). More recently, Morton Hunt (1974) asked men and women the same questions in a survey funded by the Playboy Foundation (funded by Playboy Magazine). One of the sexual indices Kinsey and Hunt asked people about was the incidence of premarital sex. From the 1940's to the 1970's, the vast majority (80 to 95 percent) of American males experienced premarital sex before age 25. Fewer women had done so, although the gap between men and women is rapidly narrowing. Only one-third of the women Kinsey interviewed, but about one-half of Hunt's female subjects, had experienced intercourse before age 25. When Hunt looked at age differences, he found that approximately 80 percent of those women under 25, 65 percent of those women 25 to 34, and one-third of women over 35 had had premarital sex. The older women, of course, represent the same women that Kinsey interviewed in the 1940's, and even then he found one-third had experienced peremarital sex. These changes in women's sexual activity over the last decades are so dramatic, that by the 1980's almost all of our young people are expected to have premarital sex.

Adolescents, like young adults, are more likely to have intercourse, and to do so at an earlier age, than ever before. One-quarter of Kinsey's college men and one-tenth of the women had had intercourse by age 17, whereas one-half of Hunt's college men and one-quarter of the women had. Sorenson (1973), in a comprehensive survey of adolescent sexual experiences, reports that 44 percent of 13- to 15-year-old boys and 30 percent of the same age girls have had intercourse. A 19-year-old girl has a 50-50 chance of having had sexual relations while a 19-year-old boy is even more likely to have done so. Adolescent sex is related to social class, education, residence, and religiosity, with intercourse being most prevalent in adolescents who reside in urban centers and come from lower socioeconomic or less educated families. Although the incidence of intercourse is increasing in all American communities, great individual variations among adolescents is still found. In the Sorenson sample just mentioned, 34 percent of the 13- to 15-year-olds had had *no* sexual experience at all, 24 percent were involved in petting, and the rest were having intercourse.

The greatest change in sexual behavior occurred after the first World War and at the end of the 1960's. After the 1920's, the actual incidence of premarital sex did not change appreciably for almost five decades. What *did* change was the willingness to talk openly about sexuality in general and one's experiences in particular (Reiss, 1960). Although your parents and grandparents may have had sex before marriage, they certainly will not talk about it!

Parents, Adolescents, and Sexuality

Parental and adolescent views about sexuality have always been at odds. After one becomes a parent, sexual attitudes become more conservative. In other words, when we are young, we tend to believe that premarital sex is acceptable as we and our friends are testing our own sexuality. When we become parents, we change our tune: adolescents are not mature enough, they will be hurt emotionally, they will be sexually stunted, they will become promiscuous, and if they are girls they will never be chosen as wives. Parental reactions to their own children's sexuality helped perpetuate the belief of a sexual revolution each generation. Adults, not wanting their adolescents to have intercourse too early, conveniently do not discuss their own adolescent experiences (Wake, 1969).

Parents and adolescents are also in conflict over the discussion of sexuality, and this is especially true for mothers and daughters. In one study by Robert Bell (1966), 83 percent of the mothers thought their daughters should answer questions about sexuality, while only 37 percent of the daughters thought they should respond to such inquiries. Parents are concerned over their teenagers' well-being, their loss of control over their children's behavior, and their need to know "what is going on." Adolescents, concerned with becoming independent from their parents, experimenting with their sexuality in private, and minimizing conflict over differences in opinion, are often reticent to discuss sexuality at home.

In some cases there is good reason for the adolescent to hesitate. Gail, a 19-year-old who became pregnant, wanted to marry the child's father and assumed her own father would agree. As she related:

> And so I told him I thought I might be pregnant. And—he hit the ceiling. He had the completely opposite reaction of what I expected. He started screaming at me and telling me I was stupid. And why didn't I use some sort of birth control? Not only that, why did I do this?

In other cases, the parents may not want to know that much about their adolescents' sexual experiences. They surmise that their children are having intercourse, or have been told so by their children, and the topic is not discussed in great detail. One 20-year-old woman of our acquaintance, with her friends, is in the throes of making decisions about her sexuality. When she brings up the topic with her older brothers and sisters after dinner, the parents unobtrusively but invariably leave the table.

Peer Groups and Sexuality

Peer groups, the arena where sexuality takes place and is discussed endlessly, also produce conflict over sexuality. These conflicts are quite different for boys and girls. Males often congregate in groups around all-male activities, especially athletics. In such groups, a favorite topic centers on sexual exploits and feats of prowess. If one listens to such a group of adolescents, it sounds as though all have had intercourse, and with a large number of women.

In contrast, girls (at least through the 1960's) are under a different pressure—to remain a virgin until marriage or at least engagement. Having intercourse may lead to ostracism from the group, to being labeled "loose." Alix Shulman describes the different attitudes of boy and girl adolescents in her amusing and poignant book, *Memoirs of an Ex-Prom Queen.* She has been crowned Queen at a high school dance and for several months has been fighting off the sexual advances of her steady boyfriend Joey, the high school hero. Joey, having just scored 40 points in a basketball game, is basking in the glory.

> The music stopped. "Great game!" said Nat Karlan, one of Joey's Keystone brothers. They twined their arms over each other's shoulders and moved away. But not before I overheard Nat whisper to Joey, with an intimacy I never achieved, "If you don't get in tonight, friend, you never will!"

> I was stung by the thought. Of course: those forty points overwhelmingly weighted the scales. Tonight Joey would have a powerful advantage. But even if I managed to resist again tonight, who would believe me?

> In the five months I had been going with Joey he'd come closer to "getting in" than anyone else, but I had always managed to resist. What happened to the girls who gave in, and even to those only suspected of giving in, was an unthinkable nightmare. I had myself sat through the now-famous S.L.T. meeting in which Renee Thomas had been expelled for allegedly going all the way. Only a year had passed and already Renee's name was legend. Girls sneered her, boys abused her, her name appeared in all the graffiti, freshmen gaped at her in disbelief. She would never marry in Baybury. She'd have been better off dead. (1972, p. 61).

An interesting paradox arises: the boys are bragging of their exploits while the girls are remaining virgins, or at least trying to do so. Since the sexually competent boys are dating the virginal girls during adolescence, someone was not telling the truth, or at least boys were having intercourse with someone other than high school girlfriends. Data from Kinsey's Institute for Sex Research suggest that in the past boys were more likely to have sexual relations with older women or with prostitutes. Coupled with earlier intercourse for girls, boys in the 1970's seemed more likely to have intercourse with girls their own age who were steady girlfriends or fiancé.

Exaggeration of sexuality certainly seems a factor in boys' discussions of experience. One of the authors has been able to "compare notes" about the sexual practices of a particular group of high school students with her husband, since both had had contact with the same group during high school. According to the husband, most of the males did have intercourse with their girlfriends; according to the author, most of the females did not have intercourse with their boyfriends during high school. When this group was queried as to their sexual experience during high school after they had become adults, the truth was found to be somewhere in between. Most of the girls were not having sex in high school, so the boys, if they were having sex, were having it with someone else!

The 1970's brought a change in peer group standards. Although boys may still brag and girls may still remain silent, most adolescents believe that premarital intercourse is all right as long as the couple is in love or going together. In the Sorenson study, the vast majority of the teenagers thought that intercourse between people in love was acceptable. That being in love is a prerequisite for intercourse, rather than engagement or marriage, is a dramatic change in sexual standards.

The Double Standard—Love and Biology

Not only were girls under constant societal and peer pressure to preserve their virginity in the face of their own and their boyfriend's sexual desires, but boys were under pressure to lose their virginity in the face of their own uncertainties and their girlfriends' resistance. Under this double standard, boys were supposed to have sex without love, and girls were supposed to have love without, or at least before, sex. The scenarios for boy and girl adolescents were as follows.

The male's first sexual experience was thought to be exploitative and self-centered. Sex was not related to intimacy or love, but to genital urges. In a 1961 study by Charles Kirkendall, college men were asked about their sexual experiences. He classified these experiences as mainly physical or emotional. Physical relationships, which almost always preceded love relationships, included intercourse with prostitutes, pickups, casual acquaintances, and casual dating partners. The first two usually involved strangers, the second two involved either "the one-night stand" or "the easy lay." The bragging of sexual exploits almost always occurred with physical relationships. Fewer men had their first sexual experience with women they loved; but when they did, they never discussed the relationship with their friends. Girls have the opposite experience. Before they have intercourse, a love relationship is usually established; sex develops after intimacy and trust are achieved.

Some people believe that dating is the mutual teaching of the physical aspect of sex to girls and the love aspects to boys. William Simon and John Gagnon point up an ironic twist in this process.

> Dating and courtship may well be considered processes in which each sex trains the other in what each wants and expects. What data is available suggests that this exchange system does not always work very smoothly. Thus, normally, it is not uncommon to find that the boy becomes emotionally involved with his partner and therefore lets up trying to seduce her, at the same time that the girl comes to feel that the boy's affection is genuine and therefore sexual intimacy is more permissible. (1969, p. 15)

The preceding discussion clearly demonstrates the sex-stereotyped nature of sexuality. The boy is expected to be aggressive, assertive, and exploitative (that is, "masculine") while the girl is expected to be passive, tender, and romantic (that is, "feminine"). Each sex is being denied the full sexual experience, the boys being denied the tender aspects, the girls the physical aspects. As in all other areas of our lives, a combination of both the masculine and feminine aspects of sexuality make for more satisfying sex lives. Thankfully, sexual behavior seems to be one area in which sex-role barriers are being broken down, albeit slowly.

Teenage Pregnancy

> It was kind of like we were taking a chance all along. I wasn't too careful as far as birth control was concerned. Sometimes we took the precautions, and then sometimes not. I don't know why, we never really got into me

> getting the pill or anything like that. And we knew we were taking this
> chance. (Maxtone-Graham, 1973, p. 385)

One in ten of all American teenage girls (aged 15 to 19) will become pregnant every year. And, of the sexually active teenage girls, one in six will become pregnant. These startling statistics are, of course, due to the increased sexuality in the 1970's teenage culture, and most of these pregnancies are unintentional. Unintentional pregnancies have several causes: pure and simple ignorance about how one gets pregnant, feelings of embarrassment about sexuality, lack of spontaneity or birth control devices, no information about clinics and physicians, little knowledge about birth control, and the belief that "it can't happen to me."

Katrina Maxtone-Graham interviewed seventeen women and girls who became *Pregnant by Mistake.* Their experiences illustrate all of the causes we have mentioned. Patti believed that it couldn't happen to her, just as one-third of all girls believe you cannot get pregnant if you don't want to. When Maxtone-Graham asked if Patti ever worried about getting pregnant, she replied:

> No, 'cause I had never used any contraceptive before and, you know, like never pulled out—withdrawal. And I have never gotten—you know, even been scared of getting pregnant. But I was late for my period . . . and all of a sudden I just knew I was pregnant.
>
> I don't believe it; you know, people try for years and years to conceive and —one time. (p. 202)

Another woman, a 45-year-old sex education counselor who became pregnant at age 22 in 1948, described her experience. Catherine believes that ignorance is as widespread in the 1970's as it was three decades ago.

> I am startled today to find out that girls who are twenty-two years old, as I was, who are in college, as I was, are as ignorant in many ways as I was— about human physiology, how you get pregnant, what you do to prevent conception, and literally what an abortion is all about.
>
> Anyway, my story is essentially that I was a twenty-two year-old girl, I was educated by nuns, Dominican nuns, in convent schools until I was eighteen—when I managed to escape, with great loud shouts and noises, and insisted on going to the University of Chicago.

Anyway, so there I was. I went off to the University of Chicago, and among other things I discovered boys; and therefore I discovered sex. And without the goofiest idea at all, literally, like most young girls, of what it was all about. Quite literally, not any real understanding. But it was just absolutely smashing. I enjoyed it thoroughly.

I knew that intercourse led to pregnancy. I just didn't know how intercourse was really done. In that sense of ignorance, I had no concept about intercourse itself. I was like most girls, including the girls of today. You can sit in on interviews upstairs and still be startled with the idea that most girls have it in their heads that intercourse is one activity, and pregnancy is another. (pp. 286–288)

This ignorance on the part of adolescents has led to the United States having one of the highest rates of teenage childbearing in the world. As of 1970, we had 58 births per 1,000 females 15 to 19 years old. Compare this to 5 in Japan, around 30 in Sweden, France, and Western Germany, and 44 in Great Britain in the same year (Callahan, 1976).

Of the 1 million American 15- to 19-year-old girls who got pregnant in 1974, 600,000 of them delivered their babies. Interestingly, most of the girls (90 percent of them) kept their babies (Zelnick and Kantner, 1974). In fact, more unmarried teenagers keep their babies than unmarried young adults in their early twenties. Unfortunately, these adolescent mothers are at risk for a number of problems: they are more likely to drop out of school, earn low wages, be unemployed, be on welfare, have large families, and, if they were married or did get married, become divorced. As Arthur Campbell pessimistically stated:

The girl who has an illegitimate child has 90% of her life's script written for her. She will probably drop out of school; even if someone else in her family helps to take care of the baby, she will probably not be able to provide for herself and her child; she may feel impelled to marry someone she might not have chosen. Her life choices are few, and most of them bad. (1968, p. 238)

How can the problem of the rise in unwanted and early pregnancies be solved? In 1976 the Alan Guttmacher Institute outlined a national program that would offer adequate sex-education courses, family planning programs, pregnancy counseling services, legal abortion centers (in *all* areas of the country, not just the urban centers), prenatal and postnatal care, social services, national health insurance, and research on new techniques of birth control. Clearly, we are a long way from the provision of such services for our young.

Sex Education

> When I got to the University of Chicago, I had credits from a high school that taught me biology and sociology. And when I got to the University of Chicago I discovered that in biology one is supposed to learn about the reproductive system. However, in my biology courses in high school we did not touch on the reproductive system, including the reproductive system of the frog! Although we had dissected the frogs, we had just never mentioned how new little frogs came into being! (Maxtone-Graham, 1973, p. 287)

Ignorance about sexuality abounds, even in a society that purports to be sophisticated in sexual matters. This ignorance is not limited to young people nor to the less educated. As recently as the 1960's, over one-half of a student population believed that masturbation caused mental illness. Well, you might say, students in the 1960's had little sex education and might be duped into believing such a thing. But these were not run-of-the-mill students; these were graduating medical students, ready to embark upon their practices. If it were not enough that half of the medical students had this misconception, one-fifth of their medical school faculty did too (Greenbank, 1961)! If even the medical profession receives little training in sexuality, it is no wonder that our adolescents are so naive.

Let's look at the questions high school students actually ask about sex to see what they know and do not know. In 1976 Barbara Greenspan met with over 1,000 high school girls in small groups to discuss their sexual concerns. After giving a brief lecture on sexual anatomy, menstruation, and intercourse, the girls were asked what they would like to know. In a permissive, open atmosphere, there was no lack of inquiries, as you can see in Table 9-1. Many of the questions concerned pregnancy: how do you know if you are pregnant; can you get pregnant with intercourse; when can you get pregnant; what is the possibility of becoming pregnant if you do not use contraception. A glance at the questions is not reassuring; high

TABLE 9-1
High School Girls' Questions about Sexuality

INTERCOURSE

What is a cherry?
How do you French?
What do you do when you go parking?
Do rubbers make it less enjoyable for the male?

Is the hymen always broken the first time?
What makes guys horny?
When can you get pregnant?
How can you tell if you are pregnant without going to a doctor?

Should we keep our babies if we are pregnant?
Can you get pregnant by French kissing?
Is sex before marriage illegal?
Can a woman have sex during her period?

Does using a tampon interfere with your virginity?
What does jerk off mean?
On your first time "doing it," does it really hurt that much?
Can you have intercourse when you are pregnant?

Will a rubber burst?
What is the possibility of getting pregnant if you use no contraception?
How can you tell if you are getting serious?
Is intercourse necessary for becoming pregnant?
Should we go all the way on a first date?

From Greenspan (1976).

school students in the 1970's are still ignorant about sexual matters.

Sex education is not as universal as one might think. Even though 80 percent of parents of adolescents in the mid-1970's favor teaching sex education and contraception to unmarried teenagers, in 1975 only one-fifth of the states mandated sex education courses for adolescents, although over one-half required health education. Even those which teach sex education either prohibit birth control education or just neglect to mention it. The whole field of sex education may be biased against females, as the girls are the ones getting pregnant, the ones rearing the children, and the ones who have "90 percent of their life's script written for them before they are 20, with most of the script being bad."

GROWN-UP EQUAL

We leave the adolescent ready to embark upon adulthood, having acquired most of the society's expectations and beliefs about sex roles through the various socialization agents. Incorporating this information into their own sex role identity, young adults may perpetuate these beliefs through their roles as parents, teachers, and community members. The less sex-typed our children are, the less sex-typed their chilren will be.

And so, even though the entire process seems sometimes slow, there *is* progress. More and more adolescent girls are on the playing field, in the electronic shop, and on an academic track. And more and more proudly report that they plan careers as lawyers, electronics engineers, and scientists. In many sections of American adolescent society, the question is no longer "What will I do until I get married or have children?" but "What career do I wish to enter?" For adolescent boys, the changes in sex-role identity seem to be more hesitant, perhaps because they are more elusive. Striving for more equal relationships and participation in child care are some time off for the adolescent boy, and being more nurturing and expressive are not stressed in the adolescent years.

CONCLUSION

chapter ten

What are little boys made of, made of?
What are little boys made of?
Love and care
And skin and hair
That's what little boys are made of.

What are little girls made of, made of?
What are little girls made of?
Care and love
And (see above)
That's what little girls are made of.

Equally haired and equally cared for, children are really more alike than different. If we wanted to divide them up and find differences, there are any number of possible criteria by which to group them. Focusing on height, we could group them into tall and short and find differences in the length of their strides, their scores on the basketball court, and the number of months they could wear a pair of jeans before outgrowing them. Focusing on dexterity, we could group them into lefties and righties and find differences in the difficulties they have cutting with a standard pair of pinking shears, the discomfort they feel sitting at a right-handed school desk, and the direction they face when they swing a bat. And, focusing on sex, we could find differences in their levels of aggression and activity, their spatial, mathematical, and verbal abilities, their self-confidence, and their achievement orientation.

Finding differences among groups of children would not, however, enable us to predict how a tall child would perform on a high jump, or how a left-handed child would handle a fly-casting fishing rod. Having actually found some differences between boys on the average and girls on the average (though far fewer than might generally be believed), we could still not predict how a girl would manage a soap box derby on a 55° angle hill or how a boy would react to his kid brother's losing a balloon. The fact is that, with all the findings we have cited on sex differences, none tell us how the *individual* child would behave.

When we attempt to learn about an individual child's general development, or about his or her sex-role development in particular, we look to a myriad of factors. First, the culture in which the child grows has an impact on the degree of sex typing to which the child is exposed and to which he or she is expected to adapt; specifically, the culture affects the behavior of persons in the child's life space and influences these persons' reactions to the child's behavior. These two factors, one analogous to modeling and the other to reinforcement, affect the child's perceptions of the actions and reactions of others, mediated, of course, by his or her own cognitive maturity. Alerted to the ways in which members of the culture "ought" to be behaving, the child nevertheless recognizes that different behaviors are expected under different circumstances and learns to alter his or her own behavior to suit the situation. Thus, the same boy who says "Flake off!" to a girl wishing to join his gang in a game of kick-the-can might appreciatively accept her advice on his tennis backhand when his peer group is not around. And the girl who makes straight A's in math through elementary and high school might nearly flunk when she shares a calculus course with her boyfriend. In adulthood, the squeamish female lays the stereotype to rest when ministering to the needs of a sick child; and the hard-nosed soldier proves his sensitivity when a new recruit falls on the battlefield. Often, though, societal demands and expectations override the situation, and people mask their individuality behind the stereotype and conform to it, and in so doing, they add to it one more kernel of truth. This is an enigmatic phenomenon, since we know that we conform to stereotypes even when we don't accept them as truly part of ourselves.

But the mediators of sex-typed behaviors and attitudes represent a formidable force in our culture. Parents, siblings, teachers, administrators, books, and television all contribute to our awareness of the expectations society holds for us. Children, by observing these mediators and by absorbing their message, soon construct a fairly accurate picture of sex roles. Their perception of sex roles is, however, always changing: with their intellectual growth and widening world comes access to new information. The toddler sees that the world divides into two groups and that mommies provide solace and daddies play. By preschool, features of the dichotomy are fleshed out: mommies also iron, cook, and care for babies; daddies go to work and take out the garbage. Children begin to classify toys, as well as people and behavior, by gender, showing a preference for boy-type play materials. Older children encompass personality characteristics, too, into the dichotomy and, by adolescence, the construction of sex roles is complete, reflecting the view of society as a whole.

Not only does the sex-role picture get filled in as the child gets older, but it becomes less inflexible, more amenable to change. Preschoolers, whose thought processes are rigid and simplistic, perceive sex roles as ironclad. Relying on the incomplete information provided by their narrow world and limited maturity, they infer that if they come from a family in which the mother drinks coffee and the father tea, that mommies, and only mommies, drink coffee and that daddies, and only daddies, drink tea. Despite even the conscious and conscientious efforts of parents to raise their children in an "equalitarian" manner, the strong sex typing almost invariably occurs at this age, lessening as the child gains the flexibility associated with more sophisticated intellectual abilities.

By adolescence, when the individual's view of sex role corresponds to the view of his or her culture, the notion of sex role represents not so much a shackle as a shroud. As adults, we are not bound by sex role, we are capable of entertaining some flexibility of thought about sex role and of accepting varying degrees of deviation from standard masculine or feminine behavior. But, we *are* influenced by it. Examining the way we and others treat children, we can see just how powerful and pervasive its influence is. Though the effort is not a concerted one, we parents, teachers, students, medical personnel, day care workers, scriptwriters, novelists, and community figures steer children into a groove on the basis of their sex.

The questions we must now ask are: Are the qualities we describe as "masculine" or "feminine" qualities that every mature adult should aspire to possess? Are the dual roles toward which we are steering children functional, or will they prove obsolete? Judging by current trends, the future will hold very different demands for our children than for us. Marriage patterns are changing. Though the percentage of women marrying remains constant, they first marry at a later age, and thus they are closer in age to their grooms than previously. Divorce rates are rising constantly, but so are the rates of remarriage, particularly for men. Family patterns are changing in another way: women are having fewer children, and later in life. This in turn leads to changes in work patterns, with women remaining in the work force longer and, if they leave it at all for childrearing, returning to it sooner.

The implications of these changes are vast. Preparing girls for pocket-money careers is already dysfunctional, since most families require two working members simply to maintain their standard of living. Its dysfunctionality in terms of the lower pay they receive and the lower status positions they occupy will become increasingly obvious in the future unless we begin to prepare girls for their expanding labor force participation. One of the ways we can be, and sometimes already are, contributing to the career development of girls is by making them aware of the predominance the role work is likely to play both in terms of their livelihood (especially in the event of divorce, widowhood, or separation) and in terms of their self-identity and self-fulfillment. While a family will continue to be of major importance to women, as to men, one's work role will prove to be of critical interest as well.

Trends that increase women's labor force participation reverberate to the home situation, where family roles, of necessity, shift to accommodate to the woman's new reponsibilities. It is becoming a fact of life that the running of a household, in terms of housekeeping, child care, and home management, is a family responsibility steadily less definable by sex role. As women enjoy increased participation in the world of work, men enjoy increased participation in the world of the family, displaying previously masked stores of nurturance, warmth, and flexibility. For this new aspect of the male role, we need to prepare boys.

Children—boys and girls alike—should embark upon their future roles as productive members of society and as self-respecting, self-assured individuals without the extra baggage of sex roles to channel them in directions indicated by little more than the presence or absence of an X chromosome! While the world continues to divide them into "he" and "she," we must remember that they are individuals first.

REFERENCES

Abel, T. E. and Jaffe, N. F. Cultural background of female puberty. *American Journal of Psychotherapy*, 1950, *4*, 90-113.

Accent on You, Tampax, Incorporated. Lake Success, NY, p. 13. Reprinted with permission.

Allport, G. W. *The nature of prejudice*. Cambridge, Mass.: Addison-Wesley Publishing Co., 1954.

Alpert, R., Stellwagen, G. and Becker, D. Psychological factors in mathematics education. *School Mathematics Study Group Newsletter*, 1963, *15*, 17-24.

Alther, L. *Kinflicks*. New York: Alfred A. Knopf, Inc., 1976.

Angrist, S. S. The study of sex roles. *Journal of Social Issues*, 1969, *25*, 215-232.

Apgar, V. A proposal for a new method of evaluation of the newborn infant. *Current Researches in Anesthesia and Analgesia*, 1953, *32*, 260-267.

Apgar, V. and James, L. Further observations on the newborn scoring system. *American Journal of Diseases of Children*, 1962, *104*, 419-428.

Apgar, V., Holaday, D., James, L., Weisbrot, I. and Bernen, C. Evaluation of the newborn infant—second report. *Journal of the American Medical Association*, 1958, *168*, 1985-1988.

Atkinson, J. W. (Ed.), *Motives in fantasy, action and society*. Princeton: Van Nostrand, 1958.

Atkinson, J. W. and Feather, N. (Eds.), *A theory of achievement motivation*. New York: John Wiley & Sons, 1966.

Atkinson, J. W. and Litwin, G. Achievement motive and test anxiety conceived as motive to approach success and motive to avoid failure. *Journal of Abnormal and Social Psychology*, 1960, *60*, 52-63.

Bandura, A. Social learning theory of identificatory processes. In D. A. Goslin (Ed.), *Handbook of socialization theory and research*, Chicago: Rand McNally, 1969.

Bandura, A., Ross, D. and Ross, S. A. Transmission of aggressive models. *Journal of Abnormal Social Psychology,* 1961, *63,* 572-582.

Barcus, E. F. Weekend commercial children's television: A study of programming and advertising to children on five Boston stations. A Report for Action for Children's Television, October, 1975.

Baruch, G. K. Maternal influences upon college women's attitudes toward women and work. *Developmental Psychology,* 1972, *6,* 32-37.

Baruch, G. K. Sex-role attitudes of fifth-grade girls. In J. Stacey, S. Bereaud and J. Daniels (Eds.), *And Jill came tumbling after: Sexism in American education,* New York: Dell, 1974.

Baruch, G. K. Sex-role stereotyping, the motive to avoid success and parental identification: A comparison of pre-adolescent and adolescent girls. *Sex Roles,* 1975, *1,* 303-309.

Baumrind, D. and Black, A. E. Socialization practices associated with dimensions of competence in preschool boys and girls, *Child Development,* 1967, *38,* 291-327.

Beckwith, L. Relationships between infants' social behavior and their mothers' behavior. *Child Development,* 1972, *43,* 397-411.

Bell, R. R. Parent-child conflict in sexual values. *Journal of Social Issues,* 1966, *22,* 34-44.

Bell, R. Q. Contributions of human infants to caregiving and social interaction. In M. Lewis and L. A. Rosenblum (Eds.), *The Effects of the Infant on Its Caregiver.* New York: John Wiley and Sons, 1974.

Bell, R. Q. and Castello, N. S. Three tests for sex differences in tactile sensitivity in the newborn. *Biological Neonatorium,* 1964, *7,* 335-47.

Bell, R. Q., Weller, G. M. and Waldrop, M. F. Newborn and pre-schooler: Organization of behavior and relations between periods. *Monographs of the Society for Research in Child Development,* 1971, *36,* (Series Number 142).

Belotti, E. *What are little girls made of? Roots of feminine stereotypes.* New York: Schocken, 1977.

Bem, S. L. Sex role adaptability: One consequence of psychological androgyny. *Journal of Personality and Social Psychology,* 1975, *31,* 624–643.

Bem, S. L. The measurement of psychological androgyny. *Journal of Consulting and Clinical Psychology,* 1974, *42,* 155–162.

Bem, S. L. and Bem, D. J. Case study of nonconscious ideology: Training the woman to know her place. In Bem, D. J. *Beliefs, attitudes and human affairs.* Belmont, Calif.: Brooks/Cole, 1970.

Bem, S. L. and Bem, D. J. Does sex-biased job advertising aid and abet sex discrimination. *Journal of Applied Social Psychology,* 1973, *3,* 6–18.

Bem, S. L. and Lenney, E. Sex typing and the avoidance of cross-sex behavior. *Journal of Personality and Social Psychology,* 1976, *33,* 48–54.

Bergman, J. Are little girls being harmed by Sesame Street? In J. Stacey, S. Béreaud, and J. Daniels (Eds.), *And Jill came tumbling after: Sexism in American education.* New York: Dell Publishing Co., 1974.

Berk. L. E. Effects of variation in the nursery school setting on environmental constraints and children's modes of adaptation. *Child Development,* 1971, *42,* 839–869.

Berry, J. W. Temne and Eskimo perceptual skills. *International Journal of Psychology,* 1966, *1,* 207–229.

Bettelheim, B. *The uses of enchantment.* New York: Alfred A. Knopf, 1976.

Block, J. H. Conceptions of sex role: Some cross-cultural and longitudinal perspectives. *American Psychologist,* 1973, *28,* 512–526.

Block, J. H. Another look at sex differentiation in the socialization behaviors of mothers and fathers. In J. Sherman and F. Denmark (Eds.), *Psychology of Women: Future Directions of Research.* New York: Psychological Dimensions, 1977.

Block, J. H., and Block J. and Harrington, D. M. The relationship of parental teaching strategies to ego-resiliency in preschool children. Paper presented at the Western Psychological Association meeting, San Francisco, April 1974.

Bock, R. D. and Kolakowski, D. Further evidence of sex-linked major-gene influence on human spatial visualizing ability. *American Journal of Human Genetics,* 1973, *25,* 1–14.

Bond, E. K. Perception of form by the human infant. *Psychological Bulletin,* 1972, *77,* (4), 225–245.

Borrow, H. Development of Occupational Motives and Roles. In L. Hoffman and M. Hoffman (Eds.), *Review of Child Development Research, Vol. 20* New York: Russell Sage Foundation, 1966.

Bowerman, C. E. & Kinch, J. W. Changes in family and peer orientation of children in the fourth and tenth grades. *Social Forces,* 1959, *37,* 206–211.

Brazelton, T. B., Yogman, M. W., Als, H., and Tronick, E. The infant as a focus for family reciprocity. In M. Lewis and L. Rosenblum (Eds.), *The child and its family: The genesis of behavior, Vol. II.* New York: Plenum, 1979.

Brindley, J. C., Clarke, P., Hutt, C., Robinson, I. and Wethli, E. Sex differences in the activities and social interaction of nursery school children. In R. P. Michael and J. M. Crooke (Eds.), *Comparative ecology and behavior of primates.* New York: Academic Press, 1973.

Brody, G. F. Sex-role differentiation in play activities of preschool children. Paper presented at the 48th Annual Meeting of the Eastern Psychological Association, New York City, April 1975.

Brophy, J. E. and Good, T. L. Feminization of American elementary schools. *Phi Delta Kappan,* 1973, *67,* 564–66.

Brooks-Gunn, J. Fear of success as a function of situation. Unpublished manuscript.

Brooks-Gunn, J. and Fisch, M. Psychological androgyny and college students' judgements of mental health. *Sex Roles,* in press, 1979.

Brooks, J. and Lewis, M. Person perception and verbal labeling: The development of social labels. Paper presented at the Society for Research in Child Development Meeting, Denver, April 1975.

Brooks, J. and Lewis, M. Infants' responses to strangers: Midget, adult and child. *Child Development* 1976, *4*, 323-332.

Brooks-Gunn, J. and Lewis, M. Early social knowledge. In H. McGurk (Ed.), *Childhood social development.* London: Methuen, in press, 1979.

Brooks, J., Ruble, D. N. and Clarke, A. E. College women's attitudes and expectations concerning menstrual-related changes. *Psychosomatic Medicine,* 1977, *39,* 288-298.

Brooks-Gunn, J. and Ruble, D. N. Socialization and menstrual distress during adolescence: Parental attitudes, first menstrual experience, and preparation for menarche. Paper presented at the Second Annual Interdisciplinary Research Conference on the Menstrual Cycle, St. Louis, May 1978.

Brooks-Gunn, J. and Ruble, D. N. Menarche: The interaction of physiological, cultural and social factors. In A. J. Dan, E. M. Graham and C. Bucher (Eds.), *The menstrual cycle: Synthesis of interdisciplinary research,* New York: Springer, in press.

Broverman, I. K., Broverman, D. M., Clarkson, F. E., Rosenkrantz, P. S., and Vogel, S. R. Sex-role stereotypes and clinical judgments of mental health. *Journal of Consulting Psychology,* 1970, *34,* 1-7.

Bruch, H. *The golden cage.* Cambridge, Mass.: Harvard University Press, 1978.

Burlage, D. C. A preliminary review of research and selected bibliography related to separated and divorced mothers. Boston, Mass.: Harvard Medical School, 1976. Report submitted to the Women's Action Project, Office of Special Concerns, DMEW.

Byrne, D. Parental antecedents of authoritarianism. *Journal of Personality and Social Psychology,* 1965, *1,* 369-73.

Callahan, D. 11 Million Teenagers: What can be done about the epidemic of adolescent pregnancies in the United States. New York: The Alan Guttmacher Institute, 1976.

Campbell, A. A. The role of family planning in the reduction of poverty. *Journal of Marriage and Family,* 1968, *30,* 2-8.

Carlsmith, L. Effect of early father absence on scholastic aptitude. *Harvard Educational Review,* 1964, *34,* 3-21.

Carlson, R. Understanding women: Implications for personality theory and research. *Journal of Social Issues,* 1972, *28* (2), 17-32.

Chafetz, J. S. *Masculine/Feminine or human?: An overview of the sociology of gender roles,* 2nd ed. Itasca, Ill.: F. E. Peacock, 1978, pp. 49-50.

Chellay, C. and Francis, S. The image of the female child on Saturday morning TV commercials. Paper presented at the annual meeting of the International Communications Association, April 1974.

Cherry, L. and Lewis, M. Mothers and two-year-olds: A study of sex-differentiated aspects of verbal interaction. *Developmental Psychology,* 1975, *12*(4), 278-282.

Chesler, P. *Woman and madness.* Garden City, N.Y.: Doubleday, 1972.

The Christian Century, October 1977, pgs. 868-869. "It seems she was guilty of being raped."

Chodorow, N. Being and doing: A cross-cultural examination of the socialization of males and females. In V. Gornick and B. K. Moran (Eds.), *Woman in Sexist Society.* New York: Basic Books, 1971, 259-291.

Clarke, A. E. and Ruble, D. N. Young adolescents' beliefs concerning menstruation. *Child Development,* 1978, *49,* 231-234.

Cohen, L. J. and Campos, J. J. Father, mother and stranger as elicitors of attachment behaviors in infancy. *Developmental Psychology,* 1974, *10,* 146-154.

Coleman, J. S. *The adolescent society.* New York: Glencoe Free Press, 1961.

College Entrance Examination Board. On further examination: Report of the advisory panel on the scholastic aptitude test score decline. New York, 1977.

Colloquy, 1973, *6,* #9.

Condry, J. and Condry, S. Sex differences: A study of the eye of the beholder. *Child Development,* 1976, *47,* 812-819.

Crandall, V. C. Sex differences in expectancy of intellectual and academic reinforcement. In C. P. Smith (Ed.), *Achievement related motives in children.* New York: Russell Sage Foundation, 1969.

Countiss, J. R. *Equity in school athletics: A guide*. New Brunswick, N.J.: The Training Institute for Sex Desegregation of the Public Schools. Rutgers University, 1977.

Cummings, J. M. Passaic County Area Vocational-Technical School, Wayne, N.J. Final Report, Program No. 31. 3995 SRES-101 Pilot Project for Women, June 2, 1975.

D'Andrade, R. G. Sex differences and cultural institutions. In E. E. Maccoby (Ed.), *The development of sex differences*. Stanford: Stanford University Press, 1966.

Davis, P. Surviving the Odds. *New York Times Book Review*. April 30, 1978, pp. 32 and 34.

Dawe, H. C. An analysis of two hundred quarrels of preschool children. *Child Development*, 1934, *5*, 139-157.

Deaux, K. and Emswiller, T. Explanations of successful performance on sex-linked tasks: What's skill for the male is luck for the female. *Journal of Personality and Social Psychology*, 1974, *29*, 80-85.

Deaux, K., White, L. and Farris, E. Skill versus luck: Field and laboratory studies of male and female preferences. *Journal of Personality and Social Psychology*, 1975, *32*, 629-636.

de Beauvoir, S. *The second sex*. New York: Knopf, 1968.

Delaney, J., Lupton, M. J. and Toth, E. *The curse: A cultural history of menstruation*. New York: Dutton, 1976.

Dinitz, S., Dynes, D. and Clarke, A. C. Preference for male or female children: Traditional or affectional. *Marriage and Family Living*, 1954, *16*, 128-130.

Doerr, M. (Untitled letter) *Newsweek*. 1973, *82*, (26), 4.

Douvan, E. Employment and the adolescent. In F. I. Nye and L. W. Hoffman (Eds.). *The employed mother in America*. Chicago: Rand McNally, 1963.

Douvan, E. New sources of conflict in females at adolescence and early adulthood. In J. M. Bardwick *et al.* (Eds.), *Feminine Personality and Conflict*. Monterey, Calif.: Brooks/Cole, 1970.

Douvan, E. The role of models in women's professional development. *Psychology of Women Quarterly*, 1976, *1*, (1), 5-20.

Douvan, E. and Adelson, J. *The Adolescent Experience.* New York: John Wiley and Sons, 1966.

Droege, R. C. Sex differences in aptitude maturation during high school. *Journal of Counseling Psychology,* 1967, *14,* 407-11.

Dunphy, D. C. The social structure of urban adolescent peer groups. *Sociometry,* 1963, XXVI, 230-246.

Dwyer, J. and Mayer, J. Psychological effects of variation in physical appearance during adolescence. *Adolescence,* 1969, *3,* 353-380.

Eaton, C. and Chase, S. Present status of sexism on Sesame Street. Report on Sex Bias in the Public Schools. New York: National Organization for Women, 1977.

Edward, C. P. and Whiting, B. B. Women and dependency. *Politics and Society,* 1974, *4,* 343-355.

Edwards, C. P. and Whiting, B. B. Sibling companions: The interactions of 2- to 3-year-old children with their next older siblings in an East African community. Symposium on Socialization and Intracultural Variation held at the Annual meeting of the American Anthropological Association, Washington, D.C., November 1976.

Edwards, H. *The sociology of sports.* Homewood, Ill.: The Dorsey Press, 1973.

Ehrhardt, A. A., Epstein, R. and Money, J. Fetal androgens and female gender identity in the early treated andrenogenital syndrome. *Johns Hopkins Medical Journal,* 1969, *122,* 160-67.

Ehrhardt, A. A., Evers, K. and Money, J. Influence of androgen and some aspects of sexually dimorphic behavior in women with the late-treated adrenogenital syndrome. *Johns Hopkins Medical Journal,* 1968, *123,* 115-122.

Ehrhardt, A. A. and Money, J. Progestin-induced hermaphroditism: IQ and psychosexual identity in a study of ten girls. *Journal of Sex Research,* 1967, *3,* 83-100.

Elkind, D. A sympathetic understanding of the child six to sixteen. Boston: Allyn and Bacon, 1971.

Emmerich, W. Young children's discriminations of parent and child roles. *Child Development,* 1959, *30,* 403-419.

Emmerich, W. Structure and development of personal-social behaviors in preschool settings. Educational Testing Service—Head Start Longitudinal Study, November 1971.

Emmerich, W., Goldman, K. S., Kirsch, B. and Sharabany, R. Evidence for a transitional phase in the development of gender constancy. *Child Development* 1977, *48,* 930-936.

Erikson, E. *Identity: Youth and crisis.* New York: W. W. Norton and Co., 1968.

Everitt, B. J. and Herbert, J. Adrenal glands and sexual receptivity in female rhesus monkeys. *Nature.* 1969, *222,* 1065-66.

Everitt, B. J. and Herbert, J. The maintenance of sexual receptivity by adrenal androgens in female Rhesus monkeys. *Journal of Endocrinilogy,* 1970, *48.*

Fagot, B. I. The influence of sex of child on parental reactions to toddler children. *Child Development,* 1978, *49,* 459-465.

Fagot, B. I. Sex-related stereotyping of toddlers' behaviors. *Developmental Psychology,* 1973, *9*(3), 429.

Fagot, B. I. Preschool sex stereotyping: Effect of sex of teacher vs. training of teacher. Paper presented to Society for Research in Child Development, New Orleans, Louisiana, March 17-20, 1977.

Fagot, B. and Patterson, G. An *in vivo* analysis of reinforcing contingencies for sex-role behaviors in the preschool child. *Developmental Psychology,* 1969, *1,* 563-568.

Fantz, R. L. and Nevis, S. Pattern preferences and perceptual-cognitive development in early infancy. *Merrill-Palmer Quarterly,* 1967, *13,* 77-108.

Farmer, H., and Bohn, M. Home-career conflict reduction and the level of career interest in women. *Journal of Counseling Psychology,* 1970, *17,* 228-33.

Fask, T. Three women, two men. *New York Times Book Review,* April 30, 1978, 48-49.

Faust, M. S. Developmental maturity as a determinant in prestige of adolescent girls. *Child Development,* 1960, *31,* 173-186.

Ferguson, L. R. Dependency motivation in socialization. In R. A. Hoppe, G. A. Milton and E. C. Simamel (Eds.), *Early expe-*

riences and the process of socialization. New York: Academic Press, 1970.

Feshbach, N. D. Empathic behavior in children. In B. A. Maher (Ed.), *Progress in experimental personality research,* Vol. 8. New York: Academic Press, 1978.

Feshbach, N. D. and Roe, K. Empathy in six- and seven-year-olds. *Child Development,* 1968, *39,* 133–45.

Feshbach, N. D. and Sones, G. Sex differences in adolescent reactions toward newcomers. *Developmental Psychology,* 1971, *4,* 381–86.

Fidell, L. S. Empirical verification of sex discrimination in hiring practices in psychology. *American Psychologist,* 1970, *25,* 1094–1097.

Fitzgerald, D. and Roberts, K. Semantic profiles and psychosexual interests as indicators of identification. *Personnel and Guidance Journal,* 1966, *44,* (8), 802–806.

Flanagan, J. C., Daily, J. T., Shaycroft, M. F., Gorham, W. A., Orr, D. B., Goldberg, I., and Neyman, C. A., Jr. *Counselor's technical manual for interpreting test scores. (Project Talent).* Palo Alto, Calif. 1961.

Fling, S. and Manosevitz, M. Sex typing in nursery school children's play interests. *Developmental Psychology,* 1972, *7,* 146–152.

Frank, A. *The diary of a young girl.* New York: Pocket Books, 1972.

Frazier, A. and Lisonbee, A. K. Adolescent concerns with physique. In R. E. Muuss (Ed.), *Adolescent behavior and society: A book of readings.* New York: Random House, 1971.

Frazier, N. and Sadker, M. *Sexism in school and society.* New York: Harper and Row, 1973.

Freedman, D. C. Film presented at the Biennial Meeting of the Society for Research and Child Development, Philadelphia, PA., 1971.

French, E. G. and Lesser, G. S. Some characteristics of the achievement motive in women. *Journal of Abnormal and Social Psychology,* 1964, *68,* 119–28.

Freud, S. Female sexuality. In *Collected Papers*, Vol. V. New York: Basic Books, 1959 (Originally published 1931).

Freud, S. Some psychical consequences of the anatomical distinction between the sexes. *Collected Papers*, Vol. V. New York: Basic Books, 1959. (Originally published 1925).

Friedan, B. *The feminine mystique.* New York: Dell Publishing co., 1963.

Frieze, I. Women's expectations for and casual attributions of success and failure. In M. T. S. Mednick, S. S. Tangri, and L. W. Hoffman (Eds.), *Women and achievement: Social and motivational analyses.* Washington, D.C.: Hemisphere, 1975.

Frieze, I. H., Parsons, J. E., Johnson, P. B., Ruble, D. N. and Zellman, G. L. *Women and sex roles: A social psychological perspective.* New York: W. W. Norton, 1978.

Frisch, R. E. Influences on age of menarche. *The Lancet*, 1973 (May 5), I, 1007.

Frisch, R. E. Menstrual cycles: Fatness as a determinant of minimum weight for height necessary for their maintenance or onset. *Science*, 1974, 949-951.

Frueh, T. and McGhee, P. Traditional sex role development and amount of time spent watching television. *Developmental Psychology*, 1975, *11*, 109.

Garai, J. E. and Scheinfeld, A. Sex differences in mental and behavioral traits. *Genetic Psychology Monographs*, 1968, *77*, 169-299.

Gesell, A. *The first 5 years of life.* Yale University Clinic of Child Development. New York: Harper, 1940.

Ginsburg, H. and Opper, S. *Piaget's theory of intellectual development: An introduction.* Englewood Cliffs, N.J.: Prentice-Hall, 1969.

Glancy, D. J. Women in Law: The dependable ones. *Harvard Law School Bulletin*, 1970, *21*, 23-33.

Goggin, J.E. Sex differences in the activity level of preschool children as a possible precursor of hyperactivity. *The Journal of Genetic Psychology*, 1975, *127*, 75-81.

Gold, M. and Douvan, E. (Eds.) *Adolescent development: Readings in research and theory.* Boston: Allyn and Bacon, 1969.

Goldberg, P. Are women prejudiced against women? *Transaction*, 1968, April, 28–30.

Goldberg, S. and Lewis, M. Play behavior in the year-old infant: Early sex differences. *Child Development*, 1969, *40*, 21–31.

Goldstein, A. and Chance, J. Effects of practice on sex-related differences on performance on embedded figures. *Psychonomic Science*, 1965, *3*, 361–362.

Golightly, C., Nelson, D., and Johnson, J. Children's dependency scales. *Developmental Psychology*, 1970, *3*, 114–18.

Goodenough, E. W. Interest in persons as an aspect of sex differences in the early years. *Genetic Psychology Monographs*, 1957, *55*, 287–323.

Gould, L. W. A fabulous child's story. *Ms.* December 1972, 74–76; 105–106.

Greenbank, R. K. Are medical students learning psychiatry? *Pennsylvania Medical Journal*, 1961, *64*, 989–992.

Greenspan, B. One day program in human sexuality: An experience in an Alabama high school. Washington, D.C.: The Population Institute, 1976.

Gregory, I. Anterospective data following childhood loss of a parent. II. Pathology, performance, and potential among college students. *Archives of General Psychiatry*, 1965, *13*, 110–120.

Gross, N. and Trask. A. E. *The sex factor and the management of schools.* New York: John Wiley & Sons, 1976.

Growing up and liking it, p. 15. Reprinted with permission. Personal Products: Milltown, N.J. 1976.

Grusec, J. F. and Brinker, D. B. Reinforcement for imitation as a social learning determinant with implications for sex-role development. *Journal of Personality and Social Psychology*, 1972, *21*, 149–158.

Guttentag, M. and Bray, H. *Undoing sex stereotypes: Research and resources for educators.* New York: McGraw-Hill, 1976.

Hacker, H.M. Women as a minority group. *Social Forces*, 1951, *30*, 60–69.

Haley, A. *Roots.* New York: Doubleday, 1976.

Hammer, M. Preference for a male child: Cultural factors. *Journal of Individual Psychology,* 1970, *26,* 54–56.

Hampson, J. L. and Hampson, J. G. The ontogenesis of sexual behavior in man. In W. C. Young (Ed.), *Sex and internal secretions.* Baltimore: Wilkins and Wilkins, 1961.

Harlow, H. F. The development of affectional patterns in infant monkeys. In B. M. Foss (Ed.), *Determinants of infant behavior, Vol. 1.* London: Methuen, 1961.

Harlow, H. F. and Zimmerman, R. R. Affectional responses in the infant monkey. *Science.* 1959, *130,* 421–432.

Harmon, L. W. The childhood and adolescent career plans of college women. *Journal of Vocational Behavior,* 1971, *I,* 45–56.

Harris, G. W. Sex differences, brain development and brain function. *Endocrinology,* 1964, *75,* 627–647.

Harrison, L. CroMagnon women—in eclipse. *The Science Teacher,* 1975, *42,* 8–11.

Harrison, L. and Passero, R. N. Sexism in the language of elementary school textbooks. *Science and Children,* 1975, *2,* 22–25.

Hartley, R. E. Sex-role pressures and the socialization of the male child, *Psychological Reports,* 1959, *5,* 457–468. Also in J. Stacey, S. Béreaud, and J. Daniels (Eds.), *And Jill came tumbling after: Sexism in American education.* New York: Dell, 1974.

Hartley, R. Children's concepts of male and female roles. *Merrill-Palmer Quarterly,* 1959–1960, *6,* 83–91.

Hartup, W. W. and Zook, E. A. Sex-role preferences in three- and four-year old children. *Journal of Consulting Psychology,* 1960, *24,* 420–426.

Hays, H. R. *The dangerous sex: The myth of feminine evil.* New York: G. P. Putnam's Sons, 1964.

Hedges, J. Women workers and manpower demands in the 1970's. *Monthly Labor Review,* 1970, 19.

Heide, F. P. *Growing Anyway Up.* New York: Bantam, 1978.

Helitzer, M. and Heyel, C. *The youth market.* New York: Media Books, 1970.

Hendrick, R. and Seal, C. Review of research and the effects of television advertising on children. Unpublished manuscript: Harvard University Graduate School of Education, Jan. 1977.

Hennig, M. Family dynamics for developing positive achievement motivation in women: The successful woman executive. *Annals of the New York Academy of Sciences,* 1973, *208,* 76-81.

Herzog, E. and Sudin, C. Children in fatherless families. In B. M. Caldwell and M. N. Ricciuti (Eds.), *Review of Child Development,* Vol. 3. Chicago: University of Chicago Press, 1973.

Hetherington, E. M. Effects of parental absence on sex-typed behaviors on negro and white preadolescent males. *Journal of Abnormal and Social Psychology,* 1966, *4,* 87-91.

Hetherington, E. M. Effects of father absence on personality development in adolescent daughters. *Developmental Psychology,* 1972, *7,* 313-326.

Hetherington, E.M. and Frankie, G. Effects of parental dominance, warmth, and conflict on imitation on children. *Journal of Personality and Social Psychology,* 1967, *6,* 119-25.

Hewitt, L. S. Age and sex differences in the vocational aspirations of elementary school children. *The Journal of Social Psychology,* 1975, *96,* 173-177.

Hill, K. T. and Sarason, S. B. The relations of test anxiety and defensiveness to test and school performance over the elementary-school years. *Monographs of the Society for Research Child Development,* 1966, *31* #104.

Hilton, T. L. and Berglund, G. W. Sex differences in mathematics achievement—A longitudinal study. *The Journal of Educational Research,* 1974, *67*(5), 232-37.

Hoffman, L. W. Early childhood experience and women's achievement motives. *The Journal of Social Issues,* 1972, *28,* 129-156.

Hoffman, L. W. Fear of success in males and females: 1965 and 1971. *Journal of Consulting and Clinical Psychology,* 1974, *42,* 353-358.

Hoffman, L. W. The value of children to parents and the decrease in family size. *Proceedings of the American Philosophical Society,* 1975, *119,* 430-438.

Hoffman, L. W. Changes in family roles, socialization and sex differences. *American Psychologist,* 1977, *32,* 644-657.

Hoffman, M. L. and Levine, L. E. Early sex differences in empathy. *Developmental Psychology,* 1976, *12* (6), 557-558.

Hollander, E. P. and Marcia, J. E. Parental determinants of peer orientation and self-orientation among preadolescents. *Developmental Psychology,* 1970, *2,* 292-302.

Horner, M. S. Femininity and successful achievement: A basic inconsistency. J. M. Bardwick, et al. (Eds.), *Feminine personality and conflict.* Monterey, Calif.: Brooks/Cole, 1970.

Horner, M. S. Toward an understanding of achievement-related conflicts in women. *Journal of Social Issues,* 1972, *28,* 157-176.

Horner, M. S. The measurement and behavioral implications of fear of success in women. In J. W. Atkinson and J. B. Raynor (Eds.), *Motivation and achievement.* New York: John Wiley and Sons, 1974.

Horney, K. The dread of women. *International Journal of Psychoanalysis,* 1932, *13,* 359.

Horney, K. *Feminine psychology.* New York: W. W. Norton, 1967.

Horney, K. The flight from womanhood, *International Journal of Psychoanalysis,* 1926, *7,* 324-339.

House Committee on Education and Labor and the Senate Committee on Labor and Public Welfare, Title IX—Prohibition of Sex Discrimination, P. L. 92-318, A Compilation of Federal Laws, As Amended through December 31, 1974 (Washington, D.C.: GPO, February, 1975), p. 43.

Hunt, M. *Sexual behavior in the seventies.* Chicago: Playboy Press, 1974.

Iglitzin, L. B. The child's eye view of sex roles. *Today's Education.* 1972, *61,* 23-25.

Jackson, P. W. and Lahaderne, H. M. Inequalities of teacher-pupil contacts. *Psychology in the Schools,* 1967, *4,* 204-11.

Jenkins, C. P. Psychological and social precursors of coronary disease: A review of recent findings. *New England Journal of Medicine,* 1971, *284,* 244-255.

Johnson, D. D. Sex differences in reading cultures. *Reading Research Quarterly,* 1973-74, *9,* 69-83.

Jones, M. C. The later careers of boys who were early- or late-maturing. *Child Development,* 1957, *28,* 113-128.

Jones, M. C. Psychological correlates of somatic development. *Child Development,* 1965, *36,* 899-916.

Kagan, J. Acquisition and significance of sex typing and sex role identity. In M. M. Hoffman and L. Hoffman (Eds.), *Review of Child Development,* Vol. I. New York: Russell Sage, 1964.

Kagan, J. The child's sex role classification of school objects. *Child Development,* 1964, *35,* 1051-1056.

Kagan, J. Reflectivity-impulsivity and reading ability in primary grade children. *Child Development,* 1965, *36,* 609-628.

Kagan, J. A conception of early adolescence. In J. Kagan and R. Roles (Eds.), *12 to 16: Early Adolescence.* New York: Norton, 1972.

Kagan, J. and Lemkin, J. The child's differential perception of parental attributes. *Journal of Abnormal and Social Psychology,* 1960, *61,* 440-447.

Kagan, J. and Moss, H. *Birth to maturity, a study in psychological development.* New York: John Wiley and Sons, 1962.

Katcher, A. The discrimination of sex differences by young children. *The Journal of Genetic Psychology,* 1955, *87,* 131-143.

Kessen, W., Haith, M. A. and Salapatek, P. H. Human infancy: A bibliography and guide. In P. H. Mussen (Eds.), *Manual of Child Psychology* Vol. 2, New York: John Wiley and Sons, 1970.

Kinsey, A. C., Pomeroy, W. B., and Martin, C. E. Sexual behavior in the human male. Philadelphia: W. B. Saunders, 1948.

Kinsey, A. C., Pomeroy, W. B., Martin, C. E., Gebhard, B. H. and Associates. Sexual behavior in the human female. Philadelphia: W. B. Saunders, 1953.

Kirkendall, C. A. *Premarital intercourse and interpersonal relationships.* New York: Julian Press, 1961.

Kohlberg, L. A cognitive-developmental analysis of children's sex-role concepts and attitudes. In E. Maccoby (Ed.), *The development of sex differences.* Stanford, Calif.: Stanford University Press, 1966.

Kohlberg, L. Stages and sequence: The cognitive-developmental approval to socialization. In I. A. Goslin (Ed.), *Handbook of Socialization Theory and Research.* Chicago: Rand McNally, 1969.

Kotelchuck, M. The infant's relationship to the father: Experimental evidence. In M. E. Lamb (Ed.), *The role of the father in child development.* New York: John Wiley and Sons, 1976.

Kuckenburg, K. G. *Effect of early father absence on scholastic aptitude.* Unpublished doctoral dissertation. Harvard University, 1963.

Labov, W. Rules for ritual insults. In D. Sudnow (Ed.), *Studies in social interaction,* New York: Free Press, 1972.

Landy, E. E. Sex differences in some aspects of smoking behavior. *Psychological Reports,* 1967, *20,* 575-580.

Lamb, M. E. The development of mother-infant and father-infant attachments in the second year of life. *Developmental Psychology,* 1977, *13,* 637-645.

Lamb, M. E. The father's role in the infant's social world. In J. H. Stevens and M. Matthews (Eds.), *Mother/child, father/child relationships.* Washington, D.C.: National Association for Education of Young Children, 1978.

Lambert, W. E., Yackley, A., and Hein, R. N. Child training values of English Canadian and French Canadian parents. *Canadian Journal of Behavioral Science,* 1971, *3,* 217-36.

LaPierre, R. T. Type-rationalizations of group apathy. *Social Forces,* 1936, *15,* 232-237.

Lasker, B. *Race attitudes in children.* New York: Henry Holt, 1929.

Lauersen, N. and Whitney, S. *It's your body: A women's guide to gynecology.* New York: Grossett and Dunlop, 1977.

Lee, P. C. Reinventing sex roles in the early childhood setting. In D. Cohen, (Ed.), *Growing Free: Ways to help children over-*

come sex-role stereotypes. Association for Childhood Education International, 1976.

Leifer, A. D., Collins, W. A., Gross, B. M., Taylor, P. H., Andrews, L. and Blacknert, E. R. Developmental aspects of variables relevant to observational learning. *Child Development,* 1971, *42,* 509-16.

Leonard, A. *Public Action Coalition on Toys Newsletter,* 1976.

Lerner, R. M. The development of stereotyped expectancies of body build-behavior relations. *Child Development,* 1969, *40,* 137-141.

Lesser, G. S., Kravitz, R. and Packard, R. Experimental arousal of achievement motivation in adolescent girls. *Journal of Abnormal and Social Psychology,* 1963, *66,* 59-66.

Levine, S. N. Sex differences in the brain. *Scientific American,* 1966, *214,* 84-90.

Levine, S. Stress and behavior. *Scientific American,* 1971, *224,* 26-31.

Levine, S. N. and Mullins, R. F. Hormonal influences on brain organization in infant rats. *Science,* 1966, *152,* 1585-1592.

Levitin, T. E. and Chananie, J. D. Responses of female primary school teachers to sex-typed behaviors in male and female children. *Child Development,* 1972, *43,* 1309-16.

Lewis, M. Parents and children: Sex-role development. *School Review,* 1972, *80* (2), 229-240.

Lewis, M. and Brooks, J. Self, other and fear: Infants' reactions to people. In M. Lewis and L. Rosenblum (Eds.), *The origins of fear: The origins of behavior,* Volume II. New York: John Wiley and Sons, 1974.

Lewis, M. and Coates, D. Mother-infant interaction and cognitive performance. Paper presented at the 6th annual meeting of the International Primatological Society, Cambridge, England, August 1976.

Lewis, M. and Freedle, R. Mother-infant dyad: The cradle of meaning. In P. Pliner, L. Kramer, and T. Alloway (Eds.), *Communication and affect: Language and thought.* New York: Academic Press, 1973.

Lewis, M. and Kreitzberg, V. The effects of gender, birth order, and social class on social and cognitive development in the first two years of life. Work in progress, Educational Testing Service.

Lewis, M. and Rosenblum, L. (Eds.). *The effect of the infant on its caregiver: The origins of behavior,* Volume I. New York: John Wiley and Sons, 1974.

Lewis, M. V. and Kaltreider, L. W. Attempts to overcome sex stereotyping in vocational education. University Park, Pennsylvania: Institute for Research on Human Resources, The Pennsylvania State University, November 1976.

Lewis, M. and Rosenblum, L. (Eds.). *The child and its family: The genesis of behavior.* Volume II. New York: Plenum, 1979.

Levy, B. and Stacey, J. Sexism in the elementary school: A backward and forward look. *Phi Delta Kappan,* 1973, *67,* 105–123.

Liebert, R., McCall, R. and Hanratty, M. Effects of sex-typed information on children's toy preferences. *Journal of Genetic Psychology,* 1971, *119,* 133–136.

Lockheed, M. E. Female motive to avoid success: A psychological barrier or a response to deviancy? *Sex Roles,* 1975, *1,* 41–50.

Looft, W. R. Sex differences in the expression of vocational aspirations by elementary school children. *Developmental Psychology,* 1971, *5,* 366.

Lorenz, K. *On aggression.* New York: Harcourt and Brace, 1966.

Luchins, A. S. Mechanization in problem-solving—the effect of einstellung. *Psychological Monographs,* 1942, *54,* no. 6.

Maccoby, E. E. et al. Hormones and behavior: First report of the Stanford longitudinal study. Symposium presented at the SRCD meetings. Denver, April 1975.

Macfarlane, A. *The Psychology of Childbirth* in *The Developing Child Series,* J. Bruner, M. Cole, and B. Lloyd (Eds.), Cambridge, Mass.: Harvard University Press, 1977.

MacLeod, J. How to hold a wife: A bridegroom's guide. *Village Voice,* Feb. 11, 1975, 5.

Manes, A. L. and Melnyk. Televised models of female achievement. *Journal of Applied Social Psychology*, 1974, *4*, 365–74.

Marshall, E. and Hample, S. (compilers). *Children's letters to God.* New York: Simon and Schuster, Pocket Books, 1966.

Martin, R. Student sex and behavior as determinants of the type and frequency of teacher-student contacts. *Journal of School Psychology*, 1972, *10*, 339–347.

Masica, D. N. and Lewis, V. G. I. Q., fetal sex hormones and cognitive patterns: Studies in the testicular feminizing syndrome of androgen insensitivity. *Johns Hopkins Medical Journal*, 1969, *123*, 105–114.

Masica, D. N., Money, J. and Ehrhardt, A. A. Fetal feminization and female gender identity in the testicular feminizing syndrome of androgen insensitivity. *Archives of Sexual Behavior*, 1971, *1*, 131–142.

Matthews, W. S. Conduites sociales et conduites d'agression: Etude différentielle des comportements relationnels des enfants en fonction de leur statut sociométrique. (Social and aggressive behaviors and their relation to the sociometric status of preschool-age children). Unpublished thesis, Université de Paris, 1972.

Matthews, W. S. Sex-role perception, portrayal, and preference in the fantasy play of young children. *Resources in Education*, August, 1977, Document No. ED 136949.

Matthews, W. S. *The nature of fantasy in the spontaneous play of young children.* (Doctoral dissertation, Cornell University, 1975). *D. A. International*, 36, (1975), p. 890–891B. (University Microfilms No. 75-17, 996).

Maxtone-Graham, K. *Pregnant by mistake.* New York: Liveright, 1973.

McArthur, L. Z. and Resko, B. G. The portrayal of men and women in American television commercials. *The Journal of Social Psychology*, 1975, *97*, 209–20.

McClelland, D. C. *The achieving society.* Princeton, N.J.: Van Nostrand, 1961.

McClelland, D. C., Atkinson, J. W., Clark, R. A. and Lowell, E. L. *The achievement motive.* New York: Appleton, 1953.

McCord, J., McCord, W. and Thurber, E. Some effects of parental absence on male children. *Journal of Abnormal and Social Psychology,* 1962, *64,* 361–369.

McCue, M. J. *How to pick the right name for your baby.* New York: Grosset and Dunlap, 1977.

Mead, M. *Sex and Temperament.* New York: William Morrow and Co., 1935.

Mead, M. *Male and Female: A study of the sexes in a changing world.* New York: Dell, 1968.

Meyer, W. J. and Thompson, G. G. Sex differences in the distribution of teacher approval and disapproval among sixth-graders. *The Journal of Educational Psychology,* 1956, *47,* 385–396.

Miller, S. M. Effects of maternal employment on sex role perception, interests, and self-esteem in kindergarten girls. *Developmental Psychology,* 1975, *11,* 405–406.

Milton, G. A. The effects of sex-role identification upon problem-solving skill. *Journal of Abnormal and Social Psychology,* 1957, *55,* 208–212.

Minton, C., Kagan, J. and Levine, J. A. Maternal control and obedience in the two-year-old. *Child Development,* 1971, *42,* 1873–94.

Minton, C., Kagan, J. and Levine, J. A. Maternal control and obedience in the two-year-old. *Child Development,* 1971, *42,* 1873–94.

Mischel, W. Sex-typing and socialization. In P. Mussen (Ed.), *Carmichael's Manual of Child Psychology,* Vol. 2. New York: John Wiley and Sons, 1970.

Mlinar, J. Sex stereotypes in mathematics and science textbooks for elementary and junior high schools. Report of Sex Bias in the Public Schools. New York: National Organization for Women, New York Chapter, 1977.

Monahan, C., Kuhn, D., and Slaver, P. Intrapsychic versus cultural explanations of the "fear of success" motive. *Journal of Personality and Social Psychology,* 1974, *29,* 60–64.

Money, J. and Ehrhardt, A. A. *Man and Woman, Boy and Girl.* Baltimore: Johns Hopkins University Press, 1972.

Money, J., Ehrhardt, A. A. and Masica, D. N. Fetal feminization induced by androgen insensitivity in the testicular feminizing syndrome: Effect on marriage and maternalism. *Johns Hopkins Medical Journal*, 1968, *123*, 160–67.

Money, J. and Raiti, S. Breasts in intersexuality and transsexualism: I. Mammary growth. *Journal of the American Medical Women's Association*, 1967, *22*, 865–69.

Morgan, M. *The total woman.* Old Tappan, N.J.: Revell, 1973.

Moss, H. A. Sex, age and state as determinants of mother-infant interaction. *Merrill-Palmer Quarterly*, 1967, *13*, 19–36.

Moss, H. A. Early sex differences and mother-infant interaction. In R. C. Friedman, R. M. Richart, and R. L. Vande Wiele (Eds.), *Sex differences in behavior.* New York: John Wiley and Sons, 1974.

Moss, H. A. and Robson, K. S. Maternal influences in early social visual behavior. *Child Development*, 1968, *39*, 401–408.

Munroe, R. L. and Munroe, R. H. Effect of environmental experience on spatial ability in an East African Society. *Journal of Social Psychology*, 1971, *83*, 15–22.

Mussen, P. H. Long-term consequences of masculinity of interests in adolescence. *Journal of Consulting Psychology*, 1962, *26*, 435–440.

Mussen, P. H. and Distler, L. Masculinity, identification, and father-son relationships. *Journal of Abnormal and Social Psychology*, 1959, *59*, 350–356.

Mussen, P. H. and Jones, M. C. Self-conceptions, motivations, and interpersonal attitudes of late- and early-maturing boys. *Child Development*, 1957, *28*, 243–256.

Newcomb, T. M. *Personality and social change.* New York: Dryden, 1943.

Newson, J. and Newson, E. *Four years old in an urban community.* Harmondworth, England: Pelican Books, 1968.

New York Times. Role of women sparks debate by congresswoman and doctor. July 26, 1970, p. 35.

Omark, D. R. and Edelman, M. Peer group social interactions from an evolutionary perspective. Paper presented at The Society for Research in Child Development, Philadelphia, 1973.

Omark, D. R., Omark, M. and Edelman, M. Dominance hierarchies in young children. Paper presented at International Congress of Anthropological and Ethnological Sciences, Chicago, 1973.

Parke, R. D. and O'Leary, S. Father-mother-infant interaction in the newborn period: Some findings, some observations, and some unresolved issues. In K. Riegel and J. Meacham (Eds.), *The developing individual in a changing world,* Vol II, *Social and environmental issues.* The Hague: Mouton, 1975.

Parlee, M. B. The premenstrual syndrome. *Psychological Bulletin,* 1973, *80* (6), 454-465.

Parsons, J. E., Frieze, I. H., and Ruble, D. N. Introduction. In D. N. Ruble, I. H. Frieze, and J. E. Parsons (Eds.), Sex roles: Persistence and change. *Journal of Social Issues,* 1976, *32* (3), 1-5.

Parsons, J. E., Ruble, D. N., Hodges, K. L. and Small, A. W. Cognitive-developmental factors in emerging sex differences in achievement-related expectancies. In D. N. Ruble, I. H. Frieze and J. E. Parsons (Eds.), Sex roles: Persistence and change. *Journal of Social Issues,* 1976, *32* (3), 47-61.

Parsons, T. An analytical approach to the theory of social stratification in *Essays in Sociological Theory.* Glencoe, Ill.: Free Press, 1949.

Pastore, N. *The nature-nurture controversy.* New York: Kings Crown Press, 1949.

Pedersen, F. A. and Bell, R. Q. Sex differences in preschool children without histories of complications of pregnancy and delivery. *Developmental Psychology,* 1970, *3,* 10-15.

Petersen, A. C. Physical androgyny and cognitive functioning in adolescence. *Developmental Psychology,* 1976, *12,* 524-533.

Piaget, J. *The construction of reality in the child.* M. Cook (trans.) New York: Basic Books, Inc., 1954.

Piaget, J. *The child's conception of the world.* J. and A. Tomlinson, trans. Totowa, New Jersey: Littlefield, Adams and Co., 1969.

Polk, B. and Stein, R. Is the grass greener on the other side? In C.

Safilios-Rothschild (Ed.), *Toward a sociology of women.* Lexington, Mass.: Xerox College Publishing Co., 1972.

Pollis, N. and Doyle, D. Sex role, status, and perceived competence among first-graders. *Perceptual and Motor Skills,* 1972, *34,* 235-238.

Preston, R. C. Reading achievement of German and American children. *School and Society,* 1972, *90,* 350-354.

Putnam, B. A. and Hansen, J. C. Relationship of self-concept and feminine role concept to vocational maturity in young women. *Journal of Counseling Psychology,* 1972, *19,* 436-440.

Rabban, M. Sex-role identification in young children in two diverse social groups. *Genetic Psychology Monographs,* 1950, *42,* 81-158.

Rabe, B. *Rass.* New York: Bantam, 1978.

Reader's Digest. March 1978, p. 134. Reprinted with permission from Joey Adams, Chris Riley, and the Reader's Digest.

Rebelsky, F. and Hanks, C. Fathers' verbal interaction with infants in the first three months of life. *Child Development,* 1971, *42,* 63-68.

Reiss, I. L. *Premarital sexual standards in America.* Glencoe, Ill.: The Free Press, 1960.

Rezler, A. G. Characteristics of high school girls choosing traditional or pioneer vocations. *Personnel and Guidance Journal,* 1967, *45,* 659-665.

Rheingold, H. L. and Cook, K. U. The content of boys' and girls' rooms as an index of parents' behavior. *Child Development,* 1975, *46* (2), 459-463.

Rimm, D. C. and Somerville, J. W. *Abnormal psychology,* New York: Academic Press, 1977.

Robbins, T. *Even cowgirls get the blues.* New York: Bantam, 1976.

Robson, K. S., Pederson, F. A. and Moss, H. A. Developmental observations of dyadic gazing in relation to the fear of strangers and social approach behavior. *Child Development,* 1969, *40,* 619-627.

Rose, R. N., Gordon, T. P. and Bernstein, I. S. Plasma testosterone levels in the male rhesus: Influences of sexual and social stimuli, *Science,* 1972, *178,* 643–645.

Rose, R. N., Holaday, J. W. and Bernstein, I. S. Plasma testosterone, dominance, rank and aggressive behavior in male rhesus monkeys. *Nature,* 1971, *231,* 366–368.

Rosenberg, B. G. and Sutton-Smith, B. Sibling age spacing effects on cognition. *Developmental Psychology,* 1969, *1,* 661–668.

Rosenthal, R. *Experimental effects in behavioral research.* New York: Appleton-Century-Crofts, 1966.

Rothbart, M. K. and Maccoby, E. E. Parents' differential reaction to sons and daughters. *Journal of Personality and Social Psychology,* 1966, *4,* 237–243.

Routh, D. D., Schroeder, C. S. and O'Tuana, L. A. Development of activity level in children. *Developmental Psychology,* 1972, *10,* 163–168.

Rubenstein, J. Maternal attentiveness and subsequent exploratory behavior in the infant. *Child Development,* 1967, *38,* 1089–1100.

Rubin, C. Cited in *In the Running.* Published by SPRINT (National organization on sex discrimination in sports). A project of WEAL Fund, 805 15th St. NW DC 20005. 1 (Spring 1978) p. 3.

Rubin, J.Z., Provenzano, F.J., and Lurin, Z. The eye of the beholder: Parents' views on sex of newborns. *American Journal of Orthopsychiatry,* 1974, *44,* 512–519.

Ruble, D. N. Premenstrual symptoms: A reinterpretation. *Science,* 1977, *197,* 291–292.

Ruble, D. N. and Brooks-Gunn, J. The menstrual cycle: A social cognition analysis of perceptions of symptoms. *Behavioral Medicine,* 1979.

Ruble, D. N. and Brooks-Gunn, J. Young adolescents' attitudes about menstruation. Paper presented at the Society for Research in Child Development meeting, Symposium on sociocultural aspects of Puberty, New Orleans, March 1977.

Ryan, B. *The Sexes: Male/Female Roles and Relationships.* New York: Scholastic Book Services, 1975.

Saegert, S. and Hart, R. The development of sex differences in the environmental competence of children. In P. Burnett (Ed.), *Women in society.* Chicago: Maaroufa Press, 1976.

Sagi, A. and Hoffman, M. L. Empathetic distress in the newborn. *Developmental Psychology,* 1976, *12* (2), 175-176.

Sameroff, A. J. The components of sucking in the human newborn. *Journal of Experimental Child Psychology,* 1968, *6,* 607-623.

Sameroff, A. J. Changes in the nonnutritive sucking responses to stimulation during infancy. *Journal of Experimental Child Psychology,* 1970, *10,* 112-119.

Sanford, N. (Ed.), Personality development through the college years. *Journal of Social Issues,* 1956, *12,* (4).

Sarason, S. B., Hill, K. T. and Zimbardo, P. G. A longitudinal study of the relation of test anxiety to performance on intelligence and achievement tests. *Monographs of the Society for Research in Child Development,* 1964, *29,* #98.

Schahter, E. E., Shore, Z., Hodapp, R., Chalfin, S. and Bundy, C. Do girls talk earlier?: Mean length of utterance in toddlers. *Developmental Psychology,* 1978, *14,* 388-392.

Schickedanz, J. A. The relationship of sex-typing of reading to reading achievement and reading choice behavior in elementary school boys. *Dissertation Abstracts,* 34 (12A Pt. 1) 7645.

Shulman, A.K. Memoirs of an ex-prom queen. New York: Bantam Books, 1976.

Sears, R. R. Influence of methodological factors in doll-play performance. *Child Development,* 1947, *18,* 190-197.

Sears, R. R. Development of gender role. In F. A. Beach (Ed.), *Sex and Behavior.* New York: John Wiley and Sons, 1965.

Sears, R. R., Maccoby, E. E. and Levin, H. *Patterns of child rearing.* Evanston, Ill.: Row, Petersen, 1957.

Sears, R. R., Rau, L. and Alpert, R. *Identification and Child Rearing.* Stanford, Calif.: Stanford University Press, 1965.

Seavey, C. A., Katz, P. A. and Zalk, S. R. Baby X: The effect of gender labels on adult responses to infants. *Sex Roles,* 1975, *1* (2), 103–110.

Seward, G. H. and Williamson, R. C. A cross-national study of adolescent professional goals. *Human Development,* 1969, *12,* 248–254.

Sexism in Textbooks Committee of Women at Scott, Foresman, and Co. "Guidelines for Improving the Image of Women in Textbooks," *NJEA Instruction,* Publication No. ID-WIE-06.

Sexton, P. C. Schools are emasculating our boys. *The Saturday Review of Education,* 1965, *48,* p. 57.

Shainess, N. A re-evaluation of some aspects of femininity through a study of menstruation: A preliminary report. *Comparative Psychiatry,* 1961, *2,* 20–26.

Sherman, J. A. Problem of sex differences in space perception and aspects of intellectual functioning. *Psychological Review,* 1967, *74,* 290–299.

Sherman, J. A. *On the Psychology of Women.* Springfield, Ill.: Charles C. Thomas, 1971.

Shipman, G. The psychodynamics of sex education. In R. E. Muuss (Ed.), *Adolescent behavior and society: A book of readings.* New York: Random House, 1971.

Siegel, A. E. and Hass, M. B. The working mother: A review of research, *Child Development,* 1963, *34,* 513–42.

Simon, W. and Gagnor, J. Psychosexual development. *Transaction,* 1969, *6,* 15–16.

Slaby, R. G. and Frey, K. S. Development of gender constancy and selective attention to same-sex models. *Child Development,* 1975, *46,* 849–856.

Slovik, P. Risk taking in children: Age and sex differences. *Child Development,* 1966, *37,* 169–176.

Smith, M. E. The influence of age, sex, and situation on the frequency of form and function of questions asked by preschool children. *Child Development,* 1933, *3,* 201–213.

Smith, S. Out of the ivory playpen. *Ms,* 1974, *2,* (Feb.), 89–92.

Sommer, B. B. *Puberty and adolescence.* New York: Oxford University Press, 1978.

Sorenson, R. C. *Adolescent sexuality in contemporary America: Personal values and sexual behavior, ages 13–14.* New York: World, 1973.

Speer, D. C., Briggs, P. F. and Gavolas, R. Concurrent schedules of social reinforcement and dependency behavior among four-year-old children. *Journal of Experimental Child Psychology,* 1969, *8,* 356–65.

St. Peter, S. Jack went up the hill . . . but where was Jill? Paper presented to the Society for Research in Child Development, New Orleans, 1977.

Stafford, R. E. Sex differences in spatial visualization as evidence of sex-linked inheritance. *Perceptual and Motor Skills.* 1961, *13,* 428.

Stein, A. and Bailey, M. The socialization of achievement orientation in females. *Psychological Bulletin,* 1973, *80* (5), 345–366.

Stein, A. H., Pohly, S. R. and Mueller, E. The influence of masculine, feminine, and neutral tasks on children's achievement behavior, expectancies of success and attainment values. *Child Development,* 1971, *42,* 195–207.

Sternglanz, S. H. and Serbin, L. A. Sex role stereotyping in children's television programs. *Developmental Psychology,* 1974, *10,* 710–715.

Stoller, R. *Sex and Gender.* New York: Jason Aronson, 1976.

Sutton-Smith, B., Roberts, J. M. and Rosenberg, B. G. Sibling association and role in violence. *Merrill-Palmer Quarterly,* 1964, *10,* 25–38.

Sutton-Smith, B. and Rosenberg, B. G. *The sibling.* New York: Holt, Rinehart, and Winston, Inc., 1970.

Tanner, J. M. *Growth at adolescence.* New York: Lippincott, 1962. (2nd ed.).

Tanner, J. M. Physical growth. In P. H. Mussen (Ed.), *Carmichael's Manual of Child Psychology,* Vol. 1. New York: John Wiley and Sons, 1970.

Tanner, J. M. Sequence, tampo and individual variation in the growth and development of boys and girls aged twelve to sixteen. *Daedalus,* 1971, 907-930.

Tanner, J. M., Whitehouse, R. H. and Takaishi, M. Standards from birth to maturity for height, weight, height velocity and weight velocity: British children, 1965. *Archives of Disease in Childhood,* 1966, *41,* 454-471; 613-635.

Tasch, R. J. The role of the father in the family. *Journal of Experimental Education,* 1952, *20,* 319-361.

Taylor, N. Date Rating. In B. Ryan (Ed.), *The Sexes: Male/Female Roles and Relationships.* New York: Scholastic Book Services, 1975.

Thomas, A. and Stewart, N. Counselor response to female clients with deviate and conforming career goals. *Journal of Counseling Psychology,* 1971, *18,* 352-357.

Thompson, S. K. Gender labels and early sex role development. *Child Development,* 1975, *46,* 339-347.

Thompson, S. K. and Bentler, P. M. The priority of cues in sex discrimination by children and adults. *Development Psychology,* 1971, *5,* 181-185.

Tidball, M. E. Perspective on academic women and affirmative action. *Educational Record,* 1973, *54,* 130-135.

Tiger, L. *Men in groups.* New York: Random House, 1969.

Tresemer, D. W. *Fear of success.* New York: Plenum, 1977.

Tyler, L. The antecedents of two varieties of vocational interests. *Genetic Psychology Monograph,* 1964, *70,* 177-227.

United States Department of Labor, Office of Information, News (77-792). September 14, 1977.

Vener, A. and Snyder, C. The preschool child's awareness and anticipation of adult sex-roles. *Sociometry,* 1966, *29,* 159-168.

Veroff, J., Wilcox, S. and Atkinson, J. The achievement motive in high school and college-age women. *Journal of Abnormal and Social Psychology,* 1953, *48,* 108-119.

Vogel, S. R., Broverman, I. K., Broverman, D. M., Clarkson, F. and Rosenkranz, P. S. Maternal employment and perception of sex roles among college students, *Developmental Psychology*, 1970, *3*, 384–391.

Vogel, S., Broverman, I. and Gardner, J. A. Sesame Street and sex-role stereotype. Updated with suggestions for eliminating objectionable features. Report to the Children's Television Workshop. Pittsburgh, PA.: KNOW, Inc., 1970.

Waber, D. Biological substrates of field dependence: Implications of the sex difference. *Psychological Bulletin*, 1977, *84* (6), 1076–1087.

Waite, L. H. and Lewis, M. Intermodal person schema in infancy: Perception within a common auditory-visual space. Paper presented at the Eastern Psychological Association Meetings, Boston, April 1977.

Wake, F. R. Attitudes of parents towards the premarital sex behavior of the children and themselves. *Journal of Sex Research*, 1969, *5*, 120–177.

Walberg, H. J. Physics, femininity, and creativity. *Developmental Psychology*, 1969, *1*, 47–54.

Waldron, I. Sex differences in longevity. Paper presented at the Epidemiology of Aging Conference, Philadelphia, 1977.

Watson, J. S. Operant conditioning of visual fixation in infants under visual and auditory reinforcement. *Developmental Psychology*, 1969, *1*, 508–516.

Waldrop, M. Longitudinal and cross-sectional analyses of seven-and-a-half-year-old peer behavior. Unpublished manuscript, National Institute of Mental Health, 1972.

Wallach, M. A. Creativity. In P. H. Mussen (Ed.), *Carmichael's Manual of Child Psychology*, Vol. II. New York: John Wiley and Sons, Inc., 1970.

Walster, E. and Pate, M. A. Why are women so hard on women? In Sue Cox (Ed.), *Female psychology: The emerging self.* Chicago: Science Research Associates, Inc., 1976.

Walters, J., Pearce, D. and Dahms, L. Affectional and aggressive behavior of preschool children. *Child Development*, 1957, *28*, 15–26.

Weideger, P. *Menstruation and menopause.* New York: Alfred A. Knopf, 1975.

Weinraub, M. Two-year-olds' responses to brief separations from their mothers and fathers. Unpublished manuscript.

Weinraub, M., Brooks, J. and Lewis, M. The social network: A reconsideration of the concept of attachment. *Human Development*, 1977, *20*, 31–47.

Weinraub, M. and Leite, J. Sex-typed toy preference and knowledge of sex-role stereotypes and 2-year-old children. Paper presented at the Eastern Psychological Association Meeting, Boston, April 1977.

Weinraub, M. and Lewis, M. Infant attachment and play behavior: Sex of child and sex of parent differences. Unpublished manuscript, 1973.

Weller, G. M. and Bell, R. Q. Basal skin conductance and neonatal state. *Child Development*, 1965, *36*, 647–57.

Whisnant, L., Brett, E., and Zegans, L. Implicit messages concerning menstruation in commercial educational materials prepared for young adolescent girls. *American Journal of Psychiatry*, 1975, *132*, 815–820.

Whiting, B. and Edwards, C. P. A cross-cultural analysis of sex differences in the behavior of children aged three through eleven. *The Journal of Social Psychology*, 1973, *91*, 171–188.

WHO Task Force on the Acceptability of Fertility Regulating Methods, *Patterns and perceptions of menstrual bleeding in ten regions.* Exeter University, Devon, England, 1975.

Will, J., Self, P., and Datan, N. Paper presented at the American Psychological Association Meeting, 1974.

Williams, J. E., Bennett, S. and Best, D. Awareness and expression of sex stereotypes in young children. *Developmental Psychology*, 1975, *11*, 635–642.

Winterbottom, M. R. The relation of need for achievement to learning experiences in independence and mastery. In J. W. Atkinson (Ed.), *Motives in fantasy, action, and society.* Princeton, N.J.: Van Nostrand, 1958.

Witkin, H., Dyk, R. B., Patersun, H. F., Goodenough, D. R., and Karp, S. A. *Psychological differentiation.* New York: John Wiley and Sons, 1962.

Wolff, H. *Stress and Disease.* New York: C. C. Thomas, 1968.

Wolf, T. M. Response consequences to televised modeled sex-inappropriate play behavior. *The Journal of Genetic Psychology,* 1975, *127,* 35–44.

Women on Words and Images, Dick and Jane as Victims: *Sex Stereotyping in Children's Readers.* Princeton, N.J.: Women on Words and Images, 1972.

Woods, M. B. The unsupervised child of the working mother. *Developmental Psychology,* 1972, *6,* 14–25.

Wood, M. M. and Greenfeld, S. T. Women managers and fear of success: A study in the field. *Sex Roles,* 1976, *2,* 375–387.

Will, J., Self, P., and Datan, N. Paper presented at the smenian Psychological Association meetings.

Yando, R. M., Zigler, E. and Gates, M. The influence of negro and white teachers rated as effective or noneffective on the performance of negro and white lower-class children. *Developmental Psychology,* 1971, *5,* 290–299.

Young, W. C., Goy, R. W. and Phoenix, C. H. Hormones and sexual behavior. *Science,* 1964, *143,* 212–18.

Zelnik, M. and Kantner, J. F. The resolution of teenage first pregnancies. *Family Planning Perspectives,* 1974, *6,* 74.

Zindel, P. *My darling, my hamburger.* New York: Bantam, 1971.

INDEX